Considered Judgment

Considered Judgment

Catherine Z. Elgin

PRINCETON UNIVERSITY PRESS

PRINCETON, NEW JERSEY

Copyright © 1996 by Princeton University Press
Published by Princeton University Press, 41 William Street,
Princeton, New Jersey 08540
In the United Kingdom: Princeton University Press,
Chichester, West Sussex

Second printing, and first paperback printing, 1999

Paperback ISBN 0-691-00523-0

The Library of Congress has cataloged the cloth edition of this book as follows

Elgin, Catherine Z., 1948–
Considered judgement / Catherine Z. Elgin.
p.   cm.
Includes index.
ISBN 0-691-02879-6 (cloth : alk. paper)
1. Knowledge, Theory of.   I. Title.
BD161.E44.   1996
121—dc20   96-21549

This book has been composed in Galliard

The paper used in this publication meets the minimum requirements of
ANSI/NISO Z39.48-1992 (R 1997) (*Permanence of Paper*)

http://pup.princeton.edu

Printed in the United States of America

3   5   7   9   10   8   6   4

ISBN-13: 978-0-691-00523-2
ISBN-10: 0-691-00523-0

For Sam

_____

CONTENTS

PREFACE

PHILOSOPHY long sought to set knowledge on a firm foundation, through derivation of indubitable truths by infallible rules. For want of such truths and rules, the enterprise foundered. Certainty is not to be had. Nevertheless, foundationalism's heirs continue their forebears' quest, seeking security against epistemic misfortune. Their detractors typically espouse unbridled coherentism or a facile cultural relativism. Neither stance is tenable. To devise a via media between the absolute and the arbitrary requires reconceiving the nature, goals, and methods of epistemology.

Considered Judgment develops and argues for a reconception that takes reflective equilibrium as the standard of rational acceptability. A system of thought is in reflective equilibrium when its components are reasonable in light of one another, and the account they comprise is reasonable in light of our antecedent convictions about the subject at hand. Such a system affords no guarantees. It is rationally acceptable, I contend, not because it is certainly true but because it is reasonable in the epistemic circumstances.

Since such a position forsakes the goals of certainty and permanent credibility, I begin by arguing that those goals cannot, in any case, be met. I then develop the positive account, showing that it has valuable resources that more familiar approaches lack. Many epistemologists now concede that certainty is a chimerical goal. But they continue to accept the traditional conception of epistemology's problematic. For them, the question remains how to justify literal, factual beliefs. I suggest that in abandoning the quest for certainty we gain opportunities for a broader epistemological purview—one that comprehends the arts and does justice to the sciences. The position I advocate thus recognizes that metaphor, fiction, emotion, and exemplification often advance understanding in science as well as in art. The range of epistemology turns out to be broader and more variegated than is usually recognized. Tenable systems of thought are neither absolute nor arbitrary. But even though they are subject to revision, they are good in the way of belief.

I have, it seems, been writing this book since the Pleistocene era. A work this long in the writing incurs many debts. Jonathan Adler, Mary Kate McGowan, Israel Scheffler, Bob Schwartz, Judy Thomson, and Bas van Fraassen read and commented on large portions of the manuscript. Although they doubtless still disagree with my position, their insightful criticisms improved the work enormously. Paul Benacerraf, Mark Bedau,

Myles Burnyeat, David Lewis, Brian Loar, Dick Moran, Amelie Rorty, Jamie Tappenden, Jill Sigman, and Dan Sperber helped locate and solve (or evade) particular problems. So, I am sure, did others whose contributions I forgot to record. My sister fellows at the Bunting believed in the project. Nelson Goodman nagged. I am grateful to you all.

I presented excerpts in a variety of venues—the Pompidou Center, the University of Bielefeld, MIT, Princeton, Columbia, Brigham Young, Rutgers, and Wesleyan Universities, Wellesley and Dartmouth Colleges, The Conference on Creativity and Cognition in Albi, Harvard's Graduate School of Education, and the Bunting Institute at Radcliffe. Comments from members of the various audiences were enormously helpful.

Three publications overlap the present text. Parts of "The Relativity of Fact and the Objectivity of Value" are incorporated into chapters 1 and 4. That paper was first published in *Relativism: Interpretation and Confrontation*, ed. Michael Krausz (Notre Dame: University of Notre Dame Press, 1989), pp. 86–98. Chapter 5 incorporates "Understanding: Art and Science," first published in *Philosophy and the Arts: Midwest Studies in Philosophy* 16, ed. Peter A. French, Theodore E. Uehling, Jr., and Howard Wettstein (Notre Dame: University of Notre Dame Press, 1991), pp. 196–208. Also incorporated in chapter 5 is "Fiction's Functions," originally published in French in *Les Cahiers du Musée National d'Art Moderne* 41 (1992): 33–44.

I acknowledge with gratitude the support of the American Council of Learned Societies, the John Dewey Foundation, the National Endowment for the Humanities, and the Mary Ingraham Bunting Institute of Radcliffe College.

Finally, there are debts of a more ineffable sort. The deepest of these are to my husband Jim and my son Sam, who make it all worthwhile.

Considered Judgment

Chapter I

EPISTEMOLOGY'S END

QUARRY

Unaccountable success, like inexplicable failure, disconcerts. Even when our undertakings achieve their avowed objectives, we endeavor to understand them. We wonder how our projects, practices, interests, and institutions fit into the greater scheme of things, what they contribute to and derive from it. Our curiosity extends beyond our limited forays into art and science, beyond our parochial concerns with commerce, politics, and law. We want to comprehend the interlocking systems that support or thwart our efforts. If we start out expecting thereby to gain fame, fortune, and the love of admirable people, many of us conclude that understanding itself is worth the candle. The epistemic quest need serve no further end.

What makes for an acceptable epistemic framework depends on the kind of excellence we are after and on the functions we expect it to perform in our cognitive economy. Agents adopt a variety of cognitive stances with different kinds and degrees of intellectual merit. In doing epistemology, we discriminate among such stances, segregating out those that are worthy of intellectual esteem. Different partitions of the cognitive realm underwrite different conceptions of epistemology's goals and vindicate the construction and employment of epistemic frameworks of different kinds.

Epistemological theories typically share an abstract characterization of their enterprise. They agree, for example, that epistemology is the study of the nature, scope, and utility of knowledge. But they disagree about how their shared characterization is concretely to be realized. So they differ over their subject's priorities and powers, resources and rewards, standards and criteria. To view them as supplying alternative answers to the same questions is an oversimplification. For they embody disagreements about what the real questions are and what counts as answering them. We cannot hope to decide among competing positions on the basis of point-by-point comparisons, for their respective merits and faults stubbornly refuse to line up. To understand a philosophical position and evaluate it fairly requires understanding the network of commitments that constitute it; for these commitments organize its domain, frame its problems, and supply standards for the solution of those problems.

John Rawls invokes a distinction between procedures[1] that extends to supply a useful classification of epistemological theories. A *perfect procedure* recognizes an independent criterion for a correct outcome and a method whose results—if any—are guaranteed to satisfy that criterion. Our independent criterion for the fair division of a cake, let us assume, is that a fair division is an equal one.[2] A cake-slicing procedure is perfect, then, just in case it yields an equal division when it yields any division. A finely calibrated electronic cake slicer that partitioned each cake it divided into equally large slices would provide a perfect procedure for fairly dividing cakes. The device would not have to be capable of dividing every cake. It might, for example, be inoperative on geometrically irregular cakes. But so long as every cake it divides is divided into equal sized slices, its use would be a perfect procedure for fairly dividing cakes. An *imperfect procedure* recognizes an independent criterion for a correct outcome but has no way to guarantee that the criterion is satisfied. The criterion for a correct outcome in a criminal trial is that the defendant is convicted if and only if he is guilty. Trial by jury, representation by counsel, the rules of evidence, and so on, are the means used to secure that result. But the means are not perfect. Sometimes a wrong verdict is reached. A *pure procedure* has no independent standard for a correct outcome. The procedure itself, when properly performed, determines what result is correct. And unless the procedure is actually performed, there is no fact of the matter as to which outcome is correct. A tournament is best construed as a pure procedure. Other construals are sometimes offered, but they are less satisfactory. If a tournament is construed as a perfect procedure for discovering the most able competitor, it is plainly defective. Anyone can have an off day or a bad series. Sometimes the best man doesn't win. And arguably, if it is construed as an imperfect procedure, it may be too imperfect. Consideration of how the parties fare overall may be a better indication of talent than hinging everything on their performance in a single game or series. But if the tournament is a pure procedure, such considerations are otiose. Winning the tournament is what makes a particular competitor the champion. The Celtics became the 1984 NBA champions by winning the playoffs. Nothing more was required; nothing less would do. A pure procedural interpretation of its function thus best explains how a tournament realizes the goal of an athletic competition: it incontrovertibly establishes a winner.

This tripartite division presents an attractive device for classifying epis-

---

[1] John Rawls, *A Theory of Justice* (Cambridge, Mass.: Harvard University Press, 1971), 85.

[2] I modify Rawls's example slightly to bring out features that are important for my purposes but not for his.

temological theories. Extended to the epistemological realm, Rawls's division enables us to classify theories on the basis of differences in the sources and strength of epistemic justification they demand. *Very roughly* the difference is this: Perfect procedural epistemologies demand conclusive reasons, ones that guarantee the permanent acceptability of the judgments they vindicate. Imperfect procedural epistemologies require convincing reasons, but they recognize that convincing reasons need not be and typically are not conclusive. Pure procedural epistemologies construe reasons as constitutive. The reasons that, if true, would support a given claim, then, collectively amount to that claim. Plainly these criteria cry out for explication. It is far from obvious what makes for a reason, much less what makes for a conclusive, convincing, or constitutive reason. Moreover, each criterion admits of multiple, divergent explications. There is, for example, an array of perfect procedural theories whose members agree in their demand for conclusive reasons but disagree about what makes a reason conclusive. I do not want to enter into internecine squabbles here. Rather, I will sketch the considerations that tell in favor of each procedural stance. For present purposes, then, a rough characterization is enough.

One point should be emphasized. Epistemology is normative. It concerns what people ought to think and why. So recognizing the normativeness of central epistemological notions is crucial. A *reason* for p is not just a consideration that, as a matter of brute psychological fact, prompts a subject to take it that p. It is a consideration that, ceteris paribus, confers some measure of obligation to do so. Other things being equal, given that reason r obtains, S would be (more or less) epistemically irresponsible if she failed to take it that p. Other things, of course, are not always equal. Reasons can be discredited or overridden. Even given r, S would not be irresponsible if she failed to believe or suspect that p, in circumstances where q also obtained. Thus, for example, symptoms that afford a prima facie obligation to think that a child has chicken pox are overridden by a blood test that discloses the absence of antibodies to the disease. Reasons, moreover, vary in strength. And reasons of differing strengths engender different epistemic obligations. A weak reason may confer an obligation to suspect that p; a weaker one, an obligation not to presume that $\sim p$. Thus red spots on a previously uninfected child's torso give a pediatrician an obligation to suspect, or at least not to exclude, that the child has chicken pox. But many other common conditions produce red spots, so it would be irresponsible to claim to know, on the basis of the spots alone, that he has the disease.

Weak reasons often persuade. That is a matter of psychological fact. But,

—if reasons are conclusive, perfect procedural epistemology contends,

—if they are convincing, imperfect procedural epistemology contends,

—if they are constitutive of *p*, pure procedural epistemology contends,

S ought to believe that *p*. Her reasons are good enough to secure the belief. Being measures of the goodness of reasons, then, 'conclusive', 'convincing', and 'constitutive' function normatively as well.

PERFECT PROCEDURAL EPISTEMOLOGY

If the truths it seeks are supposed to be antecedent and indifferent to our beliefs about them, and the test for truth affords a conclusive reason to accept its results, an epistemological theory construes itself as a perfect procedural position. The standard is rigorous. If *p* is true and *p* entails *q*, *q* is also true. Still, *p* may fail to be a conclusive reason for *q*. Suppose, for example, 'A calico cat swallowed the canary' is true; then, 'A cat swallowed the canary' is also true. But the mere truth of 'A calico cat swallowed the canary' does not convert Sam's belief that the cat is the culprit into knowledge. If Sam is ignorant of the truth in question, that truth is for him epistemically inert. Unless he has other reasons to fall back on, Sam's belief that a cat swallowed the canary is but a lucky guess. For all he knows, the canary could have been eaten by a hawk. According to perfect procedural epistemology, Sam does not know. For a perfect procedure provides a guarantee. Having satisfied its standard, the sentences it sanctions are immune to falsity and invulnerable to luck.

Both form and content have been thought to confer such immunity. Where form is the sole criterion, logic is supposed to be the guarantor of truth. Being a matter of form, the truth of

Either flamingos fly or flamingos do not fly

carries over to

Either molybdenum is malleable or molybdenum is not malleable.

Ornithological and metallurgical facts are irrelevant; logic alone decides. But logic's indifference to the way the world is invites the charge of vacuity. Such sentences, being about nothing, convey no information.

No such charge can be brought if content is involved. Sentences of a variety of kinds have been thought to owe their epistemic security to content.

Analytic sentences. 'Vixens are female foxes'; 'No bachelors are married'.

Synthetic a priori sentences. '7 + 5 = 12'; 'Every event has a cause'.

Some *fundamental laws*: 'Every integer has a successor'; 'You ought always act in such a way that you could will the maxim of your action to be a universal law'.

In these cases, epistemic standing seems to stem from, or to be intimately related to, necessity. Being necessarily true, the sentences in question could not have been false.

Some contingent sentences are also considered unimpeachable. For instance,

Some *self-ascriptions*: 'I am angry'; 'I seem to see a purple patch'; 'I think, therefore I am'.

Although contingent, these sentences are supposed so to relate to their objects that the conditions of their sincere utterance are the conditions of their truth. Incontrovertibility here attaches to tokens, not to types. Some assertions of 'I am elated' are true; others, false. The true ones, it is held, are certainly true; the false ones, lies. There is room for deception, but none for error. If I know what the sentence means, I know whether in asserting it I speak the truth.

Incontrovertibility is also claimed of

Some *sentences involving indexicals*: 'I am here now'; 'Yesterday's gone'; 'Tomorrow is another day'.

Such sentences are inevitably true; but different tokens of their indexical elements have different referents—Monday's tokens of 'yesterday' denote Sunday; Sunday's denote Saturday. So it is best to focus on tokens in these cases too.

I have culled the foregoing examples and the rationales for them from the history of philosophy. I do not contend that the categories are exclusive or exhaustive. Nor am I prepared to argue that every entry deserves its place on the list. Indeed, whether any sentence is genuinely unimpeachable remains to be seen. Still, there was traditionally a consensus that undeniable truth is a criterion of epistemic acceptability—a consensus that survived prolonged and bitter disagreements about how that criterion is to be satisfied.

Form and content are held jointly responsible for the unimpeachability of claims of a third kind—namely, the consequences of nonvacuous, unimpeachable truths. Perfect procedural epistemology contends that knowledge consists largely of claims of this kind. Unimpeachable claims are not all obvious. Some are revealed by explication and analysis; others are products of evidence and argument. Explication and analysis function archaeologically, uncovering claims that stand on their own. Rather than marshaling evidential support for a theory or practice, they articulate its presuppositions and commitments, dispel confusions in or about it, filter out what is false or untenable in it. By successive refinements, they hope to uncover the fundamental truths that underlie it. If the theory or practice in question is well-founded, the results of these processes are supposed to be obviously acceptable. In that case, we need only consider them to recognize that they are warranted. Manifestly, most of our knowledge is not obviously acceptable. But according to perfect procedural epistemology, it is unimpeachable; for its justification derives ultimately from obviously acceptable sentences.

Arguments function electronically, transmitting warrant from some sentences to others. Warrant-preserving inferences effect transmission without distortion. If our evidential base consists exclusively of warranted claims, and our methods prevent us from drawing unwarranted conclusions from warranted premises, our conclusions are secure. It follows that if knowledge is restricted to obviously acceptable claims and their consequences, and the methods for generating consequences are restricted to warrant-preserving inferences, knowledge meets the strictures of a perfect procedure: it obtains its justification in a way that no unwarranted sentence can, and its chain of justification serves as the test for warrant.

This picture of things is plainly foundationalist. Justification starts with sentences that are self-sustaining and is transmitted to other sentences by inferential chains. The conclusions require the support of the premises; without it, they are untenable. The premises, however, are epistemically autonomous; they derive no epistemological benefit from their relation to their consequences. Justification is a one-way street.

Austerity of resources and methods might seem to restrict knowledge unduly. But the matter is not altogether clear. To determine the scope of a perfect procedural theory, we must settle the criteria for obvious acceptability and for warrant-preserving inference. If only overtly incontrovertible sentences are obviously acceptable, and only first-order predicate calculus preserves warrant, our means are meager indeed. If, however, any initially credible sentence counts as obviously acceptable, and modal logic, inductive logic, and transformation rules of a language are valid inference tickets, our resources are greater. Still, once we set our sights on a specific cognitive goal, little choice remains. For a perfect procedure is characterized by a test that yields no false positives. If we seek truth, we have but one test that fits the bill: derivation by truth preserving means from known truths. To be sure, we can relax our objective and our standards in tandem. We might, for example, settle for plausibility, and evaluate candidates by a test that no implausible statement can pass. But we could assure that our test yielded no false positives only if we began with inherently plausible claims and inferred others from them in a way that does not dilute plausibility. So the structure of the positions is the same. Defects that are endemic to one are apt to have counterparts in the other.

Instead of considering defects here, however, I want to sketch what might be called the ideology of the program—the constellation of metaphysical and evaluative commitments that motivate perfect procedural epistemology and render its enterprise intelligible. Perfect procedural epistemologies doubtlessly differ over important details. What makes a sentence obviously acceptable and what inferences transmit acceptability are plainly subject to debate. But for present purposes, similarities are more significant than differences. If the procedure is vindicated, specific disagreements among perfect procedural positions become salient; if not, differences in detail hardly matter.

Metaphysically, perfect procedural epistemology is committed to the view that the facts are independent of anything we know or believe about them. Just what those facts are is, of course, hotly disputed. They may concern what is the case or what ought to be the case; they may consist of matter in motion, each of many monads reflecting the world from its own point of view, ideas in the mind of God. The crucial point is that because the identity and character of the facts is independent of what we think, we can be right or wrong about them; we can have true or false beliefs about the way the world is. The aim of perfect procedural epistemology is to learn those facts—not by chance, as Columbus happened on America, but in such a way that we are entitled to and secure in our beliefs about them. Otherwise, like Columbus, we might never realize what we have found, and so never stand to profit from it.

Perfect procedural epistemology demands cognitive security. To count as knowledge, a belief must be highly credible, and certifiable as such. Preferring ignorance to error, it excludes from knowledge anything that cannot pass its stringent tests. A variety of cognitive states, functions, and abilities fail to measure up. Being nonsentential, a painter's sense of color, a farmer's feel for the land, a poet's sensitivity to nuance can neither be evaluated in terms of truth nor justified by inference. Such sensibility is thus not knowledge. Nor is every truth bearer a candidate for knowledge. Those that are neither intrinsically credible nor susceptible of inferential justification are out of the running. Neither the insight an apt metaphor affords nor the understanding a great fiction engenders count as knowledge; for they are not backed by appropriate guarantees. And, of course, inadequately supported literal truths are excluded as well. A perfect procedure prevents falsehoods from passing for truths. It need not be, and is not, sensitive enough to discriminate truth from falsehood in every case. Some truths (along with all falsehoods) fail its test and are thus denied the status of things known.

The justification for such severe constraints lies in the power of the system that results. Any claim that passes a perfect procedural test is secure. We need never look back; for new findings are impotent to undermine credibility.[3] This allows for the incremental growth of knowledge. A limited range of considerations is relevant to the evaluation of any hypothesis—namely, those that figure in its derivation from obviously acceptable claims. These being settled, the epistemic standing of the hypothesis is secure. As they pass the perfect procedural test, sentences are incorporated one by one into the body of knowledge. The position is absolutist. Acceptability is not relative to background information, available evidence, or other contextual factors. Whatever passes its test, and nothing else, is epistemically acceptable. And the test itself makes no concession to context. A perfect procedural epistemology guarantees that if a sentence satisfies its standards, that sentence is permanently credible. But it cannot guarantee that any sentence satisfies its standards. If none does, inquiry is abortive. Compromise being impermissible, the perfect proceduralist is then forced to skepticism.

Certain prima facie virtues of the position are plain. It respects what one might call the realist intuition—the view that the facts are independent of what we think about them, and that our beliefs and theories are right only if faithful to the facts. It respects Plato's conviction that knowledge differs from (mere) true opinion in having a tether—in being, that is, appropriately tied to the facts it concerns. And it respects the conviction, common among philosophers since Descartes, that its tether protects knowledge from hypothetical as well as actual counterexamples, that genuine knowledge is cognitively estimable come what may. Perfect procedural standards, then, echo a dominant theme in epistemology. Whether these convictions are consonant with our cognitive practice, of course, remains to be seen. And if they are not, whether we ought to reform theory or practice is not obvious. But before investigating the matter in detail, we should consider the conceptions of knowledge that pure procedures and imperfect procedures employ.

IMPERFECT PROCEDURAL EPISTEMOLOGY

We can't, it seems, have everything. If objectives are settled independently of the mechanisms for realizing them, means may be exhausted before ends are reached. Should our methods prove grossly inadequate, we devise others or abandon the quest. Sometimes, however, we manage to

---

[3] Of course, new information can undermine the credibility of a contention we falsely believe has passed a perfect procedural test, but that is another matter.

design procedures that are generally successful, though not invariably so. Being imperfect, these procedures yield some defective products or sometimes fail to produce in circumstances where they should. Still, they get things right often enough to be worth using. Although we have reason to think that conscientious, impartial juries are usually right, they are not infallible. Some juries convict the innocent, some acquit the guilty, and some fail to reach a verdict. Plainly this state of affairs is unsatisfactory. Our only excuse for employing such a procedure is that we have no better. Society has a legitimate interest in fairly and accurately assigning criminal responsibility. Trial by jury, for all its defects, is the best way we know to make such assignments. We settle for an imperfect procedure for want of a better way to achieve a worthy end.

Induction is perhaps the most familiar imperfect epistemic procedure. Truth is its objective and ampliative inference its means. To draw the requisite inferences we marshal a large and varied body of evidence, describe that evidence in terms of projectible predicates, utilize refined statistical techniques, and so on. But the gap between premises and conclusions is not thereby bridged. The conclusion of a sound inductive argument may yet be false.

If the fallibility of induction is a manifestation of our general epistemological predicament, our best methods for securing knowledge are apt occasionally to fail. They may, like a hung jury, yield no verdict, leaving us in ignorance about the matter at hand. But sometimes they do worse. In counting undetected errors as knowledge, they yield false positives. Although there remains a presumption in favor of their products, these procedures, being fallible, are not intrinsically reliable. Still, the procedures we employ are the best ones available. So we have no way to differentiate their right answers from their wrong. On the principle that like cases should be treated alike, we ought to accord all products of the same procedure the same epistemic status. The problem is to decide what that status should be.

Impressed by a procedure's capacity to produce right answers (and acknowledging our inability to detect its errors), an epistemic fatalist might advocate accepting its products without reservation. We should treat our procedures as though they were perfect but recognize that in doing so we are vulnerable to epistemic misfortune. The fatalist then accepts the perfect procedural conception of the epistemic enterprise but concedes that without luck error is unavoidable. This is no small concession. To acknowledge the perennial possibility of error is to abandon hope of certainty. And certainty is the linchpin of the perfect procedural conception of knowledge. We are willing ruthlessly to restrict candidates for knowledge, forswear modes of justification, reorder epistemic priorities, and revise cognitive values, if by doing so we can achieve certainty. Security against error is a prize worth considerable epistemic sacrifice. The end of perfect procedural epistemology justifies the means.

But when the end is forsaken, the means lose their justification. Imperfect procedural philosophy must reform epistemology, legitimating both goals and methods. The considerations that led to perfect procedural stringency seem less compelling when certainty is not in the offing.

Instead of rejoicing in the general level of success of our epistemic ventures, and trusting luck to do the rest, the imperfect procedural stance I advocate adapts itself to the unfortunate propensity for error. Then even when a product appears unexceptionable, we do not accept it without reservation. Rather, we accord it provisional credibility, realizing that further findings may yet discredit it. Henceforth I shall use the phrase 'imperfect procedural epistemology' for such a position. Forced to admit fallibility, the imperfect procedural epistemologist demands corrigibility. Knowing that some well-founded conclusions are erroneous, she incorporates into her epistemology mechanisms for reviewing and revising or rejecting previously accepted claims.

Methods, too, are revisable. The best we could do yesterday need not be the best we can do today. So imperfect procedural epistemology is prepared to criticize, modify, reinterpret, and—if need be—renounce constituent ends and means.[4] If, for example, we discern a bias or limitation in inductive reasoning, we attempt to correct for it. There is, of course, no assurance of success. We might find no modification that does the trick. Or we might find one that does so only by creating more serious problems than it solves. Still, if we succeed, inductive reasoning improves. Although the procedure remains imperfect, it is less defective than it used to be. Imperfect procedural epistemology thus construes justification as inherently provisional. Reasons emerge from a self-monitoring, self-critical, self-correcting activity. Rather than deriving from a static system of uncompromising rules and rigid restrictions, they belong to and are vindicated by a fairly loose and flexible network of epistemic commitments, all accepted for the nonce as the best we can do, each subject to revision or revocation should defects emerge or improvements be found.

Perfect procedures confer permanent credibility. Nothing less than permanently credible claims can support their results, lest ineliminable error creep in. But imperfect procedures yield only provisional credibility. They are free to adduce a wider range of considerations to support their contentions, for both conclusions and arguments are subject to review. Being our best guesses as to how things stand, our considered judgments are

[4] See John Dewey, *Human Nature and Conduct* (New York: Random House, 1957), 25–35.

initially credible. Should they prove inadequate, we round them out with hypotheses and hunches that we have less faith in. Clearly the method is risky, for considered judgments can be the repository of ancient error; unsupported hypotheses may be insupportable; hunches, wild. Still, the risk is bearable, since initial credibility is revocable. If our considered judgments lead to an untenable conclusion—if, for instance, it generates false predictions or conflicts with more highly warranted claims—we retrench, retool, and try again.

Since its results are revisable, imperfect procedural epistemology is free to use arguments, sources of evidence, and linguistic forms that perfect procedures cannot. An appreciation of the ways useful analogies, sensitive emotional responses, and apt metaphors enlighten might lead it to countenance some types of analogical, metaphorical, and emotive reasoning. Their acceptance is, of course, subject to revocation should they do more harm than good. But in this they do not differ from other modes of argument. Nor is there an order of absolute epistemic priority. Claims pertaining to physical objects may warrant or be warranted by sensation reports. Rules may be validated by yielding credible results, and results vindicated by being products of reasonable rules. Still, justification is not circular, since some elements possess a degree of initial credibility that does not derive from the rest. Justification is holistic. Support for a conclusion comes not from a single line of argument but from a host of considerations of varying degrees of strength and relevance. Indirect evidence and weak arguments, which alone would bear little weight, may be interwoven into a fabric that strongly supports a conclusion. Each element derives warrant from its place in the whole.

The aim of inquiry on the imperfect procedural model is a broad and deep understanding of its subject matter. And a measure of the adequacy of a new finding is its fit with what we think we already understand. If the finding is at all surprising, the background of accepted beliefs is apt to require modification to make room for it; and the finding may require revision to fit into place. So advancement of understanding is not an incremental growth of knowledge. A process of delicate adjustments takes place, its goal being a system in wide reflective equilibrium. Coherence alone will not suffice. A system is coherent if its components mesh. Reflective equilibrium requires more. The components of a system in reflective equilibrium must be reasonable in light of one another, and the system as a whole must be reasonable in light of our antecedent commitments about the subject at hand.

Considerations of cognitive value come into play in deciding what modifications to attempt. If, for example, science places a premium on repeatable results, a finding we cannot reproduce is given short shrift and one that is easily repeated may be weighted so heavily that it can under-

mine a substantial body of accepted theory. Equilibrium is not guaranteed. We may be unable to construct a system that accommodates our
considered convictions and realizes our cognitive values. Considerable alteration may be necessary even to come close. Moreover, appearances can
be deceiving. We may believe, with reason, that a system is in equilibrium
when in fact it is not.

Imperfect procedural epistemology prefers error to ignorance. It risks
error to achieve understanding. But it hedges its bets. Because accepted
beliefs are corrigible, methods revisable, values subject to reappraisal,
error is eliminable. Aware of its own inadequacies, imperfect procedural
philosophy looks back as well as forward, reviewing, revoking, altering,
and amending its previous conclusions, methods, and standards in light of
later results. It considers nothing incontrovertible. What vindicates an
individual statement, rule, method, or value is its incorporation into a
network of cognitive commitments in wide reflective equilibrium. What
vindicates such a network is its mesh with our prior understanding of the
subject matter and the methods, rules, and values appropriate to it. Exact
correspondence is neither needed nor wanted. Realizing that our previous
position is incomplete, and suspecting that it is flawed, we would be unwise to take it as gospel. But we would be equally unwise to ignore it. We
treat it as a touchstone, being the best independent source of information
about its subject we have.

To go from a motley collection of convictions to a system of considered
judgments in reflective equilibrium requires balancing competing claims
against one another. There are likely to be several ways to achieve an acceptable balance. One system might, for example, sacrifice scope to
achieve precision; another, trade precision for scope. Neither invalidates
the other. Nor is there any reason to believe that a uniquely best system
will emerge in the long run. So imperfect procedural epistemology is plu-
ralistic, holding that the same constellation of cognitive objectives can be
realized in several ways, and that several constellations of cognitive objectives may be worthy of realization. A sentence that is right according to
one acceptable system may be wrong according to another. There is no
straight and narrow path to truth.

Still, it does not follow that every statement, method, or value is right
relative to some acceptable system. Among the considered judgments that
guide our theorizing are convictions that certain things—for example, affirming a contradiction or exterminating a race—are just wrong. We are
epistemically obliged to respect such convictions unless we find powerful
reasons to revise them. There is no ground for thinking that such reasons
are in the offing. So it does not follow from imperfect procedural philosophy that anything goes.

Nor does it follow that systems can be evaluated only by standards they acknowledge. An account that satisfies the standards it sets for itself might rightly be faulted for being blind to problems it ought to solve, for staking out a domain where there are only trivial problems, for setting too low standards for itself, and so forth. Sociobiology's fondness for 'just-so stories', for example, affords prima facie reason to doubt that its findings are epistemically estimable. An inquiry that succeeds by its own lights may yet be in the dark.

Imperfect procedural epistemology construes inquiry as a matter of pulling ourselves up by our bootstraps. The considered judgments that tether today's theory are the fruits of yesterday's theorizing. They are not held true come what may but accorded a degree of initial credibility because previous inquiry sanctioned them. We may subsequently revise or reject them, but they give us a place to start. Such an epistemological stance recognizes neither a beginning nor an end of inquiry. As epistemic agents, we are always in medias res.

Imperfect procedural epistemology finds a middle ground between the absolute and the arbitrary. Our convictions rarely if ever satisfy the standard for certainty or maximal credibility. But some are soundly backed by cognitively creditable reasons. Imperfect procedural epistemology gives such convictions their due. By denying that cognitive success requires anything like certainty, it avoids consigning well-founded convictions to the realm of ignorance. And by insisting that standards must be met, it avoids counting every conviction (or every widely held conviction) as knowledge. Moreover, in imperfect procedural epistemology, the perennial possibility of error leads to fallibilism, not to skepticism. It leads, that is, to the admission that any result is revocable, not to the conclusion that no result is tenable. Imperfect procedural epistemology affords no guarantees. It admits no criterion whose satisfaction assures that we could not be wrong. But it does offer a consolation: although our best efforts may fail, any failure can be regarded as a temporary setback. So a failure, should it occur, amounts not to a decisive defeat but to a challenge to do better next time.

PURE PROCEDURAL EPISTEMOLOGY

Pure procedures do not purport to disclose what is already the case. They do not claim to generate correspondence to a mind-independent reality or to realize antecedently accepted values. What makes the outcome of a pure procedure right is simply its being a product of that procedure. Because it is a pure procedure, a footrace determines what it takes to win; the winner is (no more and no less than) the runner who has what it takes.

A constellation of norms, conventions, rules, and objectives constitutes a practice and defines the pure procedures belonging to it. Together its components specify what counts as performing the procedures and what counts as doing so successfully. The criteria set the stage but do not identify the players. Only if the procedure is actually carried out are its performers and products determinate. For a pure procedure does not merely reveal its results; it generates them. That is what makes its products incontrovertible.

Perfect procedures and imperfect procedures are supposed to answer to something beyond themselves. So it is reasonable to ask whether they do what they claim—whether, that is, they are reliable. But pure procedures generate their results. Until the race is run, there is no winner. So we have no perspective from which to raise the question of reliability. For nothing more is required in the way of reliability than that the procedure be carried out in accordance with the rules it sets for itself. The result of that procedure, whatever it turns out to be, is ipso facto correct. Since there is nothing more to being right than being produced—and thereby certified—by the procedure, the product of a pure procedure is unimpeachable. One need only run a fair race and come in first in order to win. And standards of fairness and criteria of winning are internal to the practice of racing—the practice that produces winners.

One field of study that lends itself to a pure procedural construal is logic. All that it takes to be a theorem of a logical system is to be derivable from the system's axioms by the system's rules. To be sure, we can make mistakes in derivation, as in the performance of any other pure procedure. But if we do not, our results are unassailable. Any formula that satisfies the system's conditions for being a theorem is a theorem. Because its axioms and rules are explicitly codified, and because formal correctness seems not to involve correspondence with the independently real, logic is easily interpreted as a pure procedural inquiry. Logic's own seal of approval is all that is required for its derivations to count as valid.

Some philosophers—notably Thomas Kuhn, Richard Rorty, and the later Wittgenstein—take inquiry in general to be a pure procedural matter. Although most fields of study are not so strictly governed by explicit rules, all are, such philosophers contend, bound by implicit conventions—conventions powerful enough to fix the field's problems, methods, goals, and standards. By mastering the relevant conventions, we learn to play the language game, participate in the form of life, or work within the paradigm that they delimit. Moreover, if we look at what we do instead of at what we say, they maintain, we discover that the aim of inquiry is consensus, not correspondence. We design our practices and frame our conventions so that our procedures produce consensus. We consider something an outstanding problem for an intellectual community if its members seek, but have not yet achieved, agreement about it. And we do not worry that convictions everyone shares might fail to correspond to reality.

An inquiry, they urge, is constructed within a framework of tacit and explicit constraints. It is subject to publicly shared criteria and evaluated in terms of intersubjectively agreed-on norms. These organize the field into problems the discipline has the resources to solve, questions it has the capacity to answer. The conventions governing the discipline include devices for deflecting or disparaging embarrassing questions by, for example, pushing them off onto another field or discounting them as nonscientific, as pseudo-questions, or as what happens when language goes on holiday. Plainly a discipline's inability to answer such irrelevant or idle questions does not impugn its epistemic adequacy.

When consensus is achieved—when, that is, the community agrees that its objectives have been realized—a result becomes part of the corpus of knowledge. And, pure procedural philosophers contend, rightly so. For consensus is the product that inquiry is designed to produce. Because a result measures up to our standards for knowledge of its kind, that result—whatever it is—qualifies as knowledge. Since the criteria, standards, methods, and objectives are community property, and since the community expels inveterate naysayers, accord is bound to occur. To be sure, members of the community can disagree. But the scope of legitimate disagreement is restricted to disputes the practice has the mechanisms to resolve. Only those who share the community's standards and acknowledge the legitimacy of its objectives qualify as critics. Since the satisfaction of those standards and the realization of those objectives are publicly discernible matters, even the most carping of qualified critics will eventually come around. Objections by others are thought to be justifiably ignored. Not knowing the rules of the game, outsiders cannot tell winners from losers, fair plays from fouls. According to pure procedural epistemology then, community consensus is all we have and all we need for knowledge.

Justification of the fundamental elements of pure procedural knowledge is holistic.[5] To justify, say, the law of excluded middle is to reveal its role in the network of mutually supporting commitments that constitute classical logic. Moreover, the justification of methods, objectives, and beliefs is of a piece. Factual judgments have no epistemic primacy. By showing how each element contributes to the practice as a whole, we demonstrate that none is an idle wheel, that each is required for and involved in the working of the mechanism.

---

[5] Some pure procedural philosophers, such as Richard Rorty, take justification to be holistic throughout. Others take only the fundamentals to be justified holistically. Nonfundamental claims are justified, as they are in perfect procedural knowledge, by their epistemic relation to fundamental claims.

Plainly, such justification does not demonstrate truth—not, at least, if truth involves correspondence to a mind- and culture-independent realm. Nor does it claim to. What it does is show that a belief, method, value, or rule is an integral part of the practice. There is nothing more fundamental that can provide such a component with additional justification. The component is not self-justifying in the way that basic elements of perfect procedural knowledge are supposed to be. It does not stand on its own. Still, without that component, the mechanism would cease to function. The practice it belongs to would fall apart. And with the disintegration of the practice comes the dissolution of a shared form of life. So from the cognitive value of a pure procedure of inquiry and its associated form of life, the individual elements derive their justification.

Relativism results. Since the justification for fundamental beliefs, methods, objectives, and standards derives wholly from their place in a practice, they are justified only relative to that practice. Their warrant does not extend beyond the limits of the practice or survive the practice's demise. A law of excluded middle, for example, is justified relative to classical logic, unjustified relative to intuitionistic logic. It makes no sense to ask whether it is justified absolutely and independently of the specific logical systems it does, or does not, belong to. The highest scorer wins in tennis, loses in golf. But there is no saying absolutely whether high scores are better than low.

Although compatible with pure procedural epistemology, pluralism does not automatically follow from it. For such a position may be monopolistic. Thus Wittgenstein can be read as claiming that the conventions that underlie our form of life are constitutive of human rationality. For us, then, there are no alternatives. Kuhn contends that monopoly is required for, and is imposed by, mature science: only what accords with the conventions of the reigning paradigm counts as science. The relativism of pure procedural philosophy thus does not guarantee that an inquiry tolerates alternatives. To be sure, pure procedural philosophy may be pluralist. According to a version like Richard Rorty's,[6] each practice recognizes the optionality of (some of) its fundamental conventions and acknowledges that other practices result from choosing different options. A literary critic, while advancing one reading of a text, may concede the legitimacy of other interpretations. A set theorist appreciates that different axioms yield separate systems of equal interest and importance. The pure procedural pluralist like Rorty maintains that the fundamental elements of a

---

[6] Rorty denies that what he does is philosophy. For he takes genuine philosophy to be a perfect procedural matter. So he contends that he has abandoned philosophy and taken up cultural criticism. I see no reason to limit the scope of philosophy so narrowly and hence no reason to doubt that Rorty is doing philosophy. See Catherine Z. Elgin, "Review: *Consequences of Pragmatism*," *Erkenntnis* 21 (1984): 423–431.

system of thought, being conventional, are to some degree arbitrary. That being so, it would be arrogant to dismiss systems grounded in other, equally arbitrary conventions. Let a hundred flowers bloom.

Pure procedural pluralism carries no threat of inconsistency. Disagreements between communities of inquiry are spurious, since each community is responsible only to the standards it sets for itself. Since, for example, Newtonian and relativistic physicists assign different meanings and referents to the word 'mass', the Newtonian contention that mass is constant does not contradict the relativistic contention that mass is variable. And since relativistic physicists set standards that apply only to relativistic physics, the failure of Newtonian findings to satisfy them no more discredits Newtonian physics than the failure of a non-Euclidian geometry to respect the parallel postulate discredits its theorems.[7] The verdicts of one community of inquiry cannot impugn those of another, for their conclusions are mutually irrelevant. There is no perspective from which the verdicts of distinct communities can be compared.

The virtues of a pure procedural construal of knowledge stem from its interpretation of inquiries as social practices. It recognizes that by our own lights—which are, after all, the only lights we've got—our inquiries sometimes succeed. And it counts such success as knowledge. Moreover, a pure procedural construal preserves and justifies disciplinary autonomy. Each community of inquiry sets its own cognitive standards and, by satisfying them, achieves its own brand of knowledge.

Skepticism is avoided. A community poses problems or puzzles that it can solve. And any solution that satisfies its criteria for knowledge constitutes knowledge for it. Since pure procedural philosophy recognizes nothing more fundamental than basic conventions, it acknowledges nothing beyond those conventions for solutions to answer to. Correspondence is not necessary. Once we satisfy community standards, there is nothing left to be skeptical about. Nor should we be skeptical about whether the relevant standards have been satisfied, for that is a question we know how to answer. To be cognitively acceptable, a conclusion must be certified by the appropriate intellectual community. What I think is acceptable may turn out otherwise. But the consensus of the community cannot be mistaken. Whatever the community takes to satisfy its standards ipso facto does so. Nor need we worry that the community might wrongly credit a thesis that fails to satisfy its standards. For the standards at issue are the ones the community actually uses; these need not be the ones it explicitly avows. Actions speak louder than words. If the conclusions a community acts on diverge from the ones it avows, we take the actions to reveal its

[7] Thomas Kuhn, *The Structure of Scientific Revolutions* (Chicago: University of Chicago Press, 1970), 101.

commitments and ignore the avowals. We look at what the members of a community do, not at what they say. So pure procedural knowledge is assured by the existence of communities that count some cognitive achievements as knowledge. And the limits of knowledge are the limits of what the communities count as knowledge. The conclusions of the community of inquiry are unimpeachable. For consensus is achieved; pure procedural knowledge requires nothing more.

APPROACH

The foregoing sketches are highly schematic. The next three chapters refine, extend, and emend them. The main purpose of this book is to develop and argue for a version of imperfect procedural epistemology. But the position I advocate sacrifices seemingly legitimate epistemic aspirations. So part of the argument for it involves showing that those aspirations cannot in any case be met. I begin therefore by examining perfect and pure procedural epistemological stances.

Positions with many advocates have many formulations. I could not, of course, take up each one. But I have tried to present as fair and powerful a construal of each stance as I could. The difficulties I uncover are, I believe, not defects peculiar to particular formulations but are endemic to the epistemological stances. They stem from shared commitments about epistemology's ends and means. If I am right, tinkering with the details will not remedy them. A more drastic revision of epistemology is called for.

Chapter II

THE FAILURE OF FOUNDATIONALISM

TO ERR is human; to do otherwise, inordinately difficult. We make mistakes even about seemingly sure things. And subjective assurance repeatedly blinds us to the untenability of our views. Is it possible to do better? In principle, the way is clear: we avoid error by sticking to what we know. The problem then is to ascertain what we know. Since the time of Descartes, the conviction that the point of having knowledge is to preclude error has structured the field of epistemology. When knowledge is seen in this light, the considerations favoring perfect procedural epistemology look powerful indeed.

Foundationalism is a perfect procedural stance. It sets its sights on an independent objective—truth—and adopts standards whose satisfaction assures that its goal has been reached. Any judgment that satisfies its standards is immune to error. In this chapter I review the case for epistemological foundationalism, seeking to identify its powers and limitations. The argument yields constraints that are unsatisfiable. But weakening them undermines the enterprise, for less stringent constraints do not insure against error. The exacting standards that traditional foundationalism sets are in fact required by its conception of knowledge. The theory is untenable, I suggest, not because its standards are too high but because its conceptual underpinnings are confused. Its formulation and justification require dualisms that have proven indefensible: analytic/synthetic, scheme/content, necessary/contingent. If, as I contend, foundationalism's fundamental defect is structural, successors that share that structure, such as reliabilism and causal theories of knowledge, fare no better. Perfect procedural epistemology cannot survive the demise of the dualisms.

REQUIREMENTS

Confidence, being so often misplaced, is a notoriously unreliable indicator of knowledge. A gambler's faith is unfounded even when his lottery ticket wins. For a fair lottery favors no ticket over the rest. He is more fortunate than his rivals but not more knowledgeable, since lucky guesses do not count as knowledge. Because the gambler has no right to his confidence, we contend that he does not know. To know something, it seems, is to be epistemically entitled to confidence about it.

Epistemic entitlement is desirable not only for its own sake but also because belief guides action: given our beliefs, we design our actions to achieve our ends. Actions based on false beliefs often go awry; those grounded in truths are more promising. It is then in our interest to act on the basis of true beliefs. To be sure, we cannot always tell true beliefs from false ones. So we often do not know where to place our trust. But when we are epistemically entitled to confidence in the relevant beliefs, we have a sound basis for action. Since we understand our situation, we are in a position to consider the genuine alternatives, weigh the real risks and rewards, and choose the best course. Even if success is not thereby guaranteed, our prospects plainly improve.

What makes for epistemic entitlement? We normally consider ourselves entitled to confidence in cogent beliefs. In view of the considerations that favor them, their truth is not accidental.[1] This suggests that justification is the source of epistemic entitlement. If so, we have a right to confidence in justified beliefs, but no right to confidence in unjustified ones.

To secure beliefs against error, justification must prevail over luck. For if the truth or falsity of a justified belief is left to chance, our epistemic situation is not markedly better than the gambler's. Despite its cogency, we have no right to confidence in such a belief. To override luck, justification must ensure that even in the worst of epistemic circumstances there is no danger of error. Knowledge is restricted to beliefs whose truth is not epistemically fortuitous.

Unwarranted claims confer no epistemic entitlement, having none to confer. Justified beliefs require the support of considerations that are themselves well-founded. This suggests that justification is serial, with later elements deriving their epistemic authority from earlier ones. But an infinite regress would be vicious. Unless some epistemic entitlement is underived, no belief is genuinely justified.[2] So the series of justifiers must be grounded.

Subjective probability and persuasiveness often strengthen confidence in a belief, but they confer no right to that confidence. A hunch supported by a bias backed by a prejudice is not a candidate for knowledge; a thesis supported by an argument backed by evidence is. Epistemic support must then be objective.

Support must also be epistemically accessible. When nothing in his ken enables an agent to tell whether his belief is tenable, he is hostage to epistemic fortune. Even if the belief is in fact warranted, he has no way to know it. So he has no right to be confident about that belief.

[1] Jonathan Adler, "Skepticism and Universalizability," *Journal of Philosophy* 78 (1981): 143–156.

[2] C. I. Lewis, "The Given Element in Empirical Knowledge," *Philosophical Review* 61 (1952): 168–175.

Moreover, the warrant for a belief can involve no considerations that are epistemically posterior to that belief. Otherwise the more tenuous could support the less. Judgments about other minds, for example, are typically thought to rest on judgments about physical objects. So the contention that John's knee hurts might be backed by the knowledge that he winces when he walks. But even if we know on other grounds that his knee hurts, that knowledge cannot be used to vindicate the claim that he winces when he walks. For to allow a statement about his mind to support a statement about his body is to reverse the order of justification. And to permit such reversals is to open the door to circular reasoning. Foundationalism need not, of course, accept the traditional order of epistemic priority. So it need not hold that knowledge of other minds is epistemically posterior to knowledge of physical objects. But to defuse the threat of circularity, it must acknowledge some justificatory hierarchy.

Nor can the support for a belief consist entirely of other beliefs of the same kind. For complete justification requires showing that the issue in contention is the sort of thing that can be known. On this matter, all instances of the kind are equally suspect. Because the purported deliverances of ESP are untenable, the support they afford each other is spurious. So if sentences about other minds are likewise untenable, they too are incapable of supporting one another. The justification for the belief that John's knee hurts cannot then consist entirely of claims like: he's afraid he's developing arthritis; he believes ice packs will help; he wonders whether to quit jogging. For it may reasonably be asked, are we justified in believing any of these? Appeals to beliefs about John's further mental states, like appeals to further deliverances of ESP, are inadequate to answer that question. A satisfactory reply must be epistemically less tendentious than talk of mental states. Foundationalism then takes knowledge to be structured as a hierarchy, with each level defining an epistemic kind. Justification for claims at a given level builds on warranted beliefs belonging to prior levels and supports those at subsequent ones. The architecture of knowledge thus precludes circular justification.

Not all warranted beliefs can derive their support from more fundamental beliefs, for the regress of reasons must end. Knowledge requires that there be a level of justification to which none is epistemically prior. Justified beliefs at this level constitute the foundation of knowledge. But what justifies these beliefs? Not epistemically prior beliefs; there are none. Nor can they support each other. If they did, justification would be, at bottom, circular. Rather, such beliefs must be intrinsically warranted. Each must be justified by the very fact that it obtains.

Foundationalist theories thus consist of a basis whose constituents are independently sanctioned and a superstructure whose constituents derive their sanction from the basis. Let us call elements of the basis foundational or basic; elements of the superstructure, lofty or elevated. The argument for such a view of knowledge contends that to transmit epistemic entitlement, chains of justification are required; to exclude luck, these chains must be accessible; to preclude circularity, they must have a unique, determinate direction; to undermine subjectivism, the order of justification must be objective; and to prevent an infinite regress, the chains must be grounded. Since the beliefs the chains are grounded in must be justified, and since they can acquire their epistemic authority from no other source, they must justify themselves. The justification they provide for themselves must, moreover, be sufficient to preclude error without relying on luck. Knowledge, on this picture, is a multistoried building. Unless the foundation is solid and the structural supports sound, the building will collapse.

BLUEPRINT

The aspirations of traditional foundationalist epistemology are worthy; its standards, exacting. It seeks to determine the scope and limits of knowledge, taking knowledge to be incompatible with error and independent of luck. It recognizes that this requires justification that is objective yet accessible, and neither infinite nor circular. The task it sets is hard; the rewards, great. In meeting its demands, we become masters of our epistemic fate. For once we ascertain what we are epistemically entitled to believe, we can achieve knowledge and avoid error. Knowledge is then incontrovertible. By satisfying foundationalist standards, a belief becomes permanently credible. No longer can it legitimately be called into question. Possessed of such knowledge, we need never look back, never reevaluate our reasons, never reconsider the epistemic standing of our justified beliefs.

How are the demands of foundationalism to be satisfied? To perform their epistemic function, the beliefs that constitute the foundation of knowledge must be presuppositionless. Being basic, they presuppose no knowledge or justified beliefs. Nor can they presuppose sentences that are not believed or sentences that are believed without justification. For such sentences might be false. False presuppositions discredit a belief. So if its presuppositions might be false, we are not entitled to full confidence in it.

Moreover, the contents of such beliefs must be logically and evidentially independent of one another. Otherwise the content of one could affect the epistemic status of another. If the belief that q enhances one's justification for p, then in the absence of the belief that q, one's justification for p is less than it might be. But when the belief that p is intrinsically justified, it follows from

S believes that p

that

S is wholly justified in believing that p.

Whether S also believes that q makes no difference. Logical atomism is then neither an idiosyncratic taste nor a simplifying assumption. It is a consequence of the requirement that basic claims fully justify themselves.

Basic beliefs do, of course, enhance or diminish the justification for lofty ones. But this cannot jeopardize their independence or epistemic authority. Since foundational beliefs are intrinsically justified, any conflict with lofty beliefs discredits the latter. The epistemic priority of the basis insures that intrinsically justified beliefs prevail over extrinsically justified ones.

A basic belief is one that is justified by the very fact that it is harbored. Few statements have this character. But certain self-ascriptions are held to fill the bill. If I have a sensation of pinkness, it is said, then if I believe I have it, I am justified in believing I have it—even if there is nothing pink nearby. Since my belief pertains exclusively to my current sensory experience, nothing beyond that experience is considered germane to the belief's justification.

Ordinarily, appearances are taken as evidence for reality. My sensation of pinkness is an indication that I actually see something pink. But appearances can be deceiving, so an isolated sensation counts for little. If, however, my sensations of pinkness display sufficient order and regularity, and if these sensations relate systematically to sensations of other shades, it is reasonable to suppose that I see something pink. But what makes it reasonable? Induction is surely part of the answer; but induction alone does not suffice. It warrants the prediction of future instances of a kind on the basis of past instances. Observed regularity among sensations sanctions expectations about future sensations. But enduring physical objects are not the same kind of thing as sensations. So, unless we define physical objects in terms of certain orders of sensations, observed regularity among those sensations does not by itself sanction inferences about sensible properties of physical objects. The orderly sequence of sensations could continue ad infinitum even if the world contained no physical objects. The difficulty, moreover, generalizes. For each level of the epistemic hierarchy admits entities of kinds not recognized at prior levels. Instantial induction does not bridge the gap between levels.

Although the existence of colored objects cannot be inferred from our color sensations, those sensations might provide grounds for a reasonable hypothesis. If colored objects exist, certain regularities among sensations are to be expected. So if we observe those regularities, we have reason to believe that colored objects exist. Novel objects, qualities, relations, and so on, are thus introduced hypothetically in such a way that evidence concerning them belongs to epistemically prior levels. If sufficient evidence is found, the hypothesis is confirmed. We are then justified in believing that the items in question are real.

What relates a hypothesis to a particular evidence class? Why think that looking pink is evidence of being pink rather than, say, of being cantankerous or bald or evenly divisible by thirteen? If the correlation is supposed to be empirical, the situation is hopeless. For evidence never demonstrates its own reliability. And we have no access to the colors of things apart from the appearances they present. So there is no standpoint from which to establish an empirical correlation between looking pink and being pink. We can, to be sure, adduce additional evidence and thereby show yet greater order and regularity among our color sensations. But this avails us nothing. For we cannot allay doubts about the reliability of evidence by supplying more of the same. We are left wondering how (indeed, whether) we know that looking pink is evidence for being pink. Still, it seems absurd to demand a reason for believing that pink things typically look pink and even more absurd to entertain doubts when no adequate reason is found.

This suggests that the problem has been misconstrued. If connections between statements at different levels of the epistemic hierarchy are necessary, the problem does not arise. For no empirical correlations are needed. Pinkness is then that property of physical objects which *of necessity* typically occasions sensations of pink. How does this move help? Isn't a necessary connection even harder to demonstrate than a contingent one? Not if the necessity in question is conceptual. Then it follows from the very concept of a pink thing that pink things ordinarily look pink. Knowing this requires nothing more than knowing what 'pink' means.

The solution looks failsafe. If you know what 'pink' means, you thereby know that pink things ordinarily look pink. If you do not know what 'pink' means, you have neither true nor false beliefs about the way pink things look. If you apply 'pink' to things that do not ordinarily look pink, you attach a deviant meaning to the word. You then have a different concept—one that establishes its own connections between levels of the hierarchy. Still, you are not mistaken. Your beliefs about the appearances a pink thing presents are different from mine, but no less correct, for you mean something different by 'pink'. Given the concept you employ, your beliefs on the matter are necessarily correct.

But surely, one might object, 'looks pink' cannot be part of the definition of 'pink', for 'looks pink' contains the term to be defined. This objection rests on a misunderstanding. 'Pink things look pink' is not circular, for the two occurrences of 'pink' have different meanings.[3] As a predicate of appearances, 'pink' designates a transient, subjective, immediately evident sensory property. An observer can tell at a glance whether something looks pink. As a predicate of physical objects, however, 'pink' designates an enduring, intersubjectively observable, sensible property—one that presents different appearances in different conditions, one whose presence cannot be settled by a glance. Not all pink things look pink; not all things that look pink are pink. Predicating 'pink' of a physical object involves conceptual commitments about how the thing looks and about how it would look under different circumstances, about how it looks and how it would look to different observers. We make no such commitments when we predicate 'pink' of appearances. Nothing follows about the way a thing looks to others from its now looking pink to me; nothing follows about the way it will look to me in the future or would look to me in different circumstances.

Conceptual commitments are often more complex and varied than my example suggests. The claim that a panel is oak, for example, carries implications about the appearances it actually presents and about those it would present were circumstances different—not only how it would appear from different perspectives and in different lights but also how it would appear if it were sawed, stained, kicked, or burned. A collection of seemingly diverse sensory beliefs is thus unified by a hypothesis about the material the panel is made of. The same thing happens at higher levels: the meanings of the terms at each stage structure a logical space; they define conditions on membership in, and on inclusion and exclusion among, the kinds recognized at that stage. And they identify the epistemically prior sentences that provide evidence that the conditions are satisfied. So the meaning of the sentence 'Hannah is prey to existential angst' consists in part of the collection of claims about physical objects and events (mainly, I suppose, Hannah's body, behavior, and environment) that constitute evidence for it. The meanings of these in turn involve claims about the appearances such physical objects and events do and would present.

Claims at different epistemic levels are connected deductively and inductively. If a lofty hypothesis H is true, then (given what H means) epistemically prior statements $C_1, \ldots, C_n$ are likewise true. For $C_1, \ldots, C_n$ are deductive consequences of H. We know this simply by knowing what H means. So if $C_1, \ldots, C_n$ are all justified, H is justified as well. Moreover,

[3] Wilfrid Sellars, "Phenomenalism," in *Science, Perception, and Reality* (London: Routledge and Kegan Paul, 1963), 92–95.

each member of the series $C_1, \ldots, C_n$ affords inductive support for H. When nothing is known about the epistemic status of $C_2, \ldots, C_n$, then if C_1 is justified, we have evidence for and hence some reason to believe H. Given the meanings of our terms, deductive arguments determine what is required for justification; inductive arguments supply evidence that the requirements are, or that they are not, met.

The blueprint of knowledge sets no limit on the height of the structure. We can always erect additional stories by introducing terms for epistemically novel individuals and kinds, fixing their meanings so that hypotheses about them are inductively and deductively connected to statements about things we already know. We can then speculate about such things as quasars, quarks, and quirks—and, in principle, discover whether our speculations are warranted.

Still, some matters are beyond the scope of knowledge. Perfect procedural epistemology requires that it be determinate precisely what and how much evidence would immunize against error. It excludes metaphors then because their meanings cannot be fully articulated. The inexhaustibility and suggestiveness, which might seem to constitute a metaphor's epistemic strength, are instead its fatal weakness. For they make it impossible fully to delineate the range of relevant evidence.

Ethics and other evaluative disciplines are exiled as well. The foundation of knowledge is restricted to descriptions of experience; the superstructure to inductive and hypothetico-deductive consequences of those descriptions. But normative conclusions follow neither inductively nor deductively from descriptive premises; nor descriptive conclusions from normative premises. The hierarchy has no room for evaluative knowledge. Since ethical judgments are evaluative, it follows that they yield no knowledge. We are never epistemically entitled to confidence in our ethical convictions.

Mathematics also raises difficulties. For the truths of mathematics are held to be necessary; its entities, abstract; its justification, a matter of proof. But inductive inferences are critical to foundationalist justification. They supply evidence, not proof. That evidence, moreover, indicates that a sentence is true, not that it is necessarily true. One might argue that mathematical truths are analytic. Then their necessity is conceptual, and proof is a matter of exhibiting relations among meanings. If so, mathematical knowledge consists in nothing more than knowing the meanings of mathematical terms. Even if we bracket Quinean qualms about analyticity, this will not do. Ascertaining whether the Goldbach conjecture is true plainly involves more than knowing what it means. For we all understand the claim that every even number is the sum of two primes, but no one knows whether it is true. Mathematics is no mere matter of spelling out meanings; it is an ampliative cognitive enterprise.[4] We might secure knowledge of mathematics by denying that its truths are necessary. Then perhaps we could incorporate its claims into the superstructure. Or we might maintain that we possess a faculty of intellectual intuition that enables us to experience mathematical reality directly.[5] In that case the basis is broader than we originally supposed. Alternatively, we might accept the foundationalist picture as sketched, hold fast to our mathematical intuitions, and concede that mathematics does not yield knowledge. Desperate situations call for desperate measures; it is not at all clear what form an adequate philosophy of mathematics should take. What is clear is that the foundationalist picture of knowledge is hard to square with widely shared, intuitively plausible views about the nature of mathematics.[6]

Emotions raise problems of a different sort. Experience plainly has an affective aspect. So expressions of and beliefs about emotions may belong to the basis. But such expressions are considered epistemically inert, and the beliefs they give rise to have little influence on the upper reaches of the epistemic hierarchy. Being volatile, emotions are considered incapable of providing reliable indications of objective states of affairs. Although atrocities frequently occasion revulsion, all too often they do not. If 'atrocity' were conceptually related to revulsion, then lack of revulsion would be evidence that the term does not apply. But the absence of revulsion can indicate instead that witnesses are callous, vengeful, ignorant, or exhausted. To incorporate occasioning revulsion into the meaning of 'atrocity' would therefore be unwise. But foundationalism finds—or forces—such an intimate relation between meaning and evidence that denying that expressions of emotion are part of the meaning of a sentence amounts to denying that they are evidence for it. The awareness that an action occasions revulsion then does nothing to warrant the belief that it is an atrocity.

Excluding issues from epistemology does not make them disappear. Problems about mathematics, metaphor, evaluation, and emotion remain. But, arguably, the strength of the theory of knowledge that results from ignoring such problems is reason to think that their solutions lie elsewhere. The cost of narrowing the scope of epistemology may be worth the benefits that accrue when foundationalist standards are met. Still, the costs are nonnegligible and should be acknowledged as such.

[4] Immanuel Kant, *Critique of Pure Reason* (New York: Saint Martin's, 1965), B 15–B 16.

[5] Kurt Gödel, "What is Cantor's Continuum Problem?" in *Philosophy of Mathematics*, ed. P. Benacerraf and H. Putnam (Cambridge: Cambridge University Press, 1983), 483–484.

[6] See Paul Benacerraf, "Mathematical Truth," in Benacerraf and Putnam, *Philosophy of Mathematics*, 403–420.

STRICT STRICTURES

Considered abstractly, foundationalism promises to generate a powerful, well-motivated theory of knowledge. To decide whether the theory lives up to its promise, we need to examine its pressure points. The identification and characterization of basic beliefs, the strength of inductive support that evidence supplies, and the conceptual necessity that connects claims at different levels—all are potentially problematic.

Most beliefs are not basic. Beliefs about other minds, physical objects, even one's own prior mental states are logically and evidentially intertwined, often unjustified, sometimes false. Plainly they do not justify themselves. But some beliefs about one's own current mental states have long been considered basic. If I think I am in pain, then ipso facto I am in pain, and am thereby justified in thinking I am in pain. If I think I have a sensation of pinkness, then I have such a sensation and am justified in thinking I have it. Since there is no difference between seeming to be in such a mental state and actually being in it, such beliefs appear to justify themselves.

Manifestly, not every true description of my current mental state yields a basic belief. Although I believe that I now feel the way Wanda felt when her guppy died, this belief cannot be foundational. For its truth depends on facts about Wanda and her fish; its justification, on access to those facts. If I am wrong about Wanda's reaction or the guppy's demise, my characterization of my own mental state is neither true nor justified. So this way of characterizing my feeling cannot be the content of a statement of basic belief. Still, I feel what I feel, whether or not I am right to identify my feeling with Wanda's. According to traditional foundationalism, I can factor out unwanted commitments and get at the feeling itself. What remains is the content of an epistemically basic belief.

By refining the characterization of occurrent mental states, reference to physical objects, other minds, and prior mental states can easily be eliminated. 'I feel what it seems Wanda felt when it appeared that her guppy died' and 'I seem to see a pink elephant' involve reference to nothing outside the speaker. Judicious use of 'seems' and 'appears' enable us to withhold ontological commitment. If this is all it takes, then suitably hedging its content transforms any self-ascription into a basic one. Unfortunately things are not so simple. For seems-statements logically and evidentially intertwine. They lack the mutual indifference that basic beliefs require. 'I seem to see a pink elephant' is not justified unless 'I seem to see an elephant' is.

To arrive at the contents of foundational beliefs, logical and evidential connections must be severed. What remains, it is argued, is the immediately felt quality of experience. Being the way experience presents itself, and being prior to all categorization, this quality is independent of linguistic convention, background knowledge, past or future experience. At this level, there is no more than meets the eye (or the ear, or the heart). The character an experience seems to have is the one it actually has. So my belief that my experience has a certain basic quality is completely justified by the experience itself. There is no room for error and no need for luck. Experience, belief, and justification are simultaneously given; they constitute the foundation on which the edifice of knowledge rests. How are such contents to be described?

Foundationalists are not always explicit about the semantic commitments underlying their position. They tend, moreover, to differ over matters of terminology. But this much is generally agreed: meaning is normally a function of natural and conventional factors, and at the basis the conventional component drops out. Early foundationalists framed the issue in terms of a distinction between relations of ideas and matters of fact. With philosophy's linguistic turn, the point was recast in terms of a distinction between analytic and synthetic sentences. C. I. Lewis recognizes, more clearly than most, what this view of language involves. In his account, lines are drawn in terms of a distinction between linguistic meaning and sense meaning. A word's linguistic meaning consists in the network of definitional relationships that settle its location in a linguistic scheme; its sense meaning consists in the sense presentable characteristics that determine its applicability or inapplicability to matters of fact.[7] Linguistic meaning then connects a word with other words; sense meaning connects it, via sensation, with the world. Linguistic meanings are conventional; sense meanings, natural. The network of linguistic meanings is a syntactical scheme. Sense meanings infuse that scheme with experiential content. Together the two modes of meaning effect an organization that enables language to express epistemically accessible empirical truths.

Definitions capture conventions, but sensory contents are inexpressible. For any attempt to say what a word means results in an expression of linguistic meaning.[8] Still, explication is not irrelevant to the discovery of content. Like maps, linguistic cues guide our search. They indicate where to look for sense meanings but cannot convey the content we will find. Teaching the sense meaning of 'puce' might involve imparting the information that puce is a shade of purple, that it has a slightly grayish tinge, that it is the color of an overripe plum. Such information cannot communicate the sense meaning to someone who has never seen the color. But it can isolate a particular perceptual quality, enabling the educated perceiver

[7] C. I. Lewis, *An Analysis of Knowledge and Valuation* (LaSalle, Ill.: Open Court, 1971), 130–168.
[8] Ibid., 140.

to identify that quality as puce. By providing a framework for differentiating among contents, conventions structure the perceptual field. They prepare us to recognize a particular experience as the sense meaning it is. Conventions frame contents.

At higher levels of the epistemic hierarchy, convention predominates; at lower levels, content. Understanding a word like 'plutonium' or 'prevarication' is mostly a matter of knowing its location in a linguistic network. Understanding a word like 'poignant' or 'puce' is more a matter of recognizing the perceptual conditions under which it applies. Still, ordinary statements about appearances, even those that seem most closely tied to sensory stimulation, conceptually intertwine. The conventions concerning predicates of apparent color, for example, mandate that whatever looks puce does not simultaneously look yellow. The basic vocabulary is different: ties of linguistic meaning do not connect its terms. The application of one basic term neither requires nor precludes the applicability of any other. It follows that basic claims are semantically independent: the truth or falsity of one is indifferent to the truth or falsity of any other. Ordinary statements about appearances then cannot be basic claims.

Both convention and content figure in the justification of most empirical claims. At the basis, only content is involved. Being semantically independent of one another, basic statements are cotenable. They neither gain nor lose support from analytic connections to one another. A basic statement is justified if and only if the qualities that constitute its sense meaning are in fact presented to the senses. So a basic belief is couched in the terms in which experience presents itself. It reflects without distortion what is given in experience.

Basic qualities are hard to characterize, for our ordinary terms do not apply. The terms of ordinary language belong to families of alternatives—families that collectively sort the items in a domain. Since the linguistic meanings of family members intertwine, the application of one member of such a family carries commitments concerning the applicability of others. But at the basis no such relations obtain. If the terms we ordinarily use belong to families, those that denote basic qualities are orphans. For any basic qualities p and q, if it basically seems that p, nothing follows about whether it basically seems that q. The basic elements of knowledge are logical atoms. Perhaps we come closest to describing the basic qualities that constitute experience by employing our ordinary sensory and affective terms in suitably restricted seems-statements. We stipulate that in such statements family ties are broken. That an afterimage basically seems pink does not entail that it basically seems nonblue. Being orphans, the terms in our basic vocabulary have to fend for themselves.

This is not the way 'seems' normally operates. Seems-statements typically respect family ties. 'Seems pink' precludes 'seems blue' just as 'is pink' precludes 'is blue'. The usual function of 'seems' is to indicate or advocate a withholding of confidence. 'The swatch seems blue' suggests that, despite the reasons for thinking it blue, circumstances are not propitious for judging its actual color. Ordinary seems-statements are thus not vehicles for abstracting from linguistic meaning; so they are not vehicles for revealing the elements of the basis.

We can, of course, stipulate what we like. So we can introduce a 'basically seems' operator to factor out linguistic meaning and transform an ordinary sensory predicate into a basic one. Then, from the applicability of 'basically seems crimson', we cannot infer the applicability of 'basically seems red' or the inapplicability of 'basically seems blue'. Being matters of convention, the connections that normally license such inferences do not obtain at the basic level.

The absence of connections between linguistic meanings renders the basis inscrutable. There is no framework within which to discriminate the meanings or referents of basic terms. Experience might be thought to determine the structure of the basis. But this suggestion proves either false or useless. For experience *as we conceive it* is informed by linguistic meanings. We do not count something as an experience of crimson if we do not consider it an experience of red or if we are prepared simultaneously to consider it an experience of blue. Without the sort of organization that linguistic meanings supply, we lack the resources to recognize and classify our own experiences. The use of familiar sensory vocabulary in basically-seems-statements occasions a feeling of fluency. But that feeling is illusory. The terms are so far removed from the contexts in which they normally operate that their ordinary usage provides no guidance. By wrenching our terms from their natural habitats, the basically-seems operator deprives them of the conditions of their comprehensibility. Rather than connecting the basis with the superstructure, it simply introduces ambiguities. 'Basically seems crimson' is no more intimately related to 'crimson' than it is to 'carburetor' or 'cucumber' or any other term in the language.

Basic terms then derive no intelligibility from their connection with ordinary language. This, for foundationalists like C. I. Lewis, is as it should be. For the basis is supposed to confer intelligibility on, not inherit it from, the superstructure. The problem of the intelligibility of the basis remains. Being infused with linguistic meaning, our conceptions of experience are not basic. And any reconception suffers the same fate. For a reconception simply orders things in terms of different categories— categories infused with different but equally conventional, linguistic meanings. Lewis concedes this but maintains that behind experience as conceptualized lies experience itself. It is experience itself, prior to any conceptualization, that determines the constitution of the basis.

Exactly what experience determines is not clear. We saw that sense meanings are ordinarily located by triangulation. The network of conventions that govern 'puce' isolates a particular sense-presentable characteristic as the content of 'puce'. Plainly the conventions involved must be conceptually related to 'puce'. Since odor is not kin to color, the vocabulary of odor is useless for isolating the contents of color predicates. But the terms belonging to the basic vocabulary are semantically autonomous. Each is as indifferent to the others as 'pungent' is to 'puce'. We cannot triangulate: no network of linguistic meanings isolates the sense meaning of a basic term. Without such a network, we lack the resources to discriminate between experiences. So we cannot individuate the sense meanings of basic terms. It might seem that we do not need to. If sense meanings are determined by the sense-presentable characteristics of the things we experience, experiences that are indiscriminable instantiate basic terms with the same sense meaning. Unfortunately things are not so simple. For the problem of imperfect community looms.[9] Even if experience a is indiscriminable from experience b, and experience b is indiscriminable from experience c, experience a may be discriminable from experience c. Unless we supply criteria specifying where to draw the lines, there will be chains of indiscriminability linking wildly disparate experiences. But any criteria we supply are conceptualized, hence infused with linguistic meaning. The foundation of knowledge is ineffable. For unless linguistic meanings frame them, sense meanings are not just inexpressible, they are inconceivable. We cannot formulate determinate conceptions of them. A commitment to their existence is a commitment to something we know not what. The epistemic level that is supposed to provide direct access to reality is itself epistemically inaccessible.

Basic beliefs are held to justify themselves. Loftier beliefs require support. The epistemic hierarchy is so designed that every elevated synthetic sentence H entails the epistemically prior claims, $C_p, \ldots, C_n$, that contribute to its confirmation. We verify H by substantiating $C_p, \ldots, C_n$. Substantiation of any one of them counts for little; for evidence often misleads. But collectively $C_p, \ldots, C_n$ are supposed to be powerful enough to warrant the belief that H. The belief that Samson is a silverback needs the support of a host of claims about the appearances the gorilla presents. If that support is forthcoming, the belief is vindicated; if not, it is discredited.

Verification is interminable. For the class of epistemically prior claims that bear on H is inexhaustible.[10] To verify 'Samson is a silverback' requires ascertaining how he looks from a variety of vantage points, to a

[9] Nelson Goodman, *The Structure of Appearance* (Dordrecht: Reidel, 1977), 117–119.
[10] C. I. Lewis, *Knowledge and Valuation*, 180 ff.

variety of viewers, under a variety of circumstances. And it requires determining how his pelt fares under a variety of tests. The evidence class may
indeed be infinite: every observer is entitled to his say; every perspective is
worthy of consideration; any alteration in lighting or atmosphere might
affect our verdict or our confidence in it; new tests can call previously
accepted results into doubt. If the class of relevant considerations is not
actually infinite, it is surely enormous.

Ordinarily, of course, we settle a few central matters and draw a conclusion. But if our goal is to preclude error without relying on luck, we
cannot afford to be so cavalier. The remotest possibility of undermining
evidence discredits our claim to epistemic entitlement. So long as relevant
evidence is unexamined, that possibility is real. Inevitably, when we want
a verdict, the jury is still out.

Skepticism results. We know no basic truths, for the basis is ineffable. We
know no lofty truths, for sentences in the superstructure are never conclusively established. We cannot preclude error without relying on luck.

Strict foundationalists like C. I. Lewis set their sights on a worthy target, being well aware of what is required to reach it. Although they deploy
the most powerful weapons in their epistemic arsenal, the target remains
out of range. They fail to achieve knowledge. But their defeat is an honorable one.

LOWER STANDARDS

Skepticism is a daunting prospect, rarely embraced with equanimity.
Without rejecting it dogmatically, we should perhaps see whether relaxing
the requirements on knowledge enables us to elude it. Let us consider
then a more lenient form of foundationalism. This view accepts the broad
outlines of the foundationalist picture: knowledge consists of basic beliefs,
which require no further justification, and lofty beliefs, which are justified
by more basic ones. But the criteria on justification are relaxed so
that basic beliefs prove epistemically accessible, and lofty ones verifiable.[11]
Lenient foundationalists thus contend that the untoward skeptical result
is due to the excessive stringency of strict foundationalist criteria of justification. Once more reasonable criteria are invoked, they maintain, the
difficulties disappear.

The ineffability of the basis stems from the mutual indifference of basic
terms. Being semantically unrelated, basic linguistic meanings do not
form a network within which sense meanings can be individuated. This

---

[11] This is the sort of foundationalism Roderick Chisholm advances. See "A Version of
Foundationalism," in *The Foundations of Knowing* (Minneapolis: University of Minnesota
Press, 1982), 3–32.

suggests that we can gain access to the basis simply by acknowledging family ties. Then some ordinary seems-statements can function as basic claims. Once we abandon the autonomy condition, 'I seem to see a purple patch' has all the earmarks of a basic sentence.

But the autonomy condition is no idle whim of strict foundationalism. If we allow family relations, we must expect family feuds. Suppose

(a) at t_1 F seems red to me.

But an instant later

(b) at t_2 F seems black to me

although

(c) during the interval between t_1 and t_2, F's color does not seem to change.[12]

Such might be the experience of seeing a cardinal flit from shade into sunlight on a cloudless day. Statements (a), (b), and (c) are not cotenable. For any two discredit the third. So I am not justified in believing that F seems red to me unless I ascertain that I have no conflicting belief with a greater or equal claim to epistemic entitlement. But if the interval between t_1 and t_2 is short enough to be comprehended in a single experience, (a), (b), and (c) all count as basic. The mere fact that they are believed then does not justify such sentences. For as lenient foundationalists construe them, basic beliefs can clash.

One might object that such problematic sequences of experiences do not actually occur. This is probably false. But even if true, it is irrelevant. If the absence of such sequences is a brute fact, it is epistemically inert. Unless we know that fact, basic beliefs must be considered potential competitors. So considerations beyond the experience itself are relevant to the justification of my belief that F seems red to me. If the problematic sequences are known not to occur, their absence is epistemically significant. But what is the status of such knowledge? Since it is supposed to vindicate our confidence in perceptual beliefs, it cannot be an inductive consequence of them. Moreover, if the knowledge underwrites my belief that (a), then (a) is not basic. It is supported by a generalization whose own source of support is difficult to discern. Retreating to a more fundamental level is futile. If the statements at that level are autonomous, they are inaccessible; if they are interconnected, the prospect of conflict recurs.

Can we dispel the difficulty by saying that the knowledge in question is not a matter of fact but of linguistic fiat? In that case, it follows from the

[12] Nelson Goodman, "Sense and Certainty," in *Problems and Projects* (Indianapolis: Hackett, 1972), 60.

meanings of the terms involved that sequences like ⟨(a), (b), (c)⟩ cannot occur. And by knowing the meanings of those terms, we know that the sequence is impossible. Statement (a) retains its status as a basic sentence, for no more fundamental factual judgment underlies it. But the matter simply is not open to legislation. We cannot stipulate the order in which appearances occur; we can only stipulate what they are to be called. Meanings are powerless to preclude untoward sequences of experiences.

The discovery that basic beliefs can conflict discredits their claim to be self-justifying. So the question of their justification recurs. It admits of three answers, none of them palatable.

1. Basic beliefs justify one another. Then, justification is at bottom circular. p is justified only if q is; q, only if r; r, only if . . . p. Our basic beliefs stand or fall together. But we have no way to tell whether they stand or fall.

2. Basic beliefs are justified by yet more fundamental beliefs. If so, an infinite regress results. Justification is always conditional. p is justified only if q is; q, only if r; r, only if . . . Since the series is infinite, the conditional cannot be discharged. So it is impossible to ascertain whether a belief is actually justified.

3. Basic beliefs lack adequate justification. We cannot avoid error without relying on luck.

Self-justification initially seems a small price to pay for epistemic access to the basis. But the loss is irrecoverable. Unless some beliefs justify themselves, no belief is entirely justified. For none of the alternatives yields a satisfactory substitute. Our most credible convictions are vulnerable to epistemic misfortune; despite their justification, they might be false. Since lofty beliefs obtain their warrant from basic ones, the superstructure inherits the epistemic vulnerability of the basis. The lenient foundationalist's knowledge is built on sand.

The lenient foundationalist moderates the criteria on verification of lofty claims as well. Although the testable consequences of a lofty sentence are inexhaustible, he contends that limited testing supplies sufficient warrant. He thus urges that we abandon the quixotic quest for certainty and recognize that knowledge demands no more than demonstrable probability. All that remains is to determine what measure of probability knowledge requires.

Easier said than done. In deciding the matter, a principle of epistemic equality constrains us: like cases should be treated alike. If probability is the determinant of epistemic entitlement, then equiprobable beliefs merit equal credence; more probable beliefs merit greater credence than less probable ones. False beliefs are not knowledge. So the level of probability required for knowledge must be higher than the level achieved by warranted false beliefs. Nor can the principle of epistemic equality be gainsaid. For if equally warranted beliefs differ in epistemic entitlement, knowledge is inseparable from luck.[13]

Such high probability is not easily achieved. If the class of H's testable consequences is infinite, the probability of H on any finite body of evidence is 0. So increasing our evidence by any finite amount does not increase the probability that H is true. And we cannot hope to generate an infinite amount of evidence. Even if the class is finite, it is sufficiently large that the support provided by any feasible number of tests is negligible, and so incapable of demonstrating that H is highly probable. Nor are the difficulties only practical. Since the size of the class of H's testable consequences is indeterminate, if finite, we have no basis for accurately assigning probabilities. We thus have no way to determine the weight of evidence that any test result supplies. And since the testable consequences of H extend indefinitely into the future, at no time can we be confident that enough evidence is in. Moreover, the testable consequences of H include counterfactuals—sentences about observations that could have been made and tests that could have been run. The truth values of such sentences are not settled by their status as contrary to fact. But observations that are not made afford no evidence. A sentence's counterfactual entailments are perennially outstanding debts against its claim to epistemic entitlement.

Demonstrable probability is as elusive as certainty. For the process of demonstrating that a lofty thesis is probable, like the process of demonstrating that it is true, is interminable. Nor do all the difficulties stem from technicalities of probability theory. Replacing 'probable' with a less regimented notion like 'supported', 'warranted', or 'evident' avails us nothing. Lenient foundationalism requires a small proportion of the evidence class to so strongly support a conclusion that no further evidence could discredit it. But the demand is unsatisfiable. To discredit a claim, evidence need not convince us that the claim is false; it need only cast doubt on its truth. Weak evidence can do that. If unfavorable findings diminish our justification, they discredit a claim. We might, of course, refuse to be moved by such findings. But to remain steadfast here is a sign of stubbornness, not of epistemic entitlement.

Unfavorable evidence cannot just be ignored. So we do not know that p unless we know that further findings will not discredit p. This is no problem for the strict foundationalist. For he maintains that we do not know that p until all the evidence is in. But the lenient foundationalist contends that limited evidence suffices. If so, that evidence entitles us to confidence that our predictions about p's consequences will be borne

---

[13] Adler, "Skepticism and Universalizability."

out. But surely our history of predictive failures overrides any pretensions to prescience. The evidence in favor of p may lead us to expect additional confirmation; it may even make us confident about doing so. But we are not epistemically entitled to such confidence; for that would require knowing what the future holds. The lenient foundationalist is in no position to know that future findings will not discredit p. So he does not know that p.

Lenient foundationalist alternatives—probability, warrant, support, and the like—are not satisfactory substitutes for certainty. A belief is epistemically vulnerable if any of its testable implications remains untested. Even if the evidence is so compelling that nothing could convince us of the falsity of a belief, unfavorable findings can and should undermine our confidence in its truth. When a belief is merely probable, we are hostage to epistemic fortune: if we are lucky, further findings will confirm it; if not, they will disconfirm it. But perfect procedural knowledge is indifferent to luck. So despite the evidence in its favor, such a belief is not knowledge.

Lenient foundationalism seeks to evade skepticism by weakening the justification requirement. But standards low enough to be satisfied at all turn out to be satisfied by falsehoods as well as truths. And justified false beliefs do not count as knowledge. Strict foundationalist standards would, if satisfied, suffice for knowledge. But they cannot be satisfied. Lenient foundationalism can perhaps set satisfiable epistemic standards. But they do not suffice for knowledge. Either way, we are forced to a skeptical conclusion. Available evidence is inevitably too weak to entitle us to full confidence in our beliefs.

This leads some theorists to treat the argument as a reductio ad absurdum. They contend that since we know knowledge is possible, skepticism must be absurd; it follows that any argument that leads to skepticism is flawed. But their premise is unacceptable. Although we might think—or hope—that knowledge is possible, it would be question begging to assume in advance of inquiry that we know such a thing. Epistemology asks: What can we know? One available answer is: Nothing. This answer, though disappointing and perhaps surprising, is in no way absurd.[14] If foundationalism's premises are sound, its argument rigorous, and its standards appropriate, we have no legitimate grounds for rejecting its conclusion. In that case our antecedent conviction that knowledge is possible marks an overestimation of our epistemic powers and an underestimation of the difficulty of achieving our goal. From the fact that it leads to skepticism, we cannot conclude that foundationalism is untenable. Skepticism may be true.

---

[14] It is, of course, absurd to contend that we know that we can know nothing. But a judicious skeptic makes no such claim.

MEANING

One final feature of foundationalism remains to be considered: the necessity that links levels of the epistemic hierarchy. It is here, I contend, that the insuperable difficulties lie.

We saw earlier that a lofty hypothesis H is doubly connected to the epistemically prior claims $C_p, \ldots, C_n$ that support it. H follows inductively from $C_p, \ldots, C_n$; $C_p, \ldots, C_n$ follow deductively from H. But not from H alone. For H is no mere generalization from the evidence. Being on different levels of the epistemic hierarchy, hypothesis and evidence are expressed in different vocabularies and are ontologically committed to things of different kinds. Hypotheses about objective, enduring, sensible objects are held to entail statements about subjective, transient, sensory states.

Logic alone does not suffice for such entailments. The strictly logical consequences of a truth are those that remain true under any reinterpretation of its nonlogical particles. The strictly logical consequences of

(H) Some roses are white

then remain true when 'roses' is reinterpreted as 'numbers' and 'white' is reinterpreted as 'prime'. Clearly nothing about how things look follows from

(I) Some numbers are prime.

The necessity that links levels of the epistemic hierarchy is thus not logical necessity. The connection between hypothesis and evidence is a connection between sentences under an interpretation.

What sort of interpretation is at issue? An extensional interpretation connects words with their referents, specifying that 'rose' denotes roses, that 'white' denotes white things, and that 'some roses are white' is true just in case some members of the class of roses are members of the class of white things. Although quite definite about matters of reference and truth, such an interpretation neither says nor entails anything about evidence. It sanctions no inference about the apparent color of any rose, hence none about the range of sensory presentations that are relevant to the confirmation of our hypothesis. Manifestly, an extensional interpretation is too weak to serve.

The solution, it is urged, is to augment extensional interpretations with considerations of meaning. Then the necessary connection between hypothesis and evidence is secure. For it is held to follow from the meaning of 'white' that white things normally look white. So it follows from the meanings of the terms involved that the sincere assertion under seemingly normal circumstances of 'That looks to be a white rose' is and is known to be evidence for H.

Since the necessity that links the levels of the epistemic hierarchy is linguistic (or conceptual), it comes at no extra epistemic cost. We need no argument for 'White things normally look white', for its truth is a direct and immediate consequence of the meanings of the terms involved. Indeed, it makes no sense to ask how we know that looking white is evidence for being white. If we do not know that, we do not know what 'white' means; if we do not know what 'white' means, we cannot intelligibly raise the question.

The power of the resulting position is plain. The meaning of a lofty hypothesis determines exactly which epistemically prior claims are evidentially relevant to it. Although verification may be difficult or even impossible, identification of verification conditions is straightforward. We have no problem recognizing what it would take to know that some roses are white. Moreover, if skepticism can somehow be defused, such an account allows for the incremental growth of knowledge. The meanings of terms at a given level constitute a scheme that organizes epistemically prior claims into discrete evidence classes. Nothing more is necessary for knowledge that p than that the members of p's evidence class be verified. By rendering evidence selectively relevant, foundationalism thus allows for the possibility of knowing something without knowing everything.

This picture relies on a sharp distinction between scheme and content. At each lofty level, linguistic meanings constitute a network that organizes data into evidence classes. A term's place in such a network determines its linguistic meaning; the epistemically prior claims that bear on its instantiation determine its content. The full meaning of a term is its content as schematized by its linguistic meaning. The structure is ideally suited to hypothetico-deductive reasoning. Since linguistic meanings are conventional, we are relatively free in the formulation of hypotheses, for conventions are easily contrived. But hypotheses are no mere figments of the imagination; their content derives from prior levels of the epistemic hierarchy and, ultimately, from the basis of knowledge in experience. Without that tie to experience, a convention would be contentless—an empty syntactical shell.

Typically, the content of a hypothesis is itself schematized. The content of a sentence about real color, for example, consists of a host of epistemically prior claims pertaining to apparent color. These too are combinations of scheme and content: the scheme being the network of linguistic meanings of appearance-terms; the content supplied by yet more fundamental sentences. The content of a sentence belonging to level L then ordinarily consists of material as schematized by the categories of L-1;

the content of that, of material as schematized by the categories of *L-2*; and so on. But since the epistemic hierarchy is grounded, it has a first lofty level. The data schematized at that level are pure content, consisting of what is given in experience, independent of and prior to all conceptualization. The schemes of conventions that structure successive levels thus impose ever more complex modes of organization on the data that experience supplies.

Language is taken to depend on experience and convention. This seems reasonable enough. For were our conventions different or our experiences different, we would say different things. But foundationalism requires more: the two components must be discriminable. Unless we can differentiate between the conventional and experiential contributions to meaning, neither the location of a sentence in the epistemic hierarchy nor its relation to a specific evidence class is determinate.

Proportions vary. Some sentences owe more to convention; others, more to content. At the limit we find sentences whose meaning derives entirely from convention and sentences whose meaning derives entirely from content. The former are analytic; their truth is assured by linguistic meaning alone. They are, moreover, a priori; one need only understand them to know they are true. And they are necessary; given the meanings of the terms involved, the sentences could not be false. Both the truth of analytic sentences and the knowledge of their truth is thus independent of experience. The latter are basic; their truth is assured by the experiences they report. They are a posteriori; one needs specific experiences to know they are true. And they are contingent; had those experiences not occurred, they would not have been true. Such sentences are independent of convention. Their truth and justification are unaffected by conventional differences.

Synthetic sentences, the bearers of empirical knowledge, are the resultants of conventional and experiential vectors. Linguistic meanings determine what it takes for such a sentence to be true; sense meanings determine how those requirements can be satisfied. A priori knowledge is needed to understand such a sentence; a posteriori knowledge is needed to ascertain its truth value. Of necessity, if such a sentence is known to be true, its justification conditions are satisfied. But whether those conditions are satisfied, hence whether its truth is known, is a contingent matter. When experience complies with the mandates of linguistic meaning, empirical knowledge results. In such knowledge, the necessary and the contingent, the a priori and the a posteriori, the conventional and the experiential intertwine.

The difficulty is that convention cannot be segregated from content. Conventions are held to be articulated by analytic sentences, contents conveyed by synthetic sentences. But no clear distinction between the analytic and the synthetic has been drawn.[15]

It might seem that linguistic competence involves knowing definitions, and that these definitions and their deductive consequences constitute the analytic sentences of the language. This suggestion is multiply problematic. The criterion of definitional equivalence is obscure. Synonymy and sameness of meaning are of a piece with analyticity. Whether 'gnu' is synonymous with 'wildebeest' is no more obvious than whether 'Every gnu is a wildebeest' is analytic. So we make no headway by specifying criteria for analyticity in terms of synonymy. As a result, it is never entirely clear whether a putative definition is a real definition. In any case, we are unable to give anything like definitions for most of our terms, even when nothing beyond coextensiveness is wanted. And our linguistic competence is not thereby undermined. Although I cannot define 'weed' or 'whim', I have no difficulty using the words or recognizing their referents. Nor can we claim that knowledge of definitions is implicit. If it were, we should at least be able to recognize definitions and their consequences as such when we encounter them. But our verdicts are variable. We might, for instance, rule 'Dogs are mammals' analytic. But we are apt to consider 'Platypuses are mammals' synthetic—the statement of an empirical discovery, and a surprising one at that. Still, it is unlikely that both verdicts are correct. For then the classification of some species into biological families would be a matter of convention; the classification of others into the same families, a matter of content. Verdicts on a single case can waver. We might vacillate between calling '$E = mc^2$' the relativistic definition of 'energy' and calling it a highly theoretical empirical law. Our uncertainty here makes no difference. So long as we recognize the importance and centrality of the formula, nothing hangs on whether we label it 'analytic' or 'synthetic'.

Semantic rules fare no better. Speakers invoke no such rules in ordinary discourse. I withhold or apply the term 'domesticated' to pigeons in the park without the aid of a rule

x is domesticated $\equiv y$.

Indeed, I cannot do otherwise, for I know no value for y. If we needed to invoke semantic rules to settle every application of our terms, a regress would result, for the rules are formulated in words. The regress is infinite; for no rule determines its own interpretation. It is vicious; for, on this account, we do not know whether a word applies unless we know that the

[15] W. V. Quine, "Two Dogmas of Empiricism," in *From a Logical Point of View* (New York: Harper Torchbooks, 1963), 20–46.

rules governing its application are satisfied. Unless the regress terminates, we know no such thing. Nor do semantic rules function juridically to decide disputed or difficult cases. Something is plainly wrong with 'Whales are fish', but blame is not easily assigned. Is the sentence incorrect because it violates the semantic rule for 'whale' or because whales are, as a matter of biological fact, not fish? Whether the error is attributable to convention or content is not at all obvious. Nor does it matter. We regularly recognize and correct errors of this kind without deciding where the responsibility lies.

The inability to answer such questions may be explained by the suggestion that awareness of semantic rules is unconscious.[16] Although we can neither articulate nor explicitly appeal to them, such rules are said to function implicitly in guiding our use and understanding of words. They enable us to differentiate between meaningful and meaningless sequences, and between analytic and synthetic sentences. The convention/content distinction is, on this view, deeply embedded in human linguistic competence. Meaningful sequences, it is held, accord with semantic rules; meaningless (but syntactically well-formed) sequences do not. Semantic rules suffice to secure analytic sentences. Synthetic ones require factual support. Unfortunately these distinctions are easier to state than to apply. And our ability to recognize their instances is exaggerated. Although it would be odd to say, 'Myrna is motivated by her own apathy', it is not clear whether the oddity is semantic or psychological. Can apathy motivate? What decides—the meanings of the words or the laws of psychology? Nor is it obvious whether the truth of 'A mule is a cross between a donkey and a horse' is settled by the meaning of the word 'mule' or by the genetic constitution of its referent. Here, too, there seems no way to tell. The semantic rules that are supposed to settle such matters yield no verdicts.

One final attempt to articulate the convention/content distinction involves construing convention as invariable under change of circumstances, and content as variable. Then an analytic sentence is one we hold true come what may; a synthetic sentence, one whose warrant alters as conditions change.[17] This is an improvement over earlier attempts, for it yields a clear, applicable distinction. Unfortunately it is the wrong distinction. 'There have been black dogs' is apt to be held true come what may, but not because it is analytic. It is plainly backed by evidence. Indeed, the reason it is likely to be held true come what may is that the evidence is

---

[16] Jerry Fodor, *The Language of Thought* (Cambridge, Mass.: Harvard University Press, 1975), 79–99.

[17] Quine, "Two Dogmas of Empiricism," 41.

overwhelming. With good reason we think it more likely that arguments to the contrary are defective than that such massive evidence misleads. 'Hold true, come what may' is a measure of the strength of a conviction, not of the source of that strength. Nor are conventions, however identified, indifferent to content. Experience can reveal that conventions conflict or that they do not settle an issue that falls within their mandate. In the one case they are jointly untenable; in the other, collectively inadequate. In both cases experience prompts modifications in systems that appeared a priori unproblematic. A distinction between constancy and inconstancy in linguistic behavior neither captures nor reflects a distinction between convention and content. Sentences seemingly grounded in experience may be clung to tenaciously; sentences that apparently function as conventions may be readily sacrificed to accommodate recalcitrant experience.

In the absence of an adequate explication of 'analyticity', the analytic/synthetic distinction is untenable. And the history of unremitting failures to formulate such an explication suggests that none can be given. But the distinction is deeply embedded in foundationalism's conception of its own project. Without its support, foundationalism totters. A priori knowledge is plainly jeopardized. According to traditional foundationalism, such knowledge is a by-product of linguistic (or conceptual) competence. We are held to know, for example, that lilacs are not lug wrenches simply by understanding the terms (or concepts) involved. When analyticity is forsworn, we lose our claim to such a priori knowledge. How we know that lilacs are not lug wrenches is no longer clear. Nor can the foundationalist account of empirical knowledge stand. Such knowledge is supposed to be grounded in experience and sustained by networks of linguistic meanings. But the ground is shaky and the meanings mythical. Matters of language are inseparable from matters of fact. So we cannot factor out linguistic conventions to arrive at the way the world presents itself in experience. The commitment to knowledge untouched by such conventions is unintelligible. The given must be given up.

Both the nature of evidence and its relation to a hypothesis become problematic. Foundationalism maintains that analytic connections determine the bearing of one sentence on the truth values of others. These connections are supposed to settle questions of cotenability and connect a hypothesis with its evidence class. If the connection between H and C_1, ..., C_n is analytic, then confirmation of $C_1, \ldots, C_n$ is automatically confirmation of H. We know this by understanding the sentences involved. Without analyticity, however, the connection between H and any particular evidence class is questionable. How do we know that $\{C_1, \ldots, C_n\}$ is H's evidence class? That is, how do we know that by confirming C_1

..., C_n, we confirm H? These are not idle questions. Unless they are satisfactorily answered, we do not know that H even when $C_p, \ldots, C_n$ are confirmed. For we do not know that $C_p, \ldots, C_n$ support H. In that case we have no right to confidence in H, for we do not know that the evidence in hand entitles us to believe it.

The necessary connection between hypothesis and evidence is broken. Contingent connections remain. Perhaps H is true whenever $C_p, \ldots, C_n$ are. There is then a correlation which—if known—justifies believing H if $C_p, \ldots, C_n$. The difficulty is this: how can such a correlation be known? We might hope to demonstrate

$$(1)\ (C_p, \ldots, C_n) \supset H$$

inductively. To that end we adduce evidence $D_p, \ldots, D_m$. If we know that

$$(2)\ (D_p, \ldots, D_m) \supset ((C_p, \ldots, C_n) \supset H)$$

then, given $D_p, \ldots, D_m$, we are justified in believing (1)—justified, that is, in believing that $C_p, \ldots, C_n$ is a reliable indication that H. But (2) is as problematic as (1), and for the same reason. Evidence of doubtful reliability is for the foundationalist epistemically inert. So unless its reliability is known, (2) contributes nothing to our knowledge that (1). If (2) is established inductively, then the reliability of the evidence for (2) must be questioned in turn. Since it transcends available evidence, induction is vulnerable to counterexample. So a correlation established by induction alone is not known to be reliable. Since no correlation demonstrates its own reliability, a regress results. If contingent connections are all we have, our convictions about the relation between hypothesis and evidence rest at some point on a correlation whose reliability is unknown.

An epistemological reliabilist need not be troubled by this. Even if knowledge requires a reliable correlation between hypothesis and evidence, it does not follow that knowledge of reliability is also required. De facto reliability might be enough.

Given the number and variety of our beliefs, it is reasonable to think that some are reliably correlated with their evidence. So, arguably, such de facto reliabilism entitles us to confidence that we know something. But since it does not enable us to identify the beliefs in question, it does not enable us to recognize our knowledge. We remain hostage to epistemic fortune. Being unable to differentiate between reliable and unreliable correlations, we cannot avoid error without luck. Unrecognizable knowledge is cognitively and practically valueless, contributing nothing of use to deliberation or action. At best, de facto reliabilism achieves a pyrrhic victory over skepticism. The knowledge it provides is not obviously preferable to ignorance.

CAUSALITY

The failure of analyticity to secure a necessary connection, combined with the fruitlessness of de facto reliabilism's attempt to forego one, leads philosophers to seek another source of necessity. Agreeing that the connection between knowledge and its object cannot be accidental and that that connection is crucial to epistemic entitlement, they attempt to discover the nature of that connection and incorporate a statement of it into the definition of knowledge. A variety of alternatives have been proposed, each giving rise to a dialectical interplay between carefully constructed conditions on knowledge and cleverly contrived counterexamples. In discussing such proposals, I focus on main lines of thought. Since the difficulties I discern cannot be remedied by delicate adjustments in detail, I neglect nuances.

One popular view is that knowledge is causally connected to its object. Then

S knows that p

just in case S's justified true belief that p is caused by the fact that p or by facts from which it follows that p.[18] Without such a causal link, S's belief, although justified and true, would be epistemically fortuitous. A causal theory of inference grafts onto a causal theory of perception. The theory of perception supplies the necessity required to secure basic beliefs. The theory of inference transmits necessity through the superstructure via valid inductive and deductive inferences. Certain advantages of the theory are plain: it reflects the idea that knowledge is responsive to the way the world is. Were circumstances different, S would know different things. It preserves the empiricist conviction that knowledge comes by way of sensation. For it takes the facts that (directly or indirectly) impinge on our sense organs to be the ones that cause our knowledge. It evades responsibility for details, maintaining that it is the business of the special sciences to discover precisely what causes beliefs. The character of the basis and its effect on the superstructure are then psychological questions.

Although convenient, foisting the details off on the sciences is not altogether legitimate. Some of the relevant issues are plainly scientific: the function of the middle ear, the operation of the optic nerve, the role of the soft palate in sensation are proper subjects for scientific study. To fully understand the production of perceptual beliefs, we need the information that such investigations can be expected to supply. But the most vexing

---

[18] Alvin Goldman, "A Causal Theory of Knowing," *Journal of Philosophy* 64 (1967): 357–372; D. M. Armstrong, *Belief, Truth, and Knowledge* (Cambridge: Cambridge University Press, 1973).

problems confronting a causal theory are not so easily eluded. Questions like "What makes a connection causal?" and "What makes a judgment warranted?" remain squarely within the province of philosophy.

The findings of science might enable us to delineate the chain of events leading to the production of a brain state. But they would not thereby suffice to identify a particular belief or to decide whether the belief is justified. For belief involves classification. And belief contents do not classify themselves. The causal chain from a gem to an event in the visual cortex does not suffice to discriminate the belief that it is green from the belief that it is grue.[19] Since the stone was perceived prior to t, the perceptual indications that it is green and that it is grue are identical. But the beliefs surely differ.

To characterize a perceived item as green requires understanding what qualifies as green and what evidence, direct and indirect, is indicative of something's being green. It requires sensitivity to circumstances in which evidence misleads, and a capacity to recognize and to discount or compensate for misleading evidence. And it requires beliefs about current conditions that bear on the applicability of 'green'. To classify an item as green then involves locating it by reference to an ever widening network of cognitive commitments. The causal ancestry of a perceptual datum does not settle its location in the network.

Causal theorists might maintain that the availability and employment of a particular system of categories are themselves to be explained causally. A more comprehensive causal account explains my classifying the stone as grue, and hence my belief that the stone is grue. But it would be hard to justify the view that our categories, however wayward, are impressed on us by nature. And it is doubtful that the resources of the causal theory are up to the task. In the absence of an adequate account of categorization, the causal history of the production of a brain state does not explain the genesis of a belief. This is not to say that a category system (or anything else) is sui generis. Even if the law of universal causality is true, it does not follow that every question has a causal answer or that every aspect of thought and reality is accounted for by a causal explanation.

Science is descriptive; epistemology, normative. Science might tell us how we come to harbor certain beliefs; epistemology seeks to determine what—if anything—justifies our doing so. Even if science could give a causal account of cognition, it would not displace epistemology. A causal theory of perception describes the effects of sensory stimulation. Such a theory of vision might reveal differences between the way an object looks at the center of the visual field and the way it looks at the periphery. And

[19] An object is grue ≡ it is examined before t and found to be green or not so examined and blue, where t is some future time. See Nelson Goodman, *Fact, Fiction, and Forecast* (Cambridge, Mass.: Harvard University Press, 1983), 73–74.

the theory might disclose differences between the way the thing looks to an astigmatic and the way it looks to an anastigmatic. It shows then how different causes are systematically connected with different effects. But however sharply delineated, such differences are just differences. The causal story the science tells has no criterion of visual accuracy. So it does not determine that one kind of visual impression is better than another. It does not find peripheral vision distorted or astigmatic vision defective. But without a criterion of visual accuracy, we cannot tell which (if any) visual perceptions merit confidence. A psychological theory of reasoning faces similar objections. It might chart trains of thought, revealing, for example, how analogical thinking differs from inferential thinking. But such information does not enable us to differentiate good reasoning from bad. To do that, we need criteria of validity and soundness, and probably of relevance and cogency as well. An empirical account of the ways we actually reason is powerless to generate such criteria.

Within the context of a normative theory, findings of empirical science may be important. Given a standard of visual accuracy, the differences between central and peripheral vision might tell against the latter. But a theory that describes the differences does not thereby set the standard. A purely descriptive account of the source of our beliefs neither supplies nor supplants an evaluation of their adequacy. Science is no substitute for philosophy.

Causality is a philosophically problematic notion. Causal necessity is said to strengthen evidential support. Simple inductive correlations are unreliable, being vulnerable to charges of spuriousness. But when backed by appropriate causal connections, the theory holds, they become reliable, for causes necessitate their effects. Justified true beliefs caused by the facts they pertain to, and the inductive and deductive consequences of those beliefs, merit our confidence. For given their ancestry, their truth is no accident.

There is a certain reluctance to populate the cosmos with occult forces—causal powers, necessary connections, and the like. Still, it may be unwise at this point to be overly fastidious about metaphysical matters. We cannot, after all, *prove* that no such things exist. It would be unfortunate to deprive ourselves of real resources by insisting on a gold standard when paper money would serve. It may be best then to countenance causal powers provisionally, to see whether the epistemological benefits they yield are worth the cost of admitting them into our ontology. As it turns out, the costs are considerable; the payoff is not.

If the causal connection must itself be known, the ghost of Hume returns to haunt us. For the evidence of such a connection is inevitably inadequate. Experience attests that particular events are temporally successive and spatially contiguous. And it attests that kindred of the first are constantly (or at least commonly) conjoined with kindred of the second. But it discerns no necessary connection among matters of fact.[20] There may, as critics charge, be more to causality than Hume recognized. But the question here is whether there is more to our epistemic access to causality than Hume recognized. Although changes might be made to present the matter in a more contemporary idiom, to accommodate the fact that we rarely have anything so strong as constant conjunction, and to avoid problems peculiar to Hume's associationism, his central insight survives.

Our sense organs are unaffected by what does not impinge on them; so they do not register events that could or would occur were circumstances different. Such events do not in fact occur, and nonoccurrences leave no perceptible trace. The senses then are insensitive to differences between causal and accidental sequences of events. Such sequences, differing only over counterfactuals, are perceptually indiscriminable.

One might think otherwise. We are not, after all, entirely passive in the reception of our sensations. We can affect the epistemic standing of an observed regularity by subjecting it to systematic testing—by bringing our senses to bear where exceptions might be found. If exceptions are found, belief in the regularity is unwarranted; if not, support for the belief increases. Testing, however, reveals not counterfactuals but additional facts. It can generate evidence of regularity. But regularity does not suffice for causality, for accidentally related events can be constantly conjoined. To vindicate the claim that ps cause qs requires evidence that the connection between ps and qs is necessary: not only do qs regularly follow ps, they could not do otherwise. Since the senses detect only what actually occurs, they are powerless to discern whether things could have happened differently. Being equally supportive of causal and coincidental regularities, the evidence of the senses affords no basis for distinguishing between them. And we have no other source of evidence to make up the deficit.

A causal judgment goes beyond a judgment of constant conjunction in contending that the relation between conjuncts is necessary. But the evidence, no matter how plentiful, supports only the claim to conjunction, not the claim to necessity. If causality involves more than Hume recognized, the remainder is epistemically inaccessible. For neither casual nor systematic observation can discern a necessary connection among matters of fact. Cause and effect are linked, according to Hume, not by necessity but by custom. A habit of mind, grounded in an observed regularity, underlies our assurance that a particular chain of events will occur. But being subjective, the habit does not entitle us to that assurance.

[20] David Hume, *A Treatise of Human Nature*, ed. L. A. Selby-Bigge (Oxford: Clarendon, 1967), Book 1, chap. 3, 161–167.

Causal considerations are introduced into epistemology to shore up inductive support by differentiating between reliable and unreliable correlations. But the evidence for a causal connection is supplied by induction. If induction is unreliable, so are our causal judgments. We may have evidence that an object antedates a belief about it, that the belief is formed in the presence of the object, and that kindred beliefs have hitherto been constantly conjoined with kindred objects. We have then evidence that the relation between belief and object instantiates a regularity. Were the regularity known to be reliable, we would be entitled to confidence about that relation. As things stand, we are not. There is no epistemic premium in instantiating a regularity of doubtful reliability. Causality avails us nothing. Either some level of inductive support suffices for knowledge or it does not. If it does, causal considerations are superfluous; if not, they are unwarranted. For we have no knowledge of causal connections except what induction supplies.

We might hope to evade the difficulty by maintaining that the causal connection between knowledge and its object need not be known. Then the existence, not the apprehension, of an appropriate causal connection differentiates knowledge from epistemic luck. Granted, we remain unable to tell where the line is drawn; so our practical and theoretical undertakings are no better for it. Still, the line is there, guaranteeing a real (if unknowable) distinction between beliefs that are worthy of our confidence and beliefs that are not. That knowers are never in a position to draw that distinction is inconvenient, but epistemically unimportant.

This maneuver looks suspiciously ad hoc. Since nothing in our ken differentiates knowledge from luck, something beyond our ken is introduced to do so. But the conviction that we know something is small comfort when coupled with the realization that we cannot tell what. The causal theorist inflates ontology by introducing an epistemically inaccessible power in order to effect an equally inaccessible distinction between beliefs. Being inaccessible, the distinction is epistemically useless. We remain unable to identify the beliefs that merit our confidence.

SUBJUNCTIVE SUPPORT

Like causal theories, subjunctive theories of knowledge take modal considerations to be crucial: the connection between knowledge and truth is counterfactually invariable; that between fortuitous belief and truth, counterfactually variable. Roughly, S's true belief that p counts as knowledge if S would believe p were p true, and would not believe p were p false. To avoid obvious objections, the definition has to be stated more precisely. In one formulation,

S knows that p

just in case:

(1) p is true;
(2) S believes, via method or way of coming to believe M, that p;
(3) If p weren't true and S were to use M to arrive at a belief whether (or not) p, then S wouldn't believe, via M, that p;
(4) If p were true and S were to use M to arrive at a belief whether (or not) p, S would believe, via M, that p.[21]

If S's true belief that p is epistemically fortuitous, then there are possible circumstances in which M would lead S to believe that p even though p was false, or not to believe that p even though p was true. The subjunctive conditions on knowledge are held to show the connection between knowledge and truth to be essential and the connection between fortuitous belief and truth to be accidental.

The knower need not be aware that the subjunctive conditions are satisfied. This, plainly, is as it should be. For we are apt to be uncertain what we would think were circumstances suitably different. And without fixed belief, there is no knowledge. The subjunctive theory maintains that despite our ignorance, there is a fact of the matter about what we would believe. That fact determines which of our true beliefs count as knowledge. The theory thus requires a realist stance toward modality: there must be objective facts about what would be, as well as facts about what is. Being objective, such facts are not relative to our interest in a situation or to the vocabulary in terms of which we describe it. Nor are such facts settled by stipulation. They are determined by what is the case in the possible worlds accessible from this one.

The theory does not take knowledge to require justification. Unlike the causal theory, it contains no explicit justification condition. Nor do the subjunctive conditions function in its stead. For justification must be epistemically accessible; and we need not, typically do not, and conceivably cannot tell whether the subjunctive conditions on knowledge are satisfied. If M would lead S to cling with the appropriate mix of tenacity and flexibility to the true belief that p, S knows that p. S's utter lack of justification for p is irrelevant.

Suppose M is

Believe what is revealed by examining the entrails of water rats,

and in all possible worlds accessible from this one, such revelations are true. Then the revelations of water rat entrails are reliable. By applying M,

[21] Robert Nozick, *Philosophical Explanations* (Cambridge, Mass.: Harvard University Press, 1981), 179; see also Fred Dretske, "Conclusive Reasons," *Australasian Journal of Philosophy* 49 (1971): 1–22.

S would believe a sentence if it were true and would not believe it if it were false. In that case, any true beliefs that S arrives at via M count as knowledge. S need not have any faith in M; he might apply it out of habit, a sense of tradition, or a desire to be thought eccentric. Indeed, S need not realize that he arrives at his beliefs via M. If idle curiosity leads him to examine entrails, as it leads others to consult their horoscopes, S may be unaware that he is influenced by what he finds. S, we may assume, realizes that we have no reason to trust M. And not being epistemically irresponsible, he does not rely on M's findings. He admits to harboring beliefs that M sanctions. But unless they have outside support, he ranks them as superstitions—slightly embarrassing for a man of his age and position, but harmless enough since he is not guided by them. Despite their dubious credentials, the subjunctive theory counts the beliefs that M yields as knowledge. But such knowledge plainly confers no epistemic entitlement. Given our best estimates of M's adequacy, S is quite right to distrust its revelations and to proceed in thought and action on the basis of more well-founded beliefs.

The subjunctive theory secures a relation between beliefs and truths that holds across possible worlds. If an adequate theory of possible worlds were forthcoming, the existence of such a relation would be unproblematic. But being epistemically inaccessible, and indifferent to matters of justification, that relation would still be cognitively and practically worthless, availing us nothing in thought, word, or deed. The means by which the subjunctive theory achieves knowledge then involves scuttling our reasons for wanting it. Our lives would be no better for the sort of knowledge the theory affords.

Like classical foundationalism, causal and subjunctive theories lead to skepticism; or they redefine 'knowledge', dodging skepticism by favoring a condition that is no better than ignorance. Still, skepticism is not a priori untenable; nor is knowledge a priori better than ignorance. So unless such theories are charged with something worse, they may yet be true.

A more serious charge is indeed outstanding: the charge that there is no objective distinction between necessity and contingency. Ignorance of modal matters does not settle the issue. We often have reason to believe a hypothesis that falls short of knowledge. In such cases, though, knowledge eludes us through an evidential deficit. The standards for knowledge are sufficiently high that available support is inadequate. The epistemic inaccessibility of necessity is different. Evidence is not merely insufficient, it is effectively nonexistent. The only evidence for a claim to necessity is evidence of a regularity. Its bearing is slight; for such evidence does not enable us to distinguish between necessary and contingent regularities. At best, investigation yields information about actuality. But modal statements transcend the actual—labeling some actuals 'necessary', others 'possible' and some nonactuals 'possible', others 'impossible'. Evidence about the appropriate application of such labels is simply not to be had.

The modal realist might reply: This only shows that we are ignorant of particular modal facts. It does not follow that we are altogether ignorant of modality. Indeed we are not. We have at least two avenues of access to the modal realm. They provide grounds for reasonable belief, if not knowledge. One is modal logic; the other, intuition.

With the development of modal logics, systems containing claims about necessity, possibility, and impossibility have been shown to be self-consistent. So there is nothing logically wrong with thinking such sentences true. Undeniably this gives us some reason to believe modal claims. But not much. For systems of false sentences, and systems that combine truths with falsehoods, need not be internally inconsistent. A valid schema yields only true conclusions from true premises. Modal logics identify certain forms as valid. But no more than other logics can they identify non-vacuous premises as true. For no logic determines its own application. So unless we can supply true premises for our arguments, modal logics cannot be counted on to yield truths. To provide the premises, we look to intuition.

According to realists, we have intuitions about modal matters: given that Aristotle was a philosopher, he could instead have been a plumber; given that he was a man, he could not instead have been a mouse.[22] Intuitions, however, are not easily distinguished from other beliefs—opinions, convictions, prejudices, and the like. So if intuitions have any special epistemic standing, it is not clear how to identify the mental states that merit it. Nor is it obvious that such a standing is deserved. For intuitions, like other beliefs, waver and clash. Could Aristotle really have been a plumber? Were there plumbers in ancient Greece? If not, how does this affect what Aristotle could have been? I am not sure what I think. My intuitions may conflict with yours, with my earlier intuitions, even with my concurrent ones. And they may conflict with considered judgments and confirmed theories. Intuition tells me that simultaneity is absolute. Intuition is wrong.

Intuitions then are not intrinsically reliable. So we cannot infer their truth from their existence. The existence of modal intuitions then does little to sustain an ontological commitment to an objective modal realm. We are not just ignorant of particular modal facts. We have found no reason to believe that there exist objective modal facts to be ignorant of.

Still, realists might argue, inference to the best explanation supports the contention that objective modal facts exist.[23] Best explanation of what?

---

[22] Saul Kripke, "Naming and Necessity," *Semantics of Natural Language*, ed. D. Davidson and G. Harman (Dordrecht: Reidel, 1972), 313–314.

[23] I am indebted to Mary Kate McGowan for this point.

Not of all modal truths. It is impossible to complete the "pre-med" sequence in three years because of the hours when the required courses meet. Revise the schedule and the project becomes possible. Because this impossibility derives from a readily revisable, clearly contingent constraint, there is no temptation to appeal to objective modalities to explain it. But scientific laws and metaphysical principles seem different. 'Electrons are negatively charged' and 'Every event has a cause' are supposed to be necessary regardless of the interests, projects, priorities, and practices of those who entertain them. The best explanation of their steadfastness, it is held, is that they reflect objective necessities. Is it?

Even laws are not utterly undeniable. Serious, substantive inquiries can be mounted to investigate the implications of revising the inverse square law or denying the identity of indiscernibles. Still, let us concede that scientific laws and fundamental metaphysical principles have a greater inertia than other modal claims. Is the existence of objective modal facts the best explanation of this?

Suppose that the fact that electrons are negatively charged is objectively necessary. This alone would not enable 'Electrons are negatively charged' to function as a scientific law. To function as a law, a generalization must play a pivotal role in theorizing. It must figure in explanations and extrapolations. It must circumscribe the alternatives that need to be entertained. It must mesh with other scientific commitments, and so on. A generalization that meets such requirements will be treated as a law, for it advances the understanding of the subject that the science seeks. A generalization whose truth is relatively peripheral to the science's concerns will be deemed accidental. Particle physics has excellent reason to consider 'Electrons are negatively charged' a law, whether or not there are objective necessities. Moreover, it has excellent reason to construe the generalization as a law even if objective necessities exist, but the fact that electrons are negatively charged is not one of them. If the generalization is a truth that advances the cognitive interests the science is committed to serve, according it the status of law is warranted. The inertia of laws stems not from their reflecting the true and ultimate structure of reality (even if they do) but from the relative fixity of purpose of the disciplines to which they belong. Given certain articulable and justifiable interests, projects, and priorities, letting the generalizations deemed laws fix the constraints makes sense. Inference to the best explanation of tenacity of laws then does not favor modal realism. The best explanation of our tendency to hold laws fixed in counterfactual reasoning is their role in science.

If we consider the roles modal language plays, we see why the expectations of realists are excessive. Reasoning in a vacuum tends to be fruitless. If everything is up for grabs, we do not know what—or how—to think about anything. We operate better within a framework. By setting constraints and limiting alternatives, we focus deliberation and provide some measure of structure for our speculations.

Thinking hypothetically typically involves holding some truths fixed and suspending judgment about others. It may also involve denying accepted truths, affirming accepted falsehoods, and ascribing truth or falsity to sentences whose actual truth value is unknown. Such exercises in imagination are often valuable—revealing unsuspected kinships, affinities, and differences, bringing to light new facts, uncovering overlooked fallacies or flaws in our thinking. But it does not follow that all hypothetical reasoning, or all valid hypothetical reasoning, proceeds within a single framework. Nor does it follow that some beliefs are intrinsically fixed and others intrinsically variable. For no discipline has a monopoly on speculation.

In some contexts it is reasonable to hold the laws of science fixed and consider the consequences of altering boundary conditions. In others, we do well to take the opposite tack—fix the boundary conditions and fiddle with the laws. Neither approach discredits the other. Elsewhere, scientific considerations are otiose. In entertaining the possibility of driving from Boston to Charleston in fifteen hours, we take account of road conditions, engine power, and the vigilance of the highway patrol. In considering the possibility of having a baby during her surgical residency, Amy focuses on the rigors of the program, the demands of parenthood, the availability of child care, and the mores of the medical profession. In debating the inevitability of increased class size given the recent budget cuts, we mention the extent of the university's resources, the alternatives available to the president, and the political acumen of the dean. Such reflective, responsible modal reasoning typically proceeds without the backing of science.

Deeming scientific laws the arbiters of modal truth, scientific realism is forced to dismiss such speculation as idle. As a result, it yields no interpretation of a significant proportion of our discourse. It reveals nothing about how to reason well or badly in nonscientific domains. Such scientism is unfounded. For science is not our sole source of understanding. Aesthetic, political, moral, and practical discourse function cognitively as well. If we hew exclusively to scientific lines, we forego the insights that other approaches afford. There is no objective reason to favor science over other modes of inquiry. Not that science is peculiarly defective in this regard. The problem is that no single framework serves every speculative need. Any statement can be treated as necessary by mandating that in the context of inquiry its falsity is not to be entertained. In a different inquiry, the same statement might be deemed contingent. Our inquiries are sufficiently diverse that no single mandate is absolute.

The interpretation of modal terminology is plagued not by vagueness but by indeterminacy. It is not just at the boundaries that the application of 'necessary', 'possible', and 'impossible' is unclear. Rather, nearly every ascription of the terms is controvertible. We can almost always find a scenario in which a seemingly necessary truth looks merely possible. If modal discourse is simply imaginative speculation, such indeterminacy is unproblematic. For in that case we do not expect to spring modal claims loose from the contexts that generate them. So the fact that what is necessary relative to one set of considerations is contingent relative to another is cause for neither surprise nor alarm.

Modal realism, however, seeks truths that are independent of our interests, inquiries, and ends. Arriving at such truths requires a way to effect detachment. If in a favored context p is necessary, it follows that p is necessary *simpliciter*. The context is merely the background that facilitates the discovery of an objective truth. But there is no uniquely favored context. For relative to another equally legitimate set of cognitive concerns, p's claim to necessity is overturned. Any item can be described in a variety of ways and investigated by multiple methods. And our findings about it can be incorporated into diverse systems of thought. Reality favors no single vocabulary, mode of inquiry, or system of thought. Nor should we. By playing favorites, we willfully deprive ourselves of alternative sources of illumination, information, and understanding.[24]

The intelligibility of appropriately relativized modal claims is not in question. We use modal locutions to distinguish between what is conceded and what is in question in a given imaginative context. So long as consistency is maintained, we can assign interpretations as suits our purposes. Since purposes vary, so do interpretations. But the intelligibility of a realist stance is a more difficult matter. Having found no objective means of adjudicating among competing modal claims, we lack determinate, identifiable, context-neutral truth conditions for ascriptions of *de re* modality. In making such ascriptions then, we do not know what we're talking about.

Collapse

Foundationalist conceptions of knowledge are constructed around a framework of objective necessity. Although they do not construe themselves as foundationalists, causal theorists, reliabilists, and metaphysical realists deploy frameworks with the same structure. If the framework is linguistic, analytic truth and falsity determine necessity and impossibility; synthetic truth and falsity determine possibility. If it is nonlinguistic, the (alleged) metaphysical order of reality determines necessity, possibility, and impossibility. The framework cannot be subjective; it cannot be set-

---

[24] See Catherine Z. Elgin, "Unnatural Science," *The Journal of Philosophy* 92 (1995): 289–302.

tled by opinion, available information, or consensus. If it were, knowledge would be subjective as well. The constellation of concepts that foundationalism presupposes is no longer in place. The 'intuitions' that render it plausible have been undermined. We have made no sense of objective modality, and without it foundationalism collapses.

Foundationalism flourished when certain traditional dualisms could be accepted. The context defined by those dualisms rendered the goals, standards, methods, and limits of epistemological inquiry clear and reasonable. But the dualisms have been discredited. We cannot rely on distinctions between convention and content, necessity and contingency, analyticity and syntheticity to shore up a faltering philosophical program. And foundationalism cannot survive without their support.

If foundationalist arguments are valid—and here, I think, they are— the analytic/synthetic distinction is required to preclude error without relying on luck. And some objective distinction between necessity and contingency is demanded by the hierarchical conception of justification. Without such distinctions, foundationalist objectives are unsatisfiable; its methods, unintelligible; its restrictions unjustifiable. Neither foundationalism nor its successors satisfy the requirements for a perfect procedural epistemology. They lack the resources to secure against epistemic misfortune.

Emotion, ethics, metaphor, and mathematics were excluded from knowledge because they failed to satisfy foundationalism's rigorous standards. Their expulsion is rescinded when the standards are overturned. Whether and how they contribute to knowledge is again a matter for investigation. We have, at this point, no reason to think them more, or less, problematic than perception, science, and literal description.

When adequate epistemic criteria cannot be satisfied, we are forced to skepticism. But foundationalist criteria are congenitally defective. The result of our investigation is thus not skepticism, just ignorance. Lacking acceptable standards, we are in no position to say what—if anything—we know. Nor does idealism result. For like realism, idealism presupposes a distinction between scheme and content—conceptual schemes being free constructions of the human mind, content being supplied by the external world. Finding no pure, unconceptualized content, the idealist concludes that all is scheme. The basis is banished. But the superstructure stands, for its elements are mutually supportive. A moral of our story, however, is that, being infused with notions like necessity and meaning, the dualism of scheme and content is untenable. So 'scheme' is as unintelligible as 'content'. Neither realism nor idealism is an option, for their shared presupposition is irreparably flawed.

Ardent realists will reject my contention that the dualisms have been discredited. If they are right, the foundationalist blueprint can be retained. Even then, though, we cannot evade skepticism except by espousing a position that amounts to the same thing. Such a position assures us that we know something but concedes that we have no way to recognize our knowledge. If I am right, foundationalist standards are unintelligible. If the realist is right, they are effectively unsatisfiable.

A desire to preclude error without relying on luck underwrites foundationalism's methods, goals, and standards. That aspiration seems destined to be unfulfilled. So the aim of epistemology must be reconceived. Such a reconception is welcome in any case. For the boundary foundationalism drew was too restrictive. By making the avoidance of error our sole or primary epistemic objective, it overlooked the importance we attach to sensitivity, relevance, informativeness, and cognitive efficacy. We regularly risk error to achieve such ends. An acceptable epistemology should explain how, when, and why it is reasonable to do so.

Chapter III

KNOWLEDGE BY CONSENSUS

THE SOCIAL CONSTRUCTION OF KNOWLEDGE

A sea change occurs when epistemology is seen as a social practice. By our own lights at least, our cognitive endeavors often succeed. Problems are solved to our satisfaction, phenomena explained, theorems proved, questions answered. We readily distinguish getting things right from getting them wrong, justified belief from rank prejudice, knowledge from ignorance and from error. And we achieve a significant measure of intersubjective agreement about such matters. By reflecting on what we do in generating and validating claims to knowledge, we can discover what we take knowledge to be and delineate the structure of the practice that makes our epistemic successes possible. This might seem at best a sociological propaedeutic to epistemology—revealing only what we take knowledge to be, not what knowledge really is. But the distinction is spurious: there is nothing for knowledge to be except what we take it to be.

Appreciation of this fact leads pure procedural philosophers to construe epistemology as the study of a social phenomenon, one that seeks to map out the complex social relations that constitute inquiry and its objects. Wittgenstein takes the culture as a whole to constitute the community of inquirers; Kuhn takes each scientific community to fix its own context; Rorty's community is rather harder to identify. Disagreement here leads to substantive differences among these thinkers, differences that reverberate throughout their theories. Before examining such disagreements, however, I want to sketch the perspective that they share.

All three construe inquiry as an institution (or a matrix of related institutions) that sustains and is sustained by social practice. Its norms and standards, criteria and rules are conventions that a community imposes on its members to structure their joint ventures and further their collective aims. Those conventions, along with the activities, functions, offices, and objectives they engender, obtain their identity and justification from their contribution to a shared form of life. If knowledge is the goal of inquiry, knowledge must be construed, not as correspondence to the independently real but as a certain type of agreement among inquirers—agreement that obtains when community standards for investigation have been met.

Wittgenstein construes social practices, including those involved in inquiry, as games. Kuhn considers normal scientific investigation puzzle solving. Rorty interprets intellectual activity as a form of play.[1] So an understanding of games, puzzles, and play is crucial if we are to adopt, or even comprehend, their perspective. In what immediately follows, I focus on a view I find in Wittgenstein, it being the most explicit, articulate, and compelling of the three. Wittgenstein scholarship is rife with controversy over what precisely his position is. I do not propose to become embroiled in it. For my objective is not exegetical. I am concerned with the merits of the position, not its pedigree. Whether or not the position is Wittgenstein's, it is a stance worth investigating. Richard Rorty and, arguably, Thomas Kuhn share the general stance, but the textual exegesis required to establish this would take us too far afield. Later in this chapter I will explore points of divergence among these thinkers.

Wittgenstein notes that games form a motley; they have no common essence. Nor do they need one: we recognize games, play games, and learn new ones without appealing to shared features. So our institutions and practices could be games, even if they have no common essence. There will be any number of similarities among our practices, but no single feature or set of features common to all. To decide whether this is so, we must investigate the similarities of our other practices to those we already recognize as games. If there are enough important affinities, it may be reasonable to apply the term 'game' to practices in general; otherwise, it will not. But neither *enough* nor *important* is easily measured. To demand agreement in essential features would be tactless. At best we may find family resemblances between obvious instances of games and practices whose status is still in doubt. Obviously, the features I adduce are not shared by all the activities we call games. But they are characteristic of a fairly wide range of cases. More important, they both conform to the pure procedural model and afford a plausible basis for projection from the playground to the rest of the social realm. Let us look at some games with a view to identifying features that might make them paradigmatic social practices.

GAMES PEOPLE PLAY

One could, presumably, describe what occurs in a game of football or chess or tag strictly in terms of matter in motion. But this would not be to describe the series of events as football or chess or tag, or as a game, or even as a sequence of intelligible actions. To do that requires describing the events in terms that relate them to the rules that structure the activity, that make it a game.

[1] See Ludwig Wittgenstein, *Philosophical Investigations* (New York: Macmillan, 1958); Kuhn, *The Structure of Scientific Revolutions*; Richard Rorty, "From Logic to Language to Play," *APA Proceedings and Addresses* 59 (1986): 747–753.

Games like football, chess, and tag are rule-governed activities. Since conformity to the rules is typical, the various instances of such a game display marked regularities. Still, rule-governedness is not the same as regularity. A single counterexample discredits a putative regularity, such as all basketball players are tall. But rules are made to be broken; they retain their authority even when violated. And the games they belong to often enforce that authority by penalizing infractions. Games that have rules then are designed with the expectation that the rules will not always be obeyed. The function of the rules is primarily normative, only secondarily descriptive. They specify what should be done, not necessarily what is done in any particular case.

By prescribing correct play, the rules of a game make it possible to play incorrectly. They create a context within which mistakes can be made and corrected, excuses and defenses offered, conduct rewarded and punished. Without the normative structure the rules provide, nothing would count as an infraction, an excuse, a penalty, or a reward. There would be no standards against which play could be found wanting.

Rules, moreover, provide a game with a telos. They define its objectives, specifying what counts as, for example, a touchdown, checkmate, home free. They delimit the opportunities for realizing these objectives, the moves that can be made, the obstacles that must be overcome. They thus organize the activity in a way that permits purposes to be framed and strategies plotted. The rules also define roles or positions with their attendant responsibilities, rights, and restrictions: they determine what a rook or a tackle must do, may do, must not do. So rules shape excellences and incompetences: by specifying exactly what the function of a queen's bishop or a quarterback is, they determine what it is to perform that function well or badly; they create the opportunity for brilliance and for bungling. Outside football there are no touchdowns, wishbone formations, quarterback sneaks; no blocked punts, ineligible receivers, two-point conversions. The rules of the game constitute the practice that alone makes such things possible.

Games are conventional; rules are introduced by stipulation and adopted by (express or tacit) agreement. Rules are, nevertheless, authoritative: in adopting them we vest them with the power to regulate play. Although a game could have been designed to permit four strikes, in baseball you only get three. So having struck three times and missed, the batter is out. In baseball this is indisputable. Particular judgments can be justified by appeal to the rules, but nothing either can or need justify the rules. The rules of the game are the final court of appeal.

Rules can be variously interpreted. So a complete specification of the rules does not completely determine how a game is to be played. In football, for example, the ball carrier is required to remain in bounds. Does he satisfy this requirement if one foot is in, the other out of bounds? If he steps on the line that marks the boundary? If his heels are in but his toes are out? Clearly we need a criterion for the rule's application, a standard for determining what counts as staying in bounds. Of course, such criteria are ready to hand. Unfortunately, any statement of criteria is prey to the same indeterminacy: it, too, can be variously interpreted. So although articulation of suitable criteria can resolve specific interpretive difficulties, it cannot solve the general problem. No statement or standard can be made clear, precise, and rigorous enough to preclude the possibility of alternative interpretations.

Normally we do not bother to articulate our criteria unless interpretive indeterminacy interferes with play. Whatever goes without saying is reasonably left unsaid. Moreover, we often cannot articulate the criteria we use. We make our ruling as an umpire does: we call them as we see them. Why think that we use any criteria in such cases? The fact that we agree about how particular cases are to be decided and how precedents apply shows, it is urged, that the members of the community bring to bear a common set of criteria. Without criteria, tacit or explicit, our verdicts would be jointly inconsistent and at odds with the verdicts of other members of the community. Indeed, if no agreement antedated our explicit statements of rules and criteria, those statements could get no purchase; for nothing could determine whether the rules and criteria governing those statements were consistently and correctly applied. Nothing would provide them with a univocal interpretation. So the possibility of playing the game ultimately rests on the brute fact that we agree—a contingent fact of human natural history.[2] The socially coordinated activity exhibited in our play provides all the evidence we have or need that shared criteria are at work. The evidence of our agreement is thus found not in what we say but in what we do, not in how we state the rules but how we play the game.

It would be misleading to picture the rules of a game as a free standing structure. For what the rules amount to depends crucially on the ways they are applied; and rules are powerless to determine their own application. Someone who knew only the rules of chess, for example, would not know the game. By this I do not mean that she would be a weak player, but that she would not know the first thing about playing chess—namely, which of the interpretations consonant with the stated rules fit the practice of playing chess. A game is better pictured as a balloon. The pressure their applications exert on the rules gives the game its shape. Without

[2] Ludwig Wittgenstein, *Remarks on the Foundations of Mathematics* (Cambridge, Mass.: MIT Press, 1978), I, 141. My reading of this passage derives from Barry Stroud's "Wittgenstein and Logical Necessity," in *Wittgenstein*, ed. G. Pitcher (Garden City, N.Y.: Anchor Doubleday, 1966), 490–492.

applications, the rules would collapse, their fabric too flimsy to stand on its own. Without the rules to constrain them, the activities that make up the game would dissipate. Together, however, rules and applications constitute a self-contained, self-sustaining enterprise.

Games must be understood holistically. Rules cannot be fully comprehended apart from applications, nor applications apart from rules. Game playing is purposive behavior; the requisite purposes can neither be framed nor recognized without the background of rules and criteria of application that specify the game's objectives and constrain the options for their realization. The moves, positions, penalties, and strategies likewise make sense only within the context of the game; they are characterized in terms of and become intelligible only by reference to their role in or contribution to the game as a whole. But the game is nothing but a complex of rules, criteria, objectives, strategies, penalties, moves, positions, and so forth. So to understand the game requires comprehending its constituents and the ways they interact.

Such holism is disquieting, for the relation between parts and wholes seems too intimate to be informative. The components of a game are defined functionally, so we can understand them only by knowing the game in which they function. Its components comprise the game, so we can understand the game only by knowing its components. To understand football, for example, requires knowing what a touchdown is; but it is impossible really to know what a touchdown is without understanding football. It thus looks impossible to learn either. For there seems no way in—no entrée into this complex social practice, nothing for the novice to learn first. He has to know everything about the game to be in a position to learn anything about it, but then there is nothing left to learn.

Were a game simply an abstract scheme of arbitrary conventions, its insularity might make it impenetrable. But games are played. So the novice has access to examples. She sees rules applied; objectives sought and sometimes achieved; obstacles encountered and sometimes overcome; infractions committed and sometimes penalized, sometimes excused, sometimes ignored; moves made; and points scored. In examples, parts and wholes are presented together. What seemed impenetrable in description becomes evident in exhibition.

Rules do not always come first. We can learn a game by picking up on what others do and attempting to do likewise, subjecting our efforts to their critical appraisal, inferring the operative norms from the course of play and the reactions of competent players. We thus become initiated into the community of players (or kibitzers), acquiring the know-how needed to play (or kibitz) competently. Such know-how sometimes antedates and always extends beyond knowing that certain articulable rules and criteria are in force. For, as Wittgenstein insists, words eventually give out, and what we mean then is determined by what we do.[3]

If we think of learning a game as acquiring justified true beliefs about it, such holism is hard to countenance. How could someone simultaneously learn all the truths of chess? But when we recognize that learning a game is acquiring a competence, the picture looks quite different. The isolated skills developed along the way do not amount to learning chess until they coalesce into an ability to play the game, just as memorizing verbs does not amount to learning French until that knowledge meshes with other skills to produce meaningful, appropriate, French sentences.[4]

To say that a game can be learned directly (without, that is, first learning its rules) and that it is learned as a unit (rather than piecemeal) is not to say that it is learned without preparation. Someone previously unacquainted with competitive board games is ill-equipped to master chess. We typically begin by learning fairly rudimentary games that supply skills and analogies needed to master more difficult ones. Gradually we work our way up from Candyland to chess. The primitive games are complete in their own right: they are not parts of their successors nor are their components inherited by their successors. Their relation to more sophisticated games is analogical. It might be useful to master hearts in preparation for learning bridge, since the games are quite similar. But the value of such preparatory exercises is entirely heuristic. Even though some of the rules are stated in exactly the same words—'Always follow suit', for example—it is not the case that the same rule governs both games. For the identity of a rule derives from its function in a game. So rules belonging to different games cannot be identical. Family resemblances among features of different games are often pedagogically valuable. But because the relevant features are defined by their functions, their identities are transformed when they are incorporated into new games. Games remain insular but not unlearnable.

Rules and criteria set the requirements for winning a game, but they do not determine who wins. For a game generates its products: it has no winners or losers, no home runs, strike outs, walks, or balks until it is actually played. So if inquiry is properly understood as a game, it produces its results; it does not reveal what was already the case. It is a pure procedure.

Games, moreover, are purposely contrived so that their objectives can be realized and so that we can tell whether and by whom they are realized. Thus the objectives of a game cannot take the form of unrealizable ideals,

[3] Wittgenstein, *Philosophical Investigations*, 211.
[4] See Wilfrid Sellars, *Science and Metaphysics* (London: Routledge and Kegan Paul, 1968), 111–112.

nor can the distinctions required for play be matters of infinite refinement. To assure determinateness and the possibility of consensus requires that the enterprise be carefully circumscribed, that certain seemingly legitimate aspirations be excluded from the game's objectives.

If the rules are correctly applied, the results of a game are unimpeachable. It makes no sense to claim that what the game counts as winning is not really winning, that something more or different is required. Security of results derives from modesty of ambitions. The game discriminates winners from losers but does not show, and does not purport to show, that the best man wins. It delivers the goods it promises but does not certify that they answer to any external standard of excellence. One may play games to build character or to lose weight or to develop self-discipline. But the status of an activity as a game or its outcome as a victory is not undermined if it fails to achieve such laudable objectives.

Playing for Real

Fun is fun. But can the frivolous activities that occupy our leisure reveal anything significant about the serious business of social life? They can. To show how, I will sketch some parallels between games and other familiar social practices. I will then turn to a discussion of what are traditionally considered epistemic practices.

Promising provides a framework for voluntarily restricting our freedom. It enables us to rely on one another and coordinate our efforts for mutual advantage.[5] It does so by creating the opportunity to undertake certain obligations, thereby making us morally accountable for certain actions. Without the practice, the words 'I promise' would be empty, and an utterance like 'I'll do it' would be but a prediction or expression of intent. Failure to act might invite charges of inaccuracy or akrasia but would be no ground for moral censure. For unless my words amount to a promise, they put me under no obligation.

My words constitute a moral commitment or an excuse because of their role in the practice. And the rules and criteria that define the practice delimit the inferences my utterance licenses and the evaluations to which my words and deeds are subject. Outside the practice, the very same words function differently: a prediction or intention is not in itself a promise; nor is an explanation an excuse.

The practice is complex;[6] it admits as promises a multitude of express avowals and tacit understandings, and incorporates mechanisms for accom-

[5] John Rawls, "Two Concepts of Rules," in *Theories of Ethics*, ed. P. Foot (Oxford: Oxford University Press, 1967), 155–156

[6] See Henry Sidgwick, *The Methods of Ethics* (Indianapolis: Hackett, 1981), 295–311.

modating misunderstandings. It recognizes a range of considerations as invalidating putative promises, as excusing promisors from fulfilling genuine ones, as grounds for exonerating or censuring promise breakers. So it involves criteria for identifying promises, deciding whether they are binding and whether they are fulfilled. These criteria are largely uncodified.

Promising is conventional: a variety of actions and utterances might count as making a promise, a variety of considerations might justify or excuse its nonfulfillment. Moreover, the scope of the practice could be delimited in a number of ways. Plausible practices could differ over whether one can promise what one cannot deliver or what one is already obliged to deliver or what one is already obliged not to deliver. Still, the rules that constitute the practice are authoritative for actions falling under it. Having promised to be home by five, I am obliged to appear, even though in a different, equally reasonable practice, my words would not have counted as a promise. What makes my utterance a promise is nothing but the social conventions in force; what makes it obligatory for me to perform is the fact that I am bound by those conventions. We learn this by being reared in a moral community constituted in part by those very conventions.

Until we master the rules pertaining to making, keeping, and breaking promising, releasing promisors from or holding them to their commitments, excusing promise breakers or blaming them for their dereliction, we do not know how to play the promising game. And the evidence of our mastery is to be found in our behavior, not in a capacity to recite the rules.

A society that repudiated the institution of promising—for instance, a society of strict act utilitarians—might be viable. But a group without a language could hardly be considered a human society. And a language requires a grammar. So when we turn to grammar, we find an unquestionably central social practice.

Chomskian arguments for innateness might seem to vitiate any attempt to treat grammar as a game. But those arguments pertain exclusively to deep structure—the logically and psychologically fundamental rules purportedly shared by all possible human languages.[7] No one denies that surface grammar is acquired—that in order to speak Italian, we have to master Italian grammar. The question that concerns me is whether surface grammar can fruitfully be construed as a game. So I use the term 'grammar' to refer to the superficial structure of a language. For my purposes, debates about the alleged innateness of deep structure are irrelevant. Still, if a Wittgensteinian account succeeds in explaining surface grammar, innate depth grammar may become an idle wheel.

---

[7] Noam Chomsky, *Aspects of the Theory of Syntax* (Cambridge, Mass.: MIT Press, 1965), 58

Grammar is plainly rule-governed: to interpret an utterance as a construction of a particular language is to take it to be subject to the rules of that language. Even though the rules change as the language evolves, they are not mainly descriptive generalizations about current usage. Like the rules of basketball or chess, they are primarily normative. They set the limits on permissible forms of expression and in so doing create the possibility of error.

Although different languages have different grammars, one may question whether grammar is conventional. For it is not altogether clear what makes for conventionality. Grammar shares some important features of familiar systems of conventions. It is, for example, a contingent social construction, not wholly determined by nature or by the function it is to perform. A variety of constructions are equally effective. The acquisition of a grammar is, moreover, a product of socialization. We become grammatically adept as we are integrated into a linguistic community. And its sanctions are social sanctions. As members of, or initiates into, that community, our utterances and inscriptions are subject to the evaluation of our peers. But unlike, say, a system of conventions that correlates military ranks with social privileges, a grammar is not something we can choose. Unless we already have a language, and thus a grammar, we could not even imagine such a choice. Nor can we choose to replace one grammar by another while keeping the rest of the language fixed. We could, to be sure, choose henceforth to speak only Finnish, and we could do so out of a fondness for Finnish grammar. But we could not decide to subject English locutions to Finnish grammar, for no such decision could be implemented. The English lexicon and Finnish grammar do not mesh.

Our grammar is, of course, influenced by our choices. We may decide, for example, to modify it in order to simplify or clarify its rules, to make it more sensitive, or to bring it into closer accord with everyday usage. What we cannot do is choose whether to have a grammar at all or whether to divorce one grammatical system and marry our lexicon to another. The available choices involve only incremental changes in an ongoing practice.

It does no harm to consider a grammar a system of conventions if we recognize that, although they admit of alternatives, not all such systems are amenable to adoption. There are some systems of conventions that we are born into. Still, whether or not it counts as conventional, grammar is authoritative. Its rules determine what constructions are acceptable in a language. Nothing, for example, is obviously wrong with splitting an infinitive except that the rules of English forbid it. But the rules are empowered to decide such matters; so there is no room for negotiation. Rightness in matters of grammar is whatever the rules legislate.

Learning explicitly formulated rules is neither necessary nor sufficient for mastering a grammar. It is not sufficient, because rules without applications are inert. If I can neither formulate nor identify German dative constructions, knowing that 'bei' in German takes the dative avails me nothing; until I have mastered the network of intertwining rules and applications, with their exceptions and the exceptions to their exceptions, I cannot speak grammatically. And knowledge of explicitly formulated grammatical rules is not necessary, since one can develop a feel for the language without being able to articulate or recognize the rules or criteria on which judgments of grammaticality are based. This, indeed, is the situation of most native speakers: we can readily and reliably tell whether a construction is grammatical, but beyond saying that it sounds right (or wrong), we cannot explain how we know. Still, a grammar can be learned, for whether or not its rules are codified, they are displayed in public linguistic behavior.

Our ability to learn grammar by observing linguistic activity requires explanation. For actual usage is full of ungrammatical utterances. By observing linguistic practice, we might easily learn which linguistic forms are in fact used. But it is harder to see how our observations could enable us to discriminate between correct and incorrect forms. The conviction that they cannot is one reason for thinking that standards of grammaticality are innate. Wittgenstein supplies a different answer. He notes the availability of a wider range of behaviors than is normally appealed to. In developing standards of grammaticality, we have access not only to individual utterances and inscriptions but also to their reception by competent speakers. Every linguistic community has characteristic behaviors that indicate whether a locution is acceptable, and if it is not, why it is deemed defective. Although ungrammatical constructions are used, they are also often disparaged and/or corrected. If we are sensitive to corrective behaviors and to other manifestations of dissatisfaction, we can learn from observations pertaining to actual linguistic practice what the community takes the standards governing that practice to be.

Such observations provide our best access to a grammar. The norms that govern a practice are the ones that are actually used in generating and evaluating its products. They are not always the ones its participants explicitly espouse. The reactions of competent speakers to constructions that are actually used reveal the community's real standards of grammaticality. These may diverge from the standards set forth in its grammar books. If so, the texts are untrustworthy. Individual judgments of grammaticality can, of course, be untrustworthy as well. Not everything that is treated as correct (or mistaken) is in fact correct (or mistaken). But the collective wisdom of the linguistic community cannot be wrong. For there is nothing for it to be wrong about: there is no more to being grammatical than being what the community considers grammatical. Consensus determines correctness; conformity determines competence. To speak grammatically we need only conform with currently accepted grammatical practice. And both consensus and conformity can be discovered by seeing what acknowledged speakers of the language say and do.

The foregoing examples illustrate why Wittgensteinians find it fruitful to construe social practices as games. Such a construal highlights the ways norms function to structure the activities that constitute the practice, and the ways public participation makes available the information required to learn and engage in it. A sketchy review of selected examples is not, of course, sufficient to demonstrate that practices in general take the form of games. But it is, I hope, sufficient to make such a suggestion plausible and to show something of the insight to be gained by thinking of practices in this way.

THE INQUIRY GAME

Suppose then that inquiry is a game, and 'knowledge' the term for victory. How would this affect our epistemology? Stereotypical games, as we saw, are constituted by conventional rules and criteria that define constituent positions, moves, resources, and objectives, as well as the standards its activities and their effects are subject to. If inquiry is such a game, determinate rules and criteria circumscribe its methodology. They specify what may be done and how it may be done. They define concepts in terms of which investigations and their products are to be conceived. Just as a touchdown would be inconceivable without the conceptual framework of football, an experiment would be inconceivable without the conceptual framework of science.

Only in the context of a game do its concepts have application. The conditions for a touchdown can be realized only in the course of a football game; and unless they are realized, there is no touchdown. Similarly, on this interpretation, the conditions for evidence can be realized only in the course of an investigation; and unless they are realized, there is no evidence. The *only* way to produce knowledge then is to play an inquiry game, to do everything that its rules prescribe and nothing that its rules forbid.

Being a pure procedure, a game generates its products. Although the standards for victory are set in advance, there are no winners until a game is played. If knowledge is victory in an inquiry game, it is created, not just disclosed, by investigation. Knowledge could no more exist without inquiry than checkmate could exist without chess. Still, all that is required for the existence of knowledge is that inquiry be successfully carried out. There is no danger of skepticism. For inquiry, like other games, is designed so that it can be won and so that we can identify the winner. Whatever wins a game of inquiry, whatever is produced by its pure procedures, counts on this interpretation as knowledge.

The suggestion that knowledge would not exist without inquiry is not altogether unpalatable. For knowledge is a matter of epistemic entitlement. Arguably, we are entitled to believe only what inquiry certifies. Investigations generate warrant or justification for beliefs, and only justified beliefs count as knowledge. Doubts may emerge, though, when this view of entitlement is married to the game model of inquiry. For it is not clear that all modes of justification can be assimilated to playing by the rules. The model fits systematic inquiry fairly well. Normal science, Kuhn contends, is conducted within fairly narrow confines, according to quite rigid rules and restrictions. Only results that satisfy its conditions are scientifically credible. Likewise, in history, sociology, or literary studies, there are antecedently determinate, publicly recognized standards that have to be satisfied before a discovery or an interpretation is incorporated into the corpus of knowledge. But knowledge, as we normally construe it, comprehends the fruits of casual as well as systematic study. It is not obvious what network of rules and criteria could result in my knowing whether the lawn needs mowing or where I left my shoes or how often guppies should be fed. For the considerations that yield such knowledge seem both too inchoate and too disparate to be constituted as warranting conditions by a system of antecedently determinate rules.

Although disquieting, this objection is not decisive. The pure procedural epistemologist might easily deny that such casual convictions amount to knowledge, arguing that they lack the warrant that only rigorous, systematic investigation can supply. Such a response is not unreasonable; even when such opinions are borne out, it is often hard to see what justifies them. An alternative and, I believe, more powerful reply is that the objection rests on an excessively narrow conception of games—one that cannot accommodate loosely organized games like stickball and catch. If we adopt a more reasonable conception, recognizing that the rules of a game need be neither explicitly codified nor narrowly confining, we find that our casual convictions, when they amount to knowledge, can indeed be construed as the fruits of an inquiry game.

Seemingly casual convictions are subject to peer review. My claim to know that the lawn should be mowed may be faulted if, for example, my reasons are irrelevant or insufficient, my experience with such matters too limited, my memory unreliable or inaccurate. Such criticisms would not be possible without applicable criteria of relevance, accuracy, and adequacy. So the fact that we make and agree about critical assessments in cases of this kind indicates that shared criteria are at work. And the fact that such criteria are considered decisive shows that the context of their application is a game if more formal inquiries are. But are they?

If pure procedural epistemology is correct, the investigations we undertake, the cognitive opportunities available to us, the methods we are permitted to employ, and the evaluations that our efforts and results are subject to are all constituted by a cognitive game whose rules and criteria the epistemic community generates and enforces.

Logic and mathematics are easily cast in this light. Axioms and rules constitute formal systems. The game is to discover what can be obtained from the axioms by correct application of the rules. Although the system supplies the resources, a problem has no solution until the axioms and rules are applied to generate one. Nothing else will do. Even though a mathematical problem is posed as a question, not every method or even every reliable method of producing the right answer counts as solving the problem. We can, for example, generate reams of inductive evidence that every even number is the sum of two primes—indeed, so much evidence that no one but a card-carrying skeptic is likely to doubt the conclusion. Still, we have no proof. Mathematics does not acknowledge the validity of instantial induction. So even if the question has been answered, the problem remains unsolved. A sequence of symbols need only satisfy the relevant standards of a formal system to be a proof, a theorem, a deduction, or a problem solution. For the standards are definitive, not just indicative, of logical or mathematical status. To comply with a formal system's criteria for proof is to be a proof in that system. We cannot intelligibly concede that the standards have been met and yet deny, or even doubt that the status is merited. Any attempt to do so would show that we do not know what words like 'proof', 'theorem', and 'deduction' mean.

The game model is fitting in another way as well. Formal systems purporting to share a subject matter often accept divergent sets of axioms and/or rules of inference. Euclidian and Lovachevskian geometries, for example, differ over the parallel postulate; classical and intuitionistic logics, over the law of excluded middle. Although the source of such disagreement can be localized, the differences reverberate. For it follows from them that the systems count different inferences as valid, different formulas as theorems, different sequences as proofs. Logical or mathematical status then is not absolute but relative to the system that confers it. And a symbol holds a particular status only when interpreted as a symbol of a given system. Interpreted according to another system, it might merit a quite different status.

The availability of divergent, independently acceptable formal systems shows that logic and mathematics provide for a variety of epistemic games. Our success with any one does not discredit the others. It may, indeed, enhance our prospects for understanding related formal systems—for, that is, playing and winning kindred epistemic games.

Are logic and mathematics representative of knowledge in general? If not, other types of knowledge may lack the very features that enable formal systems to be treated as games. Indeed, there is reason to think this is the case. For there appear to be significant differences between formal and factual knowledge.

Formal systems are rigorous. They are constituted by explicit rules that determine necessary and sufficient conditions for the instantiation of their categories. Such systems, moreover, are powerful. They yield proofs. Since proof is unimpeachable, once we have ascertained that it meets the requisite standards, we are epistemically entitled to accept a result. Investigations in factual disciplines are not subject to such rigorous restraints. Their governing principles seem closer to tacit rules of thumb than to explicit rules of inference. Not even the most firmly established laws have the status of axioms. Empirical inquiry traffics in warrant, not proof. It generates support for the conclusions it countenances but is powerless to demonstrate that they are correct. In investigations into matters of fact, correctness is typically held to involve truth; truth, correspondence to a theory-independent reality. But satisfaction of standards within a system of thought is impotent to guarantee correspondence to something outside it. Such, anyway, is the prevailing stereotype.

Like other stereotypes, this one is naive. It credits formal inquiry with too much rigor; factual inquiry with too little. It fails to appreciate the extent to which ill-advised views about truth vitiate theories of formal knowledge as well as theories of factual knowledge. Once such oversimplifications are remedied, we find that the differences between the two, although real, are neither so extreme nor so significant as the stereotype pretends.

The prestige of proof derives in large measure from its putative relation to truth. If the premises of an argument are true and the form deductively valid, the conclusion is proven. It cannot be false, for deductive rules are truth-preserving.

The guarantee is conditional though, obtaining only if the premises are true and the argument forms valid. How can this be established? Some claims and rules may derive from other, more fundamental ones. But chains of justification eventually end. Basic rules and axioms are insusceptible of proof, there being nothing more fundamental from which they could derive. The conditional can be deferred but never discharged. All proof depends ultimately on unproven premises and unvalidated rules of inference.

This does not discredit formal systems. Like other pure procedures, they deliver precisely what they promise. But just as we may become less enamored with football when we realize that it fails to build character, we may become less impressed with logic when we realize that it fails to guarantee truth. Or stripped of our illusions, we may be better placed to assess its real epistemic worth.

Although indemonstrable, the bases of acceptable formal systems are not arbitrary. Only some statements are permitted to serve as axioms, only some directives as rules. But we saw in the previous chapter that there are no indubitable truths or infallible rules. So what makes for an acceptable basis? The answer, it seems, is this:

> Principles of deductive inference are justified by their conformity with accepted deductive practice. Their validity depends upon accordance with the particular deductive inferences we actually make and sanction. If a rule yields inacceptable inferences, we drop it as invalid.[8]

In constructing a formal system, as in codifying a surface grammar, we test theory against patterns already deemed correct. Proof thus rests firmly on a bed of consensus. Community accord underwrites rigor.

PUZZLE SOLVING

In *The Structure of Scientific Revolutions*, as I read it, Kuhn construes normal science as pure procedural inquiry.[9] He contends that ordinary scientific investigation occurs within a framework of accepted laws, concepts, applications, methods, and standards that delimit the legitimate problems and the range of permissible solutions.[10] Normal science does not debate fundamentals, for the framework or 'paradigm' is definitive of the science and its subject matter. Any entity that does not instantiate its concepts lies outside the scope of the discipline; any investigation that does not satisfy its strictures is unscientific. To be sure, such an investigation might satisfy the strictures of, and so be counted scientific by, another paradigm. But scientific communities are closed societies; each recognizes no authority to confer scientific standing but its own.

Kuhn's position is holistic in much the way Wittgenstein's is. In structuring a science, laws are given pride of place; they function almost as tautologies, their denial being practically inconceivable. But like the rules of a game, laws without applications are not fully determinate. So to ascertain what, say, the second law of thermodynamics amounts to, we must see how it enters into explanations, how it bears on experimental design,

---

[8] Goodman, *Fact, Fiction, and Forecast*, 63–64.

[9] Here, as with Wittgenstein and Rorty, I am concerned more with the merit of the position than with its pedigree. *The Structure of Scientific Revolutions*, like Wittgenstein's and Rorty's works, admits of numerous readings, not all of which take it to adopt a pure procedural stance.

[10] Kuhn, *The Structure of Scientific Revolutions*, 10.

how it is integrated into theory, and so on. We must see, that is, how unquestioning allegiance to it affects the ongoing activity of a scientific community.

Expressions do not fix their own interpretations. In science, as elsewhere, criteria of application must be supplied. Different criteria may be equally reasonable. So different paradigms can apply the same formula differently. Then the formula means different things in the different sciences; it constitutes distinct laws. For the meaning of a law and of the terms occurring in it are determined by their use—their application in the context the paradigm defines. Just as 'always follow suit' means different things in bridge and in hearts, the Schrödinger equation means different things in solid state and field theoretic physics.[11] Its acceptance commits the two scientific communities to different applications. According to Kuhn then, it is only in the context of a paradigm that a scientific term or law has determinate meaning, and the role it plays determines its meaning.

Several important consequences follow: First, not every seemingly significant question about its subject falls within the purview of a science. Only those construable as puzzles count as scientific. Indeed, Kuhn suggests that social inquiry is less successful than natural science precisely because it insists on addressing important questions—how to alleviate poverty or bring about peace—rather than restricting its efforts to the more trivial puzzles that it obviously has the resources to solve.[12]

Second, not every way, or even every reliable way, of arriving at a correct answer counts as solving a scientific problem. For once a problem has been construed as a puzzle, the methods for solving it are severely restricted.[13] So even when folk remedies are effective, they do not belong to medical science. For the science mandates that cures must be effected in particular ways, ways that are informed by its conception of health and disease.

Third, puzzles are so designed that the existence of a solution is assured. So failure to solve a puzzle tells against those working on it, not against the puzzle itself or the institution that generates it. My inability to solve the *Times* crossword puzzle diminishes my standing as a puzzle-solver; it does not discredit that particular puzzle or the conventions regulating the construction and solution of crossword puzzles in general. Similarly, when scientific investigations are framed as puzzles, investigative failures tell against individual scientists, not against the paradigm that produces the puzzles or the laws it presupposes in framing them.[14] The laws

[11] Ibid., 187.
[12] Ibid., 36–37.
[13] Ibid., 38.
[14] Ibid., 35.

and methods of normal science, according to Kuhn, are like the axioms and rules of a formal system and like the rules of a game in that those working with them unquestioningly accept their adequacy.

Normal science then seeks to solve puzzles it sets for itself. If we call the solutions true, we must recognize that truth consists in the settled opinion of the scientific community, not in correspondence to nature. If, on the other hand, we insist that truth is correspondence, then normal science, as Kuhn describes it, is indifferent to truth.

Much of a paradigm is tacit, being captured in methodology, instrumentation, experimental design, and execution. Explicit articulation of laws counts for little. Until we know how the laws are applied, what explanations they figure in, what phenomena instantiate them, and how their instantiation is discerned, we do not understand them; for we do not know what accepting them commits us to. Once we know such things, explicit statement of the laws adds little to our understanding.[15] Here again the analogy with games is helpful. What we need to know to do science or to play chess is how the rules are realized in practice. The ability to state them correctly is less important than the ability to mold our behavior to conform to their restrictions and realize their objectives.

Examples are cognitively crucial for Kuhn for the same reasons they are for Wittgenstein: they are able to show aspects of a practice that cannot be said. A paradigm, according to Kuhn, is designed around a particular scientific achievement that serves as a model for future inquiry. The challenge is to articulate and extend the insights implicit in that achievement without violating the (equally implicit) standards responsible for its success. The paradigm presents its practitioners with an achievement that exemplifies its theoretical, conceptual, methodological, and instrumental commitments; it instructs them to go and do likewise.

But how do they tell what doing likewise consists in? The exemplary achievement has any number of features; scientists bent on developing its promise need to know which ones to model their practice on. Moreover, if that achievement is to serve as the basis of a coherent research tradition, members of the scientific community must agree about its salient characteristics. Otherwise, individual efforts at paradigm articulation would radiate from the focal achievement in all directions; research would lack direction.

The fear of radical divergence in paradigm articulation is groundless. For the nucleus of a paradigm is an example, not just an instance, of scientific practice. Plainly we have no recipes for interpreting examples; even rules of thumb are lacking for those that revolutionize a practice. Rather, interpretation depends on function—on what is done with a symbol, on

[15] Ibid., 142.

how understanding and action within a practice are affected by it. For pure procedural philosophers, the meaning of an example, like the meaning of a word, is its use. So we cannot correctly interpret the nucleus of a paradigm if we isolate it from its cognitive environment. We need to understand its function in the context of the science it guides. The way the community uses it thus determines its interpretation.

The commitment to a paradigm is a commitment to develop a network of scientific results with the features the paradigm's focal achievement exemplifies. So in concurring on the interpretation of that achievement, scientists agree about which features are exemplified and about how to determine whether putative results have those features. This enables them to build on one another's work, for they can be confident that established results have the properties the paradigm prescribes. Univocal interpretation of the example at its heart thus gives a paradigm direction. It makes progress possible by enabling scientists to collaborate—to work together and to take what has already been done as a basis for future research. To be sure, there is no guarantee that a univocal interpretation will emerge. If it does not, an achievement, however noteworthy in itself, is incapable of seeding a paradigm. It is a mere curiosity, for the scientific community does not know what to make of it. The possibility of normal science—and thus, if Kuhn is right, of the cumulative growth of scientific knowledge—is grounded in the contingent fact that scientists agree on the interpretation of the example at the core of their science.

Although contingent, such agreement is not entirely accidental; it is aided by acculturation and enforced by fiat. Scientific education, according to Kuhn, is largely a matter of indoctrination, the ethos of the community being transmitted from one generation to the next as scientists train their successors. Though loaded, the term 'indoctrination' is apt. Reasoned argument cannot convince a novice to accept a paradigm, for he lacks the requisite conceptual resources. Being ignorant of the paradigm's concepts, methods, and standards, he can neither comprehend its arguments nor appreciate their force. Only after he has thoroughly assimilated the paradigm's worldview is he in a position to be moved by its reasons. So a student acquires a paradigm as a child acquires his first language. As he learns his way about in an environment in which it is used, his efforts meet with encouragement and resistance. Eventually, if his training succeeds, he conforms to the mores of the community; he does what is expected of him as a scientist.

Members of a scientific community manage to agree despite their inability to articulate the basis of their agreement. This is no surprise, Kuhn contends, for their education is designed to foster conformity. Initiates into a paradigm all receive the same training: they read the same textbooks, perform the same experiments, solve the same problems. These texts, experiments, and problems are carefully contrived to inculcate the community's vision of its subject matter. Moreover, students are taught and graded by professors who received much the same training. Even though there are indefinitely many ways to interpret a data set or continue a series, only one—or at most a few—will be counted correct. Kuhn maintains that scientific education actively discourages innovation and originality. Students who fail to conform are ostracized; they haven't got what it takes to be scientists. In the end then, agreement among scientists is assured by the power of a scientific community to determine its own membership. A scientific community is exclusive; it determines its own constitution and standards of conduct. Although it cannot compel individuals to conform, it can and does expel nonconformists. Moreover, since it has a monopoly on its subject, all and only the views about that subject that the community accepts are scientifically acceptable. There is no independent standpoint from which its verdicts can be challenged. The scientific community thus effectively silences dissidents by declaring their pronouncements unscientific.

Like logic and mathematics then normal science is quite rigid. A paradigm so structures its subject matter that seemingly plausible approaches to its problems are foreclosed. By restricting the scientist's options, it assures that its game can be won. To succeed, the investigator need only do what the paradigm prescribes; he need not pursue every imaginable line of inquiry nor answer every conceivable objection. A paradigm, like a formal system, is grounded in consensus about what the subject matter is and how it is legitimately reasoned about. The collective wisdom of the community cannot be wrong. Since the community, in constructing a paradigm, constitutes its subject matter, consensus makes for correctness. There is nothing for the community to be wrong about.

Incommensurability of scientific languages follows immediately from the insularity of normal science. Scientific terms obtain their meaning and reference from their function in scientific practice. The rules governing their application are determined by a paradigm and extend only as far as the paradigm does. So syntactic replicas belonging to different paradigms are homonyms: they express distinct concepts, bear distinct meanings, refer to distinct states of affairs. The magnitude denoted by 'mass' in Newtonian mechanics is not the one denoted by 'mass' in relativistic mechanics. For the two exhibit different regularities, are captured in different laws, are revealed by different observations. Nor does any other Newtonian concept denote the magnitude relativistic mechanics calls 'mass'. According to Newtonian mechanics, there is—indeed, there could be—no such thing as relativistic mass. There is no room for it in the world the Newtonian paradigm describes. So the languages of the two paradigms are not intertranslatable, for the central concepts of the one have no coun-terpart in the other.[16]

Proponents of separate paradigms are thus mutually unintelligible; each lacks access to the concepts the other employs and the world the other describes. Nor can a neutral framework afford access to both. Since para-digm-dependent laws and applications are integral to the meanings of sci-entific terms, retreat to agnosticism about those laws and applications marks a change of meaning. Whatever may be conveyed in a neutral lan-guage, the commitments of separate scientific paradigms cannot.

WIDENING THE FIELD

Kuhn's account applies only to science; Wittgenstein's is unrestricted. The *Philosophical Investigations* attempts to expose the forces that structure institutions, delimit practices, set standards, and frame inquiries and other activities generally. Like Kuhn, Wittgenstein takes these forces to be so-cial; unlike Kuhn, he believes them to be generated by the culture as a whole, not by diverse subcultures. Plainly, the story Wittgenstein has to tell is more complicated than Kuhn's, for a culture does not display the unity of purpose that Kuhn finds in a scientific community. Still, the out-lines of the two accounts are surprisingly similar. Indeed, Kuhn's normal science is a microcosm of Wittgenstein's form of life.

The culture is the arbiter of linguistic correctness. Like grammaticality, applicability of terms is a matter of conformity with linguistic practice. 'Dog' correctly applies to just those animals the community counts as dogs. Any other literal application is mistaken. If the community does not consider coyotes to be dogs, then for all their similarities, coyotes are not dogs. The conditions on the application of our terms settle the identities of their objects. All and only entities satisfying the criteria for 'dog' are in fact dogs. A community's authority over its language amounts to authority over the constitution of its world. Since the assertibility of a sentence depends on its grammatical form and on the applicability of its terms, it too is socially determined. We are warranted in asserting a sentence in just those circumstances in which the linguistic community counts it assertible. Regardless of the strength of, or reasons behind, the personal convictions that motivate it, an assertion is unwarranted un-less it satisfies the relevant community standards. If, as seems reasonable, we are epistemically entitled to believe any sentence we are warranted in asserting, then satisfaction of community standards generates epistemic entitlement.

[16] Ibid., 101–103.

This relation between language and cognition is general; it is not peculiar to science or a product of the special structure of scientific communities. But it would be wrong to think that the public at large determines the correct use of specialized vocabularies. Standards of applicability of terms and assertibility of sentences may be variously located. Familiar locutions like 'dog' and 'The bus is late' are common currency. More recondite ones tend to be the province of particular specialties. We defer to astronomers the authority to determine the applicability of 'quasar' and to musicians the authority to determine the assertibility of 'He's singing off key'. So a Wittgensteinian account can accommodate the division of linguistic labor.[17] Even though the meaning of an expression is its use, that use is not always settled by majority rule. Within a shared form of life a variety of language games may be played.

Learning, Wittgenstein insists, is a public enterprise. Whether or not we are schooled, we are subject to peer review, our efforts being shaped by the encouragement and criticism we receive. An individual counts as having mastered physics (or photography or planting pachysandra) when her relevant beliefs and actions satisfy the community's criteria for knowledge of physics (or photography or pachysandra planting). The mark of an educated person is conformity to the cognitive mores of her culture. Linguistic competence is at one with factual knowledge. To master the term 'rutabaga', for example, is to learn what can correctly be said about and done with rutabagas; that is, to learn what rutabagas are and how they relate to other sorts of things. We know rutabagas when we are competent to apply the term 'rutabaga' and its cognates and to respond correctly to talk of rutabagas.

That knowledge of rutabagas is acquired from others is no surprise, for the instructional scenario is easily imagined. We point out rutabagas to a child, identify their salient features for him, and applaud or correct his attempts to use the term. And we consider him to have mastered 'rutabaga' when he consistently employs the term as we do—when he makes the right moves in the language game.

Wittgenstein's insight is that language learning is of a piece. We learn 'pain' in the same way we learn 'rutabaga'. The public manifestations of pain are identified; early efforts to use the term are rewarded or reproved; and linguistic behavior is gradually molded until the novice comes to use the term as competent speakers do. Only then does he know what pain is. This is surprising indeed. Even if knowledge of rutabagas is inseparable from mastery of rutabaga-talk, knowledge of pain hardly seems to require linguistic competence. Isn't learning the word 'pain' just learning a label

---

[17] Hilary Putnam, "The Meaning of 'Meaning,'" in *Mind, Language, and Reality* (Cambridge: Cambridge University Press, 1975), 227–229.

for a sensation I know all too intimately already? Wittgenstein thinks not. He contends that without the schematization that language supplies, I can get no purchase on pain, no fix on the flux of experience. I have no way to differentiate among my mental states, no basis for considering diverse throbs and twinges the same sort of thing.

What enables us to ascribe mental states is the existence of regularities in publicly observable behavior. These generate criteria for the correct application of mental terms. To be sure, the regularities in question are subtle, complex, and interconnected; the criteria we employ defy articulation. To say that we ascribe pain on the basis of behavior is not to say that we ascribe pain by the rote application of a formula:

x is in pain $\equiv$ x displays behavior y.

Still, we do recognize people as being in pain, and it is their behavior that tips us off. Were there no regularities in pain behavior, were individual manifestations of pain utterly idiosyncratic, we could never have learned the term; indeed, there could be no such term. And we could have developed no conception of pain. "An 'inner process' stands in need of outward criteria."[18]

Competence with a term thus coincides with knowledge of its object. But linguistic competence is a product of socialization. So knowledge of objects must be a product of socialization as well. Knowledge on this account consists not in correspondence to a mind-independent reality but in conformity to societal norms, and learning consists not in securing a match between mind and the world but in bringing our words and deeds up to par.

Two lines of argument support this position. The first is a sustained critique of correspondence. It notes that the connection allegedly linking knowledge and its object is obscure. We have no criterion to mark out the right relation, no basis for ruling out impostors. Moreover, no such correspondence could secure the normativeness of knowledge. Knowing that p entitles us to believe that p. But a mere connection between thought and object is powerless to establish cognitive norms, and a connection unmediated by norms can convey no entitlement. If we require that the existence of the relevant correspondence or the relevant norms and the conditions for their realization be known, the problem arises anew, and an infinite regress begins. Finally, a correspondence theory divorces the learning process from its product. We learn by being brought to think as our mentors do. A student counts as having learned geography when her beliefs about geographical matters agree with those of acknowledged experts. If knowledge consists in such agreement, it is a direct product of

[18] Wittgenstein, *Philosophical Investigations*, 580.

learning. If, however, knowledge is or involves correspondence, the connection between learning and correspondence—between a process that generates agreement and a product that relies on correspondence—remains to be explained.

The second line of argument is summarized in the slogan, 'Look at what we do, not at what we say'. If we avow that knowledge is correspondence, our actions belie our words. A correspondence that disregards the community's cognitive standards is epistemically impotent. Were we to discover such a correspondence we would (and should) treat it as a curiosity. Being indifferent to our cognitive norms, it could convey no epistemic entitlement. The cognitive demands of the community of inquiry structure the quest for knowledge. Investigations are designed around community standards of evidence, relevance, and reason. They terminate when consensus is reached. If everyone agrees that willow trees are deciduous and that the criteria for deciding such matters have been satisfied, we treat the question as closed. We unhesitatingly accept and confidently act on the conclusion that willow trees are deciduous.

Perhaps knowledge requires both correspondence and consensus. Then knowledge might be construed as a form of justified true belief, justification deriving from the satisfaction of community standards and truth from correspondence to the world. Although this proposal fits our intuitions, our behavior tells against it. For when our socially established standards are met, inquiry ends; we do not suspend judgment until correspondence has also been established. Community standards are authoritative. Nothing more than their satisfaction is required for knowledge, and nothing less will do. Knowledge is whatever the community takes it to be, whatever passes the community's tests for knowledge.

We might be reluctant to endorse such a position, thinking it threatens to trivialize knowledge. Rather than the product of the arduous, lonely task of wresting the world's secrets from it, knowledge turns out to consist in conformity—in thinking what our peers believe we should. Even so, knowledge is not easily achieved. For society's cognitive standards are multiple, diverse, and often devilishly difficult to satisfy. Opinions intertwine. It may be an exaggeration to say that you cannot know anything without knowing everything, but it is no exaggeration to say that you cannot know anything without knowing a lot. Wittgenstein's position is holistic. Knowledge is achieved not by piecemeal learning of individual truths but by mastering complex networks of cognitive commitments—networks that contain practical as well as theoretical nodes. A good deal of botany, carpentry, ecology, and commerce is implicated in correct talk about trees. So satisfying the relevant standards, knowing the role of 'tree' in the language game(s) it belongs to is no mean trick. Indeed, the outstanding problems in any field of inquiry attest to the difficulty of satisfying the cognitive standards we set for ourselves.

'Look at what we do, not at what we say' gives prominence to examples. Every utterance is subject to multiple interpretations. The problem is to decide which of them is correct. Appeals to speakers' intentions avail us nothing, for intentions are couched in words. And the interpretation of a statement of intention is at least as problematic as the interpretation of the original remark. Nor can definitions of constituent terms settle the matter. Even if we had them, they too would bear divergent interpretations. It is actual usage—what we do with words, not what we say about them—that determines their role in a language. And it is that role which a correct interpretation is supposed to reflect. In examples of actual usage then, a term's function is exhibited. Such examples show what cannot be said—how an expression functions in the language.

Examples are thus pedagogically and epistemologically central to Wittgenstein as they are to Kuhn. For competence with a term consists in playing its language game correctly, not in being able to recite a formula that characterizes correct play. And competence with a term, which is learned from and exhibited in examples, amounts to knowledge of its object. There is, to be sure, no a priori guarantee that the examples at the heart of our practices will be interpreted univocally. That they are is a contingent fact of human natural history.[19] That fact is responsible for the existence of a culture, a shared form of life.

Although contingent, agreement is not altogether fortuitous. Wittgenstein recognizes that our pedagogical practices are designed to foster conformity. What he regards as contingent is the fact that our efforts succeed. Although there are infinitely many ways to continue the series: '1, 2, 3, . . .', we manage to agree about which one is right. Deviance is not tolerated. If, after suitable training, a child cannot continue the series as we do, he "is separated from the others and treated as a lunatic"[20]—even though we recognize that his way of continuing the series instantiates some self-consistent mathematical rule. Diagnosis and treatment appear drastic, given the seeming innocuousness of the aberration. But since our practices intertwine, such an aberration is indicative of a serious, systemic disorder. The child who cannot continue the series correctly cannot count; nor can he take measurements, perform calculations, use money, or tell time. Once we appreciate the gravity of his cognitive disorder, labeling him mentally defective does not seem an overreaction. And separating

---

[19] Wittgenstein, *Remarks on the Foundations of Mathematics*, I, 141.

[20] Ludwig Wittgenstein, *The Blue and Brown Books* (New York: Harper Torchbooks, 1958), 93.

him from his peers seems inevitable, for someone so severely disabled would be incompetent to participate in our form of life.[21] Wittgenstein, like Kuhn, thus believes that consensus is achieved by silencing dissidents. In the one case, dissenters are denied the status of scientist; in the other, they are denied the status of rational agent. Disagreement over fundamentals is preempted. Anyone who attempts to mount such a disagreement can safely be ignored, for his very attempt shows him to be incompetent.

DIVERGING PATHS

Normal science, I have urged, is a microcosmic form of life. But normal science is not the whole of science. In Kuhn's account of scientific revolutions, his differences with Wittgenstein emerge. According to Kuhn, the orderly process of normal science is interrupted by revolutions marked by disagreements so profound that the very nature of the discipline and its subject matter are called into question. Rival paradigms vie for the allegiance of the scientific community, the stakes being the future course of inquiry. Paradigm disagreements, Kuhn maintains, cannot be rationally adjudicated, for the canons of rationality are themselves in dispute. Standards of evidence, relevance, fruitfulness, and the like, determine what counts as justification within a paradigm. They vindicate particular scientific judgments if the paradigm's adequacy is presupposed. But since they presuppose the paradigm, they cannot justify it; nor can they vindicate particular findings when the paradigm's adequacy is in doubt. So long as the Newtonian paradigm is controversial, Newtonian results are questionable and Newtonian methods powerless to justify them; for if the paradigm is untenable, its results and methods are unfounded. Paradigm disputes thus cannot be resolved by appeal to standards internal to the contending parties; for each begs the question in favor of its own side.

Nor can matters be resolved at the metalevel. For metatheoretical adjudication would be possible only if clashing paradigms were subject to common principles. But they are not. Without applications, rules are indeterminate; so metatheoretical principles diffuse when divorced from the sciences to which they apply. And a formula without a settled interpretation is incapable of guiding practice. Moreover, divergence in application marks a difference in principles. Paradigms that disagree about whether the results of two experiments are mutually consistent are ipso facto committed to different standards of consistency. By their acceptance of different methods, results, and modes of argument, rival paradigms reveal themselves to be answerable to different standards. For what is acceptable to a paradigm is a function of what is accepted by its practitioners. To be

[21] Stroud, "Wittgenstein and Logical Necessity," 487–488.

sure, rival paradigms may couch their express metatheories in the same words. But this just shows again that words admit of divergent interpretations, that actual applications are needed to tie them down. By ascending to the metalevel, we hope to discover commonality; what we find instead is vagueness, ambiguity, or outright disagreement.

Rational resolution of paradigm disputes remains out of reach. For although metatheory can synthesize or organize or articulate the principles implicit in scientific practice, it has no critical function. Practice can correct theory, but theory is powerless to correct practice. For the very meaning of a theoretical claim derives from the practices it describes. Theory cannot, without sacrificing its content, obtain enough distance from its subject to look at that subject critically.

In our discussion of games we saw that a framework of rules, criteria, and goals creates the possibility of objective evaluation. By determining what should be done, how, and to what end, it enables us to distinguish between correct and incorrect, right and wrong, success and failure; it enables us to recognize mistakes and rectifications. But the framework does not provide resources for criticizing the practice itself. If Kuhn is right, the same goes for science. No more than the resources of baseball determine whether the designated hitter rule is an abomination do the resources of physics determine whether acceptance of irreducibly probabilistic laws is apostasy. We can and do discuss the wisdom of the designated hitter rule and the acceptability of irreducibly probabilistic laws. But disputes about such matters tend to be interminable. For there is no shared sense of how they could be resolved or even of what considerations bear on their resolution.

Being incapable of resolving their differences by reason, Kuhn maintains, revolutionary adversaries resort to persuasion. Each side tries to convert its rivals by adducing considerations that are psychologically appealing, though not rationally compelling. Each seeks to display its favored form of scientific life in such a desirable light that its opponents will come to prefer its brand of science. Where reasons cannot convince, enticements may allure. The method works. Eventually one party wins enough converts to dominate the field. Normal science begins anew under the aegis of the victorious paradigm. The victors entrench their power by expelling remaining rivals. Whatever those people are doing, it is not science; for science is now defined by a paradigm they reject. The successful paradigm cements its power by securing a monopoly on scientific education. Future generations will be reared in the scientific tradition it defines, learning little and caring less about its vanquished predecessor. In time, the old guard dies out; its vision of science is lost as the victors rewrite the history of their discipline. Such is Kuhn's picture of scientific revolution.

Richard Rorty takes Kuhn to have shown that intersubjective agreement is the product of identifiable social forces, not an indication of truth,
objectivity, or other epistemically favored status. Indeed, according to
Rorty, there is no such status, for 'true', 'objective', 'rational', and the
like, are just "compliment[s] to sentences that seem to be paying their
way."[22] Rorty recognizes that regimentation is not peculiar to science. So
he extends Kuhn's usage, considering inquiry in any field normal if it consists in the routine application of antecedently accepted methods to clearly
delimited problems. Normal inquiry is thus a staple of history, political
science, and literary studies as well as of science.

In Rorty's work, the sociologization of epistemic values is taken to
the limit. Recognizing nothing outside our practices against which their
adequacy could be measured, he identifies acceptability with whatever a
practice counts as acceptable. As we have seen, the actions of practitioners,
not their words, determine what a practice counts as acceptable. So acceptability turns out to be whatever our peers let us get away with.[23] The
only interesting difference between normal and abnormal inquiry is this:
in normal inquiry we know in advance what we can get away with; in
abnormal inquiry we do not. But normal inquiry is not cognitively preferable to abnormal inquiry, for the criteria that make normal inquiry possible are "just temporary resting-places introduced for specific utilitarian
ends."[24] Rorty thus urges that literary and cultural criticism be understood on the model of revolutionary science. It proceeds without agreement about what vocabulary to use, what questions to ask, what methods
to employ, what standards to invoke. With no common ground and no
common goal, there is little prospect of consensus in interpretation and
little desire for it.[25]

In its indifference to consensus, criticism is unlike revolutionary science. But the drive to resolve scientific revolutions derives, Rorty contends, from the practical advantages of agreement in science.[26] These in
turn result from the place of science in our culture (for instance, from
its bearing on technology). They do not demonstrate that agreement is
better than creative disagreement. So critics' perennial failure to resolve
their differences does not show criticism to be intellectually inferior to

[22] Richard Rorty, "Introduction," in *The Consequences of Pragmatism* (Minneapolis:
University of Minnesota Press, 1982), xxv.

[23] Richard Rorty, "Pragmatism, Relativism, and Irrationalism," in *Consequences of Pragmatism*, 165; and *Philosophy and the Mirror of Nature* (Princeton: Princeton University
Press, 1979), 385.

[24] Rorty, "Introduction," xli.

[25] Rorty, "Nineteenth Century Idealism and Twentieth Century Textualism," in *Consequences of Pragmatism*, 142.

[26] Rorty, "Introduction," xli.

science, for the goal of criticism is not to produce accord but to enliven interpretation.

Normal discourse, Rorty contends, takes the form of argument. It aims to answer a well-defined question, making further discussion of the issue unnecessary. Its prospects are promising, since interlocutors agree on the rules of the language game they are playing and the initial positions of the various players. Discussion thus proceeds along a well-marked path toward a common goal.[27] But normal inquiry requires criteria. And criteria are artificial restrictions on intellectual freedom. They are introduced "because some particular social practice needs to block the road of inquiry, halt the regress of interpretations, in order to get something done. So rigorous argumentation—the practice which is made possible by agreement on criteria, on stopping-places—is no more *generally* desirable than blocking the road of inquiry is generally desirable."[28] Normal inquiry, Rorty believes, is straitjacketed abnormal inquiry.

We should, he contends, construe inquiry—particularly abnormal inquiry—as conversation rather than argument. We can converse without agreeing on fundamentals. We need share no perspective, no methodology, no criteria of relevance, no vision of success. All we require is a modicum of civility. In conversation we are free to reverse ourselves, go off on tangents, entertain wildly implausible suggestions, change the subject or our approach to it entirely. We can satirize or caricature positions we disparage, attack straw men, take cheap shots. So if Rorty's conversational construal is correct, inconsistency, irrelevance, impropriety, and irresolution are not necessarily defects in inquiry. They are only defects in the normal inquiries that proscribe them.

Conversation has no goal. The value of a conversation resides in features inherent in it, not in conclusions it generates. We converse, Rorty maintains, not to find answers (and thereby bring conversation to a close) but simply because conversation is enjoyable. So if intellectual discussions are conversations rather than arguments, their objective is not to find answers or solve problems or resolve disagreements. At their best, they stimulate yet further conversation; that is all they are supposed to do. Rorty thus maintains that inquiry is subject to no constraints but conversational ones. And conversational constraints vary from one discussion to the next, being determined by the liberties interlocutors allow one another to take. A discussion in which every unsubstantiated assertion is challenged is bound by a fairly severe justification condition; one in which unsupported claims are unopposed is not. There are, Rorty believes, no general constraints on conversation. Even consistency is not universally required, for

[27] Rorty, "Pragmatism, Relativism, and Irrationalism," 170.
[28] Rorty, "Introduction," xli.

in some conversations, inconsistencies pass unchecked. And it is only in a practice that its operative norms are located.

It follows that there are no global constraints on inquiry. To be sure, individual investigations, like individual conversations, are bound by local constraints. Normal scientific inquiry, for example, subjects itself to fairly rigorous requirements that the parties involved antecedently understand and accept. In criticism and other abnormal inquiry, however, the constraints are looser and more variable, and are apt to evolve in the course of discussion.[29] There are then neither universal canons of rational acceptability nor any principled distinction between idle and edifying conversations.

Abnormal inquiry cannot be construed as a game, but it can be construed as play. No rules, objectives, or standards of sportsmanship shape its activities. Rather, its course is directed by a lively appreciation of current circumstances and the events that led up to them, along with an awareness of the opportunities open to us and the resources at our disposal. Responsiveness is grounded in the specifics of the situation; it is not backed by the authority of a framework of regulations and objectives. Unlike competitors, playmates accommodate one another directly, neither having nor needing recourse to rules of right conduct. And if we do not want to accept the domination of the neighborhood bully, we simply stop playing with him.

Play, however enjoyable, accomplishes nothing. Having no goal, it lacks a standpoint to distinguish success from failure, gain from loss, good moves from bad. Changes can occur in the course of play, but no improvements; alterations, but no accomplishments. For an aimless activity embodies no conception of what an accomplishment or an improvement would be. So to see inquiry as conversation, and conversation as play, is to abandon the idea that inquiry leads to an objectively certifiable enhancement of understanding or advancement of knowledge. Rather, "in the process of playing vocabularies and cultures off against one another, we produce new and better ways of talking and acting—not better by reference to any previously known standard, but just better in the sense that they come to seem clearly better than their predecessors."[30] For Rorty, seeming better is good enough.

NORMALIZING RELATIONS

Rorty and Kuhn maintain that revolutionary adversaries can communicate with one another. Despite the incommensurability of their languages and the disparity of their worldviews, they have the resources to converse with and (perhaps) persuade their opponents. They are at odds because

---

[29] Rorty, "Pragmatism, Relativism, and Irrationalism," 165.
[30] Rorty, "Introduction," xxxvii.

neither party can demonstrate that its own position is right and its rival's is wrong. But once communication is conceded, abnormal inquiries are hard to distinguish from normal ones. In both, arguments for and conclusions of opposing positions are readily conveyed; opinion remains divided, neither side being able to convince the other. The crucial distinction between the two is that abnormal differences are supposed to be irreconcilable; normal ones, reconcilable. Normal adversaries agree about how the issue between them ought to be resolved, about what considerations are relevant and how they should be weighted. And they agree that conclusive reasons are not at hand. All it would take then to resolve their disagreement is the discovery of evidence that settles the question. Both sides agree about what sort of evidence that would be. Abnormal adversaries disagree about which considerations are germane to their dispute and how such considerations should be weighted. They thus take different methods to be useful and different demonstrations to be compelling. So discord may persist even after one side has adduced reasons it considers conclusive. It is unclear then what, if anything, could satisfy all parties to an abnormal dispute.

It follows that revolutionary adversaries use terms of epistemic appraisal differently. They apply words like 'conclusive', 'justified', 'reason', and 'evidence' to different items, and do so by appeal to distinct criteria. Neither party's usage is merely mistaken, for each usage is consonant with criteria its advocates accept. Epistemic terms thus diverge in reference and meaning. Moreover, application of descriptive terms depends on epistemic appraisal. Criteria for 'mass', 'time', and 'trope' determine the conditions under which we are entitled to use the terms. What makes particular conditions qualify as criteria is that they realize our epistemic standards. So if rival schools accept divergent criteria of epistemic appraisal, they are bound to be committed to different criteria for their descriptive vocabularies. Having, for instance, separate criteria for conclusiveness, rival paradigms differ over what would count as conclusive evidence of quasars—over, that is, the conditions under which 'quasar' definitely applies.

Recognizing that express differences reverberate, Kuhn concludes that adherents of rival paradigms talk past each other, that communication between them is inevitably partial.[31] Is this position tenable? Or does a revolutionary reconception effect a chain reaction, the revision of one concept entailing the revision of its neighbors until the entire language is transmuted? If so, none of the revolutionary's words has the same meaning for his rivals. Then any appearance of communication is misleading. The challenge is to produce a controlled chain reaction—one powerful enough to spark a revolution, yet limited enough to preserve contact between opposing factions.

[31] Kuhn, *The Structure of Scientific Revolutions*, 109.

To that end, Rorty invokes Davidson's version of the principle of charity: most of a person's beliefs must be true, for nothing could show the majority of them to be false. Any ostensible indication of overwhelming falsity is actually evidence of misinterpretation.[32] He takes Davidson's principle to show that revolutionary adversaries are largely in agreement, for all parties harbor predominantly true beliefs. Moreover, their agreement affords the basis for translation; as far as possible (and that is guaranteed to be fairly far), claims held true by one side map onto claims held true by the other. When consistency of translation requires that claims held true be mapped onto claims held false, disagreement is isolated. The principle of charity thus assures that the languages of rival factions are intertranslatable. To communicate, advocates of rival paradigms simply translate each other's statements into their own language.

Since the two languages overlap to a considerable degree (being dialects of a common tongue), charity often involves construing seemingly shared terms as ambiguous. To make most Newtonian claims come out true, relativity theorists take 'mass', 'distance', 'simultaneity', and the like, to be ambiguous—each term having one meaning (and reference) in their own dialect, another in their rival's. The appearance of incompatibility thus derives from an unwise application of the homophonic rule—from the rash assumption that since rival paradigms use the same terminology, they must be talking about the same thing. Once this misapprehension is removed, no real disagreement remains.

'Mass is constant'

does not conflict with

'Mass is variable'

unless 'mass' has the same reference throughout. Otherwise, the two are compatible. Relativity theory then no more conflicts with Newtonian mechanics than it does with Freudian psychology. The three theories simply treat of different subjects.

If we invoke the principle of charity, with its power to dispel discord by conjuring up ambiguity, different paradigms become commensurable. Proponents of each can communicate with proponents of the other, can appreciate the force of the other's arguments, can even accept the other's position without abandoning or compromising their own. For putatively antagonistic paradigms turn out to be talking about different things. There is no reason why an informed thinker cannot have sound, well-supported views on a variety of subjects. So each paradigm that succeeds

---

[32] Richard Rorty, "The World Well Lost," in *Consequences of Pragmatism*, 5–6; Donald Davidson, "On the Very Idea of a Conceptual Scheme," in *Inquiries into Truth and Interpretation* (Oxford: Oxford University Press, 1984), 183–198.

by its own lights can be accepted. If one fails by its own lights, the problems it faces are the stuff of normal inquiry.

Rorty's invocation of the principle of charity thus achieves communicability by sacrificing incommensurability. Relations between warring factions are normalized by construing what had been considered profound and irreconcilable differences in belief as easily accommodated differences in dialect. When we apply the principle of charity, we recognize our rivals as members of our community. Individuals working in separate paradigms are then simply playing different language games. If Kuhn is right, there are strong social pressures to minimize the number of scientific games people play at any one time. If Rorty is right, those pressures are not present in literary and cultural criticism. Revolutionary practice is then a part of our shared form of life. Abnormal discourse is simply discussion about which games we prefer to play.

DOES CHARITY END AT HOME?

Perhaps we were too quick to infer general agreement from the principle of charity. That principle maintains that most of a person's beliefs must be true, since nothing could show them to be false. But it does not follow that something can show them to be true. A translation is acceptable only if it yields overwhelming agreement between speakers of the two languages. Still, nothing guarantees that an acceptable translation can be produced. If it cannot (and the Davidsonian principle of charity is true), we have genuine incommensurability. Speakers of each language believe and speak truths. But the truths couched in one language are inaccessible to speakers of the other. In that case, of course, there would be no communication, no possibility of conversation or persuasion.

Alienation would be complete. Since systematic correlations among speakers' utterances, their behavior, and their environment would afford a basis for translation, it is only in the absence of such correlations that translation is impossible. But without such correlations, individuals would be utterly inscrutable. We could have no idea what they think or want or intend at any given time. Moreover, if we cannot ascribe particular beliefs, desires, and intentions to them, we have no reason to credit them with beliefs, desires, and intentions at all. If translation fails then, we have no reason to think that their vocalizations constitute a language or their bodily movements actions. Having found no way to construe their behavior as rule-governed, we are not justified in believing them to participate in practices or adhere to a form of life. If languages are genuinely incommensurable then, speakers of one could not recognize the other as a language.[33]

---

[33] Rorty, "The World Well Lost"; Wittgenstein, *Philosophical Investigations*, pp. 226–227.

They would inevitably consider its speakers as brutes or madmen—producing much sound and fury but signifying nothing.

Wittgenstein is under no illusions about this point. "If a lion could talk, we could not understand him."[34] For the leonine form of life with its predatory, pride-bound practices would be so remote from our experience that we could find no foothold in it. We cannot interpret a speaker's words without an understanding of his beliefs, desires, and actions. For the meaning is the use—and the use involves expressing, avowing, and describing beliefs and desires; performing, motivating, reporting, and reacting to actions; and misrepresenting—out of malice or mistake—what one believes, desires, and undertakes. Without an entrée into the form of life that shapes it, we cannot understand a language; without access to the language that gives it expression, we cannot enter into a form of life. So if a language is genuinely incommensurable with our own, the world its speakers inhabit is as inaccessible to us as the world of the lion.

We could, to be sure, study its inhabitants but only as we do lions; we could, that is, employ ethological methods to discover and explain regularities in their (animal) behavior. In this way we might learn, say, that one vocalization is characteristic of fear, another of hunger; that one posture is adopted during dominance disputes, another when status relations are clear; that one facial expression occurs in the vicinity of predators, another in the vicinity of prey. The regularities we find would enable us to understand them as natural phenomena. We could then predict and perhaps control their behavior. But we could not by these methods come to understand them as persons, as members of a community, as beings who are and take one another to be responsible to rules that bind a society together. We could treat their various behaviors as natural indications but not as socially constituted symbols.

Are we left then with yet another intractable form of the problem of other minds? Might the world be rife with unrecognizable intelligences? Could the dances of bees or the vocalizations of dolphins be languages untranslatable into our own? Could the interactions within a pack of wolves or a colony of ants be manifestations of an incongruous form of life? Could people who appear not to be playing with a full deck actually be playing a game that requires a different deck? As possibilities multiply, vertigo becomes acute. We feel ourselves losing all touch with reality as we thought we knew it.

Relief is at hand; for the possibilities just described are, according to pure procedural epistemology, unreal. They presuppose that whether someone speaks a language, plays a game, or participates in a form of life is a question whose answer is independent of anything we know, and may

[34] Wittgenstein, *Philosophical Investigations*, p. 223.

be independent of anything we can know. It forgets that linguistic correctness is a matter of conformity with local practice. If a sequence of behavior displays no discernible resemblance to the activities we count as games, if that behavior does not satisfy our criteria for 'game', we do not (and should not) call it a game. Since the meaning is the use, it follows from our collective refusal to call it a game that it is not a game. *Our* word 'game' does not apply to it. Similarly, activities that do not satisfy our criteria for 'language', 'practice', and 'form of life' are ipso facto not languages, practices, or forms of life. The world then could not be rife with unrecognizable intelligences, for beings would not be intelligences if we did not recognize them as such.[35]

Pure procedural epistemology precludes incommensurability. If translation is possible, languages are commensurable. Real disagreements are resolvable, and seemingly irresolvable disagreements are, for that very reason, unreal. So if Wittgenstein is right about language, he is wrong about lions. If a lion could talk, we could understand him; for if we cannot understand him, it follows that he cannot talk. If translation is impossible, the phenomenon we confront is not a language. Our language then is comprehensive: we can be confident that it captures every possibility, for whatever is inexpressible is inconceivable; and whatever is inconceivable is impossible. So the adequacy of language is assured. Whatever its limits, nothing is left out.

Summing Up

As Wittgenstein's work demonstrates, pure procedural philosophy has the capacity to yield powerful, integrated, and in many ways attractive theories. Social dimensions of philosophical problems, so often obscured by other approaches, fall neatly within its purview. The epistemological benefits are evident. Pure procedural philosophy conceives of inquiry as something we engage in; knowledge, as something we achieve. And it treats epistemic status as conceptually inseparable from the actions and achievements of epistemic agents. It appreciates the normativeness of epistemic categories—'knowledge', 'justification', 'evidence', and the like—and explains how the operative norms derive from, and owe their authority to, their function in the cognitive life of the community. It connects the process of acquiring knowledge with the product acquired. It acknowledges that education engenders conformity and that investigation terminates when consensus is reached. If knowledge requires correspondence to a mind-independent reality (as, for example, definitions of knowledge in terms of justified, true beliefs or reliable mechanisms maintain), our epi-

[35] Rorty, "The World Well Lost".

stemic efforts appear inadequate and perhaps irrelevant to the task. But if knowledge is identified with the settled opinion of the community of inquiry, no such difficulty arises. To settle opinion, to produce consensus, is to generate knowledge; to come to share settled opinion is to acquire the knowledge our compatriots already have. Intersubjective agreement on this view is constitutive, not merely indicative, of knowledge.

Pure procedural epistemology defeats skepticism. For knowledge consists in satisfying the community's epistemic standards, and those standards can be, and often are, satisfied. This might be challenged; at least we might doubt that we can ever tell whether the relevant standards have been met. And second order doubt is enough to generate skepticism. For a vicious regress threatens. If we must justify a judgment by appeal to social standards, and justify the claim that they have been satisfied by appeal to further standards, and . . . , we are not entitled to confidence unless we have ascertained that all members of an infinite series of standards have been met. We are then never in a position to know that a judgment is correct. But Wittgenstein denies that we appeal to further standards to tell whether our initial standards for knowledge have been satisfied. We look instead, he insists, to community practice. If the community treats a matter as settled, it is settled. We easily determine that by looking at what its members say and do. So the criteria for knowledge are satisfied when our community treats them as satisfied, for the standards are embodied in the practices of the community.

The defeat of skepticism does not, however, determine the scope of knowledge. Unlike other theories, pure procedural epistemology does not legislate that certain intellectual activities—ethical debate, metaphorical description, mathematical reasoning—are incapable in principle of yielding knowledge. For it takes the issue to be one of practice, not of principle. If the community that sustains an activity treats its products as knowledge, if those products function in the cognitive life of the community as knowledge does, then they amount in that community to knowledge. Otherwise they do not. So to determine whether, for example, insights captured in apt metaphors count as knowledge, we must ascertain what the community thinks about and does with apt metaphors. There is no saying independently of practice whether a given judgment will count as knowledge, or whether a given procedure will count as generating knowledge. Epistemology, on this view, is responsive to, and an outgrowth of, the cognitive life of an actual community.

Pure procedural philosophy thus appreciates the ways epistemological theory is answerable to our pedagogical, investigatory, and justificatory practices. Rather than setting remote, Olympian requirements on any acceptable claim to knowledge, pure procedural theories are rooted in local soil. They explain how people go about knowing around here.

But the relation they find between principal and practice is not reciprocal. Practice can challenge principle but cannot be challenged by it. Pure procedural epistemology is entirely descriptive. It describes and explains our cognitive practices and, in so doing, identifies the norms and values embodied in them. But it has no evaluative function.[36] It can no more fault an inductive strategy, for example, than anthropology can fault an initiation rite, or chemistry a molecular bond. Epistemology is just sociology of knowledge.

Must pure procedural philosophy treat practice as invulnerable to criticism? Surely an astute epistemologist could discern, say, that participants in a practice regularly commit the gambler's fallacy. She ought, it seems, to be able to explain why it is a mistake to do so, and to recommend doing otherwise. But this is precisely what she is in no position to do. If avoiding the fallacy is already demanded by the practice, its participants need no epistemological advice. If not, the criticism is unfounded, the recommendation impertinent. For in that case, the gambler's fallacy is a permissible move in their language game. And the players ought not be faulted for doing what it is within their rights to do.

Still, couldn't the epistemologist argue that by committing the fallacy they undermine their own enterprise, that the game would be better were the fallacious move forbidden? If she can, epistemology retains an evaluative role. But the language game is constituted by the rules that govern it. So the critic cannot say that *it* would be better if the move were forbidden. For it would not be the game that it is if the rules were revised. We cannot then correct a given practice by changing the rules, for such changes create new practices. And we cannot intelligibly recommend correcting the rules that constitute a practice, for in such recommendations language is on holiday; the applications of its terms are removed from the network of norms and objectives that render their workaday uses and referents determinate.

It might seem that the epistemological critic can still make her point if she chooses her words more judiciously. Can't she just say that since the game that permits the gambler's fallacy leads to unsatisfactory results, we would do better to play a different game instead? Unfortunately, things are not so simple. For to make her case, indeed even to make her case intelligible, the critic needs words. But on a pure procedural account, she has none that will serve. Norms derive both their content and their authority from their place in a practice. So when the epistemologist purports to apply normative terms from a standpoint outside the practice, as she

---

[36] "There cannot be a question whether these rules or other rules are the correct ones for the use of 'not'. . . . For without these rules the word has as yet no meaning; and if we change the rules, it now has another meaning (or none), and in that case, we may just as well change the word too" (Wittgenstein, *Philosophical Investigations*, p. 147).

must if she is to criticize it, she deprives them of the conditions of their intelligibility. Words fail her. Removed from their role in a language game, they are empty and impotent. Evaluations within a practice do not produce evaluations of the practice. And outside of a practice, there is no basis for evaluation.

This does not make language games, practices, or forms of life static. Institutions change; standards are not what they once were. But without overarching normative criteria, changes can be counted neither advances nor declines, neither progress nor degeneration. Alterations are thus powerless to make things better or worse; they can only make things different. To be sure, we prefer our own practices to those of our ancestors on the grounds that ours seem better (to us, of course). But "not better by reference to any previously known standard, . . . just better in the sense that they come to *seem* clearly better than their predecessors."[37] When inquiry is conceived as a pure procedure, when all criteria of evaluation are internal to whatever game we happen to be playing, there can be no perspective from which to ask whether a game that seems better actually is better. Seeming better is all we have and, according to pure procedural philosophy, all we need.

Of course, we expect our successors to participate in different practices and to consider theirs better than ours. But our practices are none the worse for that. If epistemic merit is whatever the community of inquiry takes it to be, then whatever satisfies the community is ipso facto satisfactory. The recognition that future generations are likely to think otherwise gives us no reason to think that our views are flawed, for they satisfy our standards. "We did the best we could, as we trust our descendants will do theirs."[38] We can afford to be complacent, since our best is bound to be good enough. Pure procedural epistemology thus achieves knowledge without relying on luck by the simple expedient of defining 'knowledge' as that which it manages, without relying on luck, to achieve.

WHAT WE DO

Knowledge then is whatever the community takes it to be, whatever satisfies the community's epistemic standards. There is no requirement that the standards be any good; indeed, on a pure procedural conception, the question of the merits of the standards or of the practices they engender cannot intelligibly be raised.

Pure procedural philosophy rests its case on the fact that we act on our findings. This is supposed to show that we treat our epistemic standards as authoritative, their satisfaction as conclusive. But we do other things with

---

[37] Rorty, "Introduction," xxxvii.
[38] Richard Rorty, "Realism and Reference," *The Monist* 59 (1975–76): 323.

our findings besides act on them—things that are hard to incorporate into the pure procedural model.

We consider established findings open to corroboration and encourage the development of new sources of support for already accepted claims. The discovery of gravitational lenses, for example, was taken to confirm the theory of relativity, even though that theory already satisfied our standards of acceptability. If those standards were authoritative, such discoveries would lack corroborative power. They would also lack the capacity to unsettle accepted findings. A negative X-ray could not undermine a diagnosis of tuberculosis if medical science treated a positive skin test as conclusive. But the X-ray would likely give us pause, even if it did not immediately refute received wisdom. Our cognitive practices thus apparently differ from games in permitting newly discovered facts, newly developed tests, newly formulated desiderata to reinforce or discredit currently accepted findings and the standards that justified their acceptance.

Pure proceduralists must deny this. Thus Kuhn maintains that a paradigm protects itself from disconfirmation by bracketing anomalies and deflecting troublesome results. He recognizes that protectionism is a temporary expedient; unresolved difficulties ultimately give rise to revolution. But even then, he insists, the original paradigm is not discredited, just replaced. Kuhn thus believes that our cognitive behavior (in science, at least) reveals no difference between changing the rules of a game and correcting them. This is doubtful. When basketball introduced the three-point shot, previous victories were not rescinded. Even if the Celtics would not have beaten Philadelphia in 1965 had the new rule then been in effect, it was not; so their victory is secure. But a change in cognitive standards carries with it a commitment to reconsider antecedently accepted results. Medical diagnoses, for example, may be revoked on the basis of new etiological findings. Whatever his symptoms, we now know that Molière did not have tuberculosis unless he was infected by *Mycobacterium tuberculosis*. Change is just prospective; correction is retrospective as well. Though old victories stand when the rules of basketball are revised, old diagnoses may fall to advances in medical science.

Moreover, cognitive standards and methods, unlike rules of a game, require validation. The IQ test is in disrepute, not because its results are irreproducible but because their relation to the magnitude they purport to measure is moot. If an IQ score were the standard of intelligence in the way a basketball score is the standard of winning, test results would speak for themselves. They do not. In demanding validation, psychology concedes that it does not consider the IQ test the authoritative measure of intelligence.

One might argue that the validation requirement is just a rule of the inquiry game. If so, comparison with basketball shows not that inquiries differ from games but that different games have different rules. This is hardly surprising. But a practice whose standards require validation allows for a type of error that games like basketball do not. A conclusion that satisfies its current standard for x may be mistaken because that standard does not afford an accurate measure of x. This is just the error that distinguishes authoritative from indicative standards. Even when nuclear power plants satisfy contemporary safety standards, reservations remain. We are not convinced that the reactors are safe because we are not confident that our safety standards are adequate. And our inability to formulate a standard we would trust does not assuage our doubts. We treat current safety standards as indicative at best.

Although we regularly act on our findings, that is not all we do. We hedge our bets. We devise safeguards to avert error and damage control mechanisms to channel the effects of errors we cannot prevent and to soften their impact. We hone techniques, refine methods, sharpen standards, and then deploy them to evaluate the continued acceptability of previously accepted results. Were satisfaction of current standards sufficient for rightness, such efforts would be otiose; were it constitutive of rightness, they would be unintelligible. They are neither. When standards function as reasonable but potentially fallible indications of rightness, such prudence makes sense. A distinction between being right and satisfying our standards for rightness is implicit in cognitive practice. It derives from the design of the practice, not the quality of its product; so it involves no admission that current standards are flawed. But in providing for the possibility that its standards are unreliable, our practice denies that they are authoritative.

Our behavior thus belies the claim that rightness is just what we treat as right or truth what we count as true or warrant what we take to be warranted. So pure procedural epistemology does not pass its own test: it is not borne out by what we do. Our cognitive endeavors and their objects may nevertheless be social constructs. But if they are, they are not constructed according to the blueprint that pure procedural epistemology supplies.

TWO CONCEPTS OF RULES

In "Two Concepts of Rules," Rawls distinguishes between justification within a practice and justification of a practice.[39] Justification within a practice conforms to the pure procedural model. Particular judgments, actions, rulings, and the like, are justified by the rules or standards that define and govern the practice to which they belong. Justification of a practice, however, appeals to considerations of utility. Although corrobo-

---

[39] Rawls, "Two Concepts of Rules," 144–170.

ration of antecedently acceptable conclusions and validation of antecedently acceptable methods contribute nothing to justification within a
cognitive practice, they are not idle wheels, I suggest, because they figure
in the justification of the practice. They provide reason to believe that the
practice's standards, rules, and methods are adequate, that the practice as
constituted promotes its epistemic ends. The characterization of differences in successive practices as corrections or refinements also figures in
the project of justifying practices. It makes sense to call an amendment a
correction or refinement only if it constitutes an improvement. That cannot be settled without knowing the good toward which the practice aims.

To be sure, our habit of demanding corroboration, validation, correction, and refinement does not show that cognitive practices can be justified. Still less does it say what the standards of justification for such practices might be. It shows only that we consider our cognitive practices
subject to justification. Unless we can find or formulate suitable standards,
unless we can identify the ends that epistemic utility promotes, our demand for justification may be futile.

Our prospects may look bleak. The failure of foundationalism deprives
us of the resources for identifying a unique goal toward which cognition
naturally aims. So practices cannot be justified by their promoting activities or producing results that realize such a goal. If we attempt to justify
our practices by embedding them in a metapractice, the problem simply
recurs. Unless the metapractice is itself justified, it is powerless to justify
the practices it authorizes.

There is a third alternative: to construct our epistemic ends out of our
actual interests and goals in theorizing. To be sure, we cannot identify the
objectives we happen to pursue with the legitimate ends of inquiry. That
would be to confuse the valued with the valuable. Moreover, our actual
epistemic goals form a disconcertingly motley crew. They are apt to be
inchoate, incomplete, mutually incompatible, and/or jointly unsatisfiable. Still, by adjudicating among them, revising and amending as required, we may bring them into reflective equilibrium. And a system of
tenable commitments in reflective equilibrium defines, I suggest, a worthy
epistemic goal. Its elements are reasonable in light of one another, and the
system as a whole is reasonable in light of the objectives we originally
espoused.

Justification on this account is a twofold process. Cognitive practices
are justified by their epistemic utility; they are answerable to standards
they need not themselves acknowledge and may be faulted for failing to
achieve ends to which they do not aspire. Individual methods, inferences,
conclusions, and the like, are justified by the standards of the practices to
which they belong, by rules they recognize as binding on them—but only
if those practices in turn are justified. Particular inductive inferences, for

example, are justified by their place in an inductive logic. The requirement
of total evidence, on the other hand, derives its justification from the point
of such a logic. It is a requirement *on* inductive logic, not a requirement
in inductive logic.[40] It reflects our conviction that a practice that permitted us to disregard inconvenient members of an evidence class would not
promote our epistemic ends. If I am right, not all epistemic norms and
concepts are wedded to particular practices. Some derive their standing
from the practices to which they belong; others, from the ends we seek by
those practices to promote.

The picture I am proposing is more complicated than the one pure
proceduralists espouse; the success of our cognitive endeavors is no longer
assured. But it does, I think, introduce a via media between the abandoned absolutes of Cartesian epistemology and the potentially arbitrary
games Wittgensteinians would have us play.

[40] I am indebted to Jonathan Adler for this example.

Chapter IV

THE MERITS OF EQUILIBRIUM

EPISTEMOLOGY'S failures prove surprisingly inconsequential. We continue the cognitive quest, undaunted by our apparent inability to properly characterize its objective. We differentiate between justified and unjustified claims as a matter of course. And we stake our lives on our assessments, even if we lack a conception of justification capable of backing our claims.

This does not mean that we are right. We might be victims of the blind confidence that lures soldiers into battle and lemmings to the sea. But perhaps not. If epistemology discredits the distinction between justified and unjustified belief, reluctance to draw that distinction should accompany philosophical sophistication. But even our best philosophers continue to distinguish the two. This suggests that the distinction we daily deploy is not the one philosophy sought (and failed) to secure—indeed, that the traditional epistemological problematic has little bearing on ordinary cognitive endeavors. So before abandoning epistemic hope, it is worth attempting to formulate an account appropriate to our cognitive activities. Even if it will not insure against epistemic misfortune, such an account might establish what is good in the way of belief.

Pure procedural philosophy canonizes the status quo. But an epistemology capable of criticizing practices cannot blithely endorse their principles. It can, however, craft its principles out of raw materials such practices supply. This is what the imperfect procedural epistemology I advocate attempts to do. The task may seem hopeless. Without a criterion of justification, we have no basis for distinguishing justified from unjustified claims. But unless we can draw that distinction, we seem unequipped to validate any proposed criterion.

We are not entirely without resources, though. Even if we cannot tell justified from unjustified claims, we readily distinguish claims we consider justified from those we do not. To be sure, we are as yet in no position to defend our convictions. But that we accept some sentences, reject others, and withhold still others is a brute fact, there for us to use.

INITIAL TENABILITY

Whether or not they are justified, we accept some sentences without reservation. Being our current best estimates of how things stand, such sentences have some claim on our epistemic allegiance. This might be doubted. The prevalence of superstition, prejudice, delusion, and ordinary error undermines any hope of identifying the accepted with the acceptable. Nevertheless, I contend, a sentence's being accepted is not epistemically irrelevant to its acceptability.

Our convictions form the basis for our actions. If projects grounded in a particular judgment often go awry, reservations develop and the courage of that conviction wanes. So confidence in a given judgment indicates that we have not yet found it an impediment to action. And that its acceptance has not obviously thwarted (and may even have advanced) our efforts is a reason to credit a judgment.

Were this an argument for the truth or permanent credibility of the sentences we accept, it would be woefully inadequate. It neglects the possibility that our complacency derives from self-deception, low standards, wishful thinking, or compensating errors. It overlooks our ability to deflect blame for failure away from cherished beliefs. It endorses sentences like

There is no greatest prime number.

whose bearing on action, if any, is so remote that their failure to derail our projects is as inconsequential as it is inevitable. But I am after smaller game. That the sentences we accept do not in general frustrate our efforts is some reason to accept them. It is reason enough, I suggest, to render them initially tenable. At the outset of any inquiry then there is some epistemic presumption in favor of the commitments we already have.

If I am right, even superstitions, delusions, and prejudices begin their careers as initially tenable beliefs. This is not so objectionable as it first appears though, for initial tenability is a modest and precarious epistemic achievement. Having some reason to accept a sentence is far from having sufficient reason. An initially tenable sentence's claim on our epistemic allegiance is slight and is easily overridden should continued acceptance prove too costly. Among those most readily and decisively discredited are the ones we come to call superstitions, delusions, and prejudices.

Initially tenable claims form a motley crew. Generalizations consort with statements of particulars; idealizations, with approximations and exact specifications. Assessments of value mingle with assertions of fact, and judgments from the upper reaches of the traditional epistemic hierarchy may be initially tenable even when their traditional supports are not.

Plainly such sentences can clash. Some may be mutually inconsistent. Though separately plausible,

It never snows at the equator;
It snows throughout the Andes;
The Andes cross the equator

form an inconsistent triad. Others, though not logically at odds, may be jointly untenable. The vegetarian's belief that her dog will readily adapt to a diet of tofu and soybeans does not square with her conviction that confirmed carnivores seldom convert. The tenability that initially attaches to individual judgments thus does not always survive their conjunction. So we cannot simply conjoin our initially tenable judgments to arrive at an acceptable theory or system of beliefs. Conflicts must be resolved, inconsistencies purged to generate an acceptable system.

How might this be done? We could simply jettison the less tenable of each pair of competing claims. This would settle conflicts but might fail to maximize overall tenability. Even if

The butler did it

is initially less tenable than

Fickle Freddy Frogmore did it,
The butler did it and only his fingerprints are on the murder weapon

is more tenable than

Freddy Frogmore did it but only the butler's fingerprints are on the murder weapon.

The tenability of the fingerprint report enhances the case against Jeeves while weakening the case against Freddy. So instead of accepting the competitor with the greatest initial tenability, we do better to accept the one that contributes most to the tenability of the theory or belief system as a whole. Sometimes an even better strategy is to reject both competitors and settle for a compromise candidate. If Jeeves had no motive and Freddy no means, we might resort to a conspiracy theory or endorse the initially less tenable case against the scullery maid. Here again, a judgment's claim to enduring tenability is a function of its contribution to the tenability of the account that emerges.

A duly curtailed collection of initially tenable claims is not yet a theory or system of thought. Typically there remain relevant cases it does not cover, questions it does not answer, problems it does not solve. It needs to be supplemented, rounded out by additional judgments that connect its fragments, smooth its rough spots, fill its holes. Clearly such judgments should be consonant with the ones we already hold. But what makes for consonance? Consistency is mandatory, for the admission of jointly inconsistent claims would subvert the epistemic enterprise. Consistency, though, is hardly enough, being automatically achieved through irrelevance. We could easily insure that our opinions were consistent by accepting only statements that have no bearing on one another. But a collection of mutually indifferent claims does not a theory make. Nor does inclusion in such a collection increase the tenability of its members. Relevance is required as well. The sentences we annex must be relevant to those we already accept. And their annexation must increase the cogency of the system as a whole.

The implausibility of a hitherto devoted servant's wantonly murdering his master may lead us to ascribe to Jeeves a deep, perhaps unconscious resentment of the late Lord Frogmore. Even if we have no independent evidence of antipathy, our ascription is reasonable to the extent that it fits with what we already have reason to believe (about the crime and about psychology) and makes sense of an otherwise senseless slaying. An initially questionable claim is then provisionally acceptable if its incorporation leads to a no less tenable account than we already had and a no less tenable one than would result from the incorporation of any of its rivals.

Our goal is to maximize the epistemic standing of the considerations we finally endorse. In forging connections among initially tenable claims, we integrate them into a mutually supportive network. This enhances their tenability, each being more reasonable in light of the others than it was alone. It also confers tenability on the sentences we annex, transforming initially doubtful claims into integral parts of an acceptable system of thought.

Individual judgments ordinarily owe some measure of their tenability to their place in a tenable system. Considerations such as consistency, cotenability, relevance, and cogency are critical in deciding which judgments belong. Tenability thus depends on the adequacy of our epistemic principles, standards, and methods. But adequacy no more attaches a priori to principles, standards, and methods than it does to judgments. Indeed principles, standards, and methods obtain their warrant in the same way factual judgments do. The ones we ordinarily use are counted initially tenable. But they may conflict with one another or with initially tenable claims; they may generate incompatible or implausible conclusions. They are, moreover, likely to be incomplete, yielding no verdict on cases within their purview. Like initially tenable claims, initially tenable principles, standards, and methods are subject to rejection, correction, and amendment in the process of systematization.

Categories too are subject to revision. Border disputes may need to be settled, boundaries redrawn, familiar distinctions repudiated, novel ones introduced. The scope of a category scheme may be expanded to cover a wider domain or shrunk to curb overweening ambition. Our goal is a category scheme that fits into a constellation of tenable commitments, a scheme that affords an order appropriate to our ends. Suppose, for example, we discover important physiological features, Φ, to be characteristic of a wide range of animals including orangutans, bats, lions, and whales but excluding turtles, robins, lobsters, and trout. If we retain the initially tenable commonsense classification of whales as fish, our findings conform to the hypothesis

All mammals and some, but not all, fish display Φ,

a cumbersome, seemingly ad hoc generalization ill suited to science. But if we reclassify whales as mammals, our findings support

All and only mammals display Φ.

By streamlining our terminology, we accommodate our findings to tenable commitments about science.

A category scheme imposes an order on a domain, classifying some elements as alike, others as unlike. Its merits depend on its utility, an effective scheme being one whose organization of its realm suits our purposes. Rightness of categorization thus consists neither in blind fidelity to tradition nor in accord with an antecedent metaphysical order, but in meshing with other tenable commitments to promote tenable ends. If our revised taxonomy proves more effective than its predecessors and competitors, if its adoption advances understanding, the suggested revision is opportune.

Cognitive activity is reflective. Theorizing is informed by (often inchoate) views about theorizing—about what constitutes evidence, argument, explanation, and the like. Such views have no special epistemic standing; they are, in principle, neither more nor less secure than other initially tenable commitments. They are vulnerable in the same ways. The principles we endorse may be at odds with one another or with the applications we accept; the methods we advocate, at odds with the ones we employ. What we practice may deviate markedly from what we preach. Adjudication often is necessary to reconcile our various first- and second-order commitments. In the process any of them may be called into question.

Strategies for design and modification are sensitive to the goals of the system under construction. Different systems have different goals. If, for example, we seek to explain Jeeves's behavior as action, we take pains to preserve the intentional idiom. We tolerate the seemingly inevitable imprecision of propositional attitude ascriptions rather than replace them with descriptions of underlying physiological mechanisms. Although mechanistic descriptions are typically more exact and may be more easily verified, they would not serve our purpose. They would not explain Frogmore's murder, though they might describe how he died.

Values come into play as well. Prizing intersubjective agreement, science favors repeatable results. In a system suited to science then, an observation report's initial tenability normally decays rapidly if the observation

cannot be repeated. A system with other designs—one appropriate to the
arts or to self-ascription, perhaps—might sustain the uncorroborated report's tenability longer, preferring sensitivity to intersubjective accord.
Here too conflicts can occur. It is not unreasonable to want both inter-
subjectivity and sensitivity. But the more refined a system's distinctions,
the harder it is to classify cases. We can maximize one or the other or settle
for something in between. But we cannot maximize both at once. To
obtain a tenable system, we must moderate initially reasonable demands.
Choosing among alternatives involves deciding what combination of features is best on balance.

A conviction's justification is not a matter of its etiology or phenome-
nology but of its fit into a tenable system of thought. Considerations that
are alike in phenomenological feel or causal history often differ in fit. Even
if, for example, premonitions and perceptions present themselves with
equal force and vivacity, their epistemic standings diverge. For deliverances of perception can regularly be integrated into tenable systems,
whereas premonitions prove unamenable to integration. Similarly, hypotheses with a common causal history differ in epistemic standing if one
meshes with our theoretical, evidential, and methodological commitments and the other does not.

REFLECTIVE EQUILIBRIUM

In building a system of thought, we begin with a provisional scaffolding
made up of the relevant beliefs we already hold, the aims of the project we
are embarked on, the liberties and constraints we consider the system subject to, the values and priorities we seek to uphold. We suspend judgment
on matters in dispute. This ramshackle structure is not expected to stand
by itself. Major improvements may have to be made. Our initial judgments are not comprehensive; they are apt to be jointly untenable; they
may fail to serve the purposes to which they are put or to realize the values
we want to uphold. And initial principles, standards, purposes, and values
are apt to be equally unsatisfactory. So our scaffolding has to be supplemented and in part reconstructed before it will serve.

We proceed dialectically. We mold specific judgments to accepted generalizations, and generalizations to specific judgments. We weigh considerations of value against antecedent judgments of fact. We synchronize
ends and means, reconcile principle and practice. A process of delicate
adjustments occurs, its goal being a system in reflective equilibrium.
Achieving that goal may involve drawing new evaluative and descriptive
distinctions or erasing distinctions already drawn, reordering priorities or
imposing new ones, reconceiving the relevant facts and values or recog-

nizing new ones as relevant. We test the construction for accuracy by seeing whether it reflects (closely enough) the initially tenable judgments we began with; we test it for adequacy by seeing whether it realizes our cognitive and practical ends. An exact fit is neither needed nor wanted. We realize that the views we began with are incomplete, and suspect that they are flawed; we recognize that our initial conception of our objectives is inchoate and perhaps inconsistent. So we treat our starting points as touchstones that guide but do not determine the shape of our construction.

Coherence alone is not enough. A system is coherent if its constituents are suitably related to one another. Then its statements, strategies, values, and priorities form a mutually supportive network, each being reasonable in light of the others and each contributing to the integrity of the whole. Plainly such a system could be a complete fiction. Aside from the support its constituents lend one another, there may be little reason to endorse any of them. And their mutual support may derive from a judicious disregard for contravening considerations.

For reflective equilibrium, independently motivated, initially tenable commitments must underwrite coherence. The components of a system in reflective equilibrium must be reasonable in light of one another, and the system as a whole reasonable in light of our initially tenable commitments. Indeed, such a system must maximize tenability. For we would not on reflection accept a system of thought if a competitor were more tenable.[1] No mere castles in the air, systems in reflective equilibrium are tethered—not to Things in Themselves but to our antecedent understanding of and interest in the matter at hand. Coherence provides justification *in* the system; the tie to initially tenable commitments, justification *of* the system.

Does reflective equilibrium then consist in coherence with a consistent, suitably comprehensive class of initially tenable commitments? This too is problematic. Since initially tenable commitments have a presumption in their favor, they are not to be given up without reason. If nothing but conflicts among themselves supplies such a reason, there is no ground for repudiating such commitments unless they clash. In that case initially tenable commitments are irrevocable if cotenable. But it is unlikely that all infelicitous initially tenable commitments succumb to conflicts with their peers. So a policy dedicated to preserving every survivor is apt to reinforce and perpetuate error. To ground acceptability in coherence with whatever initially tenable commitments happen to survive thus subverts the goals of a reflective, self-correcting epistemology.

---

[1] Israel Scheffler, "On Justification and Commitment," in *Inquiries* (Indianapolis: Hackett, 1986), 293–302.

The remedy is to recognize that considerations with no initial tenability sometimes dislodge initially tenable commitments. The cure, however, may look worse than the disease. For it implies that statements we have no reason to believe can discredit statements we have reason to believe. And it seems intuitively obvious that even minimally tenable commitments override nontenable ones. But when we recall that initial tenability is determined by what we actually accept, and that what we actually accept is fraught with idiosyncrasy and vulnerable to vagaries of history and personality, confidence in this intuition wanes.

Initially tenable commitments are apt, individually and collectively, to have unanticipated consequences. Being unforeseen, such consequences are not at the outset accepted. They are then not initially tenable. When brought to light, however, they may reflect well or badly or indifferently on the commitments that engender them. Unless on due deliberation we can endorse their consequences, our commitments—initially tenable or not—are discredited. Meno's slave rightly repudiated his initially tenable geometric beliefs once he recognized their implications.

Sustaining and underwriting initially tenable commitments may require additional commitments we are loath to make. Since, for example, the initially tenable convictions that motivate Cartesian dualism need to be filled out with an account of mind-body interaction, the manifest untenability of available accounts threatens to dislodge those convictions. We might, of course, treat the difficulty as an outstanding problem, expecting that in due course it will be solved. Often this is a reasonable attitude to adopt. But in the long run our inability to formulate an account we are willing to endorse (or a tenable reason for thinking none necessary) casts doubt on the commitments we began with. Ultimately, their failure to seed a system we can countenance discredits such commitments.

Success, like failure, may unseat initially tenable commitments. When, for example, a highly plausible, robust, and fruitful principle skirts our initially tenable commitments, we may endorse it enthusiastically and reevaluate those commitments, perhaps reconstruing them as approximations. And when a powerful principle shuns some initially tenable commitments, we may repudiate those commitments outright, trading a complete match with our previous convictions for the power and elegance of the resulting account. To reap the rewards of the theory of relativity, for instance, we willingly sacrifice commonsense judgments about simultaneity.

Considerations of elegance, breadth, economy, and the like, can also prevail over initially tenable judgments. That

Some p are q

follows from

All p are q

is initially tenable. It seems obvious that some buses are late if all buses are late. But when we realize how much such a principle would complicate logic and how easily we can do without it, we readily drop it. An epistemic system is built with an eye to initially tenable commitments but need not be built upon them.

If our revisions were required to hew as closely as possible to initially tenable commitments, novel hypotheses would find it hard to gain a hearing. But maximizing tenability is not always a matter of minimizing deviation. A system that incorporates a radical hypothesis may be more tenable than its conservative rivals. Even if the hypothesis has no initial tenability of its own, its incorporation might, for example, enable a system to accommodate a higher proportion of our initially tenable commitments; or fruitfully extend beyond its current domain; or avoid ad hoc, implausible, or otherwise untenable assumptions that its competitors have to make. By replacing an initially tenable commitment to determinism with the Heisenberg uncertainty principle (and making suitable adjustments in the background theory), for example, quantum mechanics was able to account for a range of phenomena that its more traditional rivals could not. We sometimes achieve a more tenable overall system then if we replace an initially tenable commitment with an initially untenable one.

The process of adjudication provides the basis for distinguishing the accepted from the acceptable. Initially tenable commitments are accepted. Elements of tenable systems are acceptable. Being accepted then neither entails nor is entailed by being acceptable. A tenable system need not accommodate every relevant initially tenable commitment. So not everything we accept is acceptable. And we may overlook a consideration's membership in a tenable system or be unwilling or psychologically unable to endorse it despite its membership. So acceptability does not guarantee acceptance. Even though construction starts from what we in fact accept, the accepted and the acceptable diverge. This is as it should be.

In *Fact, Fiction, and Forecast*, Nelson Goodman poses the notorious grue paradox. He defines 'grue' as follows:

x is grue $=_{df}$ x is examined before time t and is found to be green, or x is not so examined and is blue,

time t being some future time. All emeralds examined to date have been both green and grue, for the predicates do not yet diverge.[2] Why then should we infer

---

[2] Goodman, *Fact, Fiction, and Forecast*, 74.

All emeralds are green

rather than

All emeralds are grue?

After discrediting a number of proposed solutions, Goodman concludes
that the preferability of 'green' derives from its entrenchment—from the
fact that 'green' and its cognates have been successfully projected far more
often than 'grue'. This might seem a weak, if not irrelevant reason, since
'grue' would have been equally successful had it been projected instead,
and since past success is no guarantor of future prospects. Marked differences in entrenchment demonstrate that we prefer 'green' to 'grue'. But
do they show that we should? They do. The entrenchment of 'green' endows its use with a measure of initial tenability that 'grue' cannot match.
So other things being equal, in current epistemic circumstances theories
employing 'green' are more tenable than their gruesome rivals. If our goal
is to maximize tenability, we should then favor 'green' over 'grue'. One
nice feature of this defense is that the presumption in favor of 'green'
evaporates if counterexamples emerge. For in that case, hypotheses
framed in terms of 'green' lose their initial tenability.

Although initially tenable claims have a measure of noninferential justification, the position that emerges is not foundationalist.[3] For initially tenable judgments function differently from foundationally basic beliefs.

Initially tenable claims are woefully uncertain, but are not defective on
that account. They are not taken as true or as incontrovertible or even as
probable, but only as reasonable starting points in a reflective, self-correcting enterprise. Adopted provisionally, they are subject to revision or
rejection as construction proceeds. Unlike the justification that attaches
to foundationalism's basic claims, initial tenability can be lost.

Systematization enhances tenability. Collectively the sentences of a system have implications that they severally lack. As these implications are
borne out, our commitment to the system's constituents is reinforced.
Our new found reason to believe all of them increases our reason to believe each of them. Foundationalism's basic beliefs, however, cannot augment their original level of justification. They supply warrant to, but do
not derive it from, the structures they support.

Being determined by current practices and convictions, a consideration's initial tenability may vary over time. But those who disagree
about a claim's initial tenability need not be permanently at odds. For
the systems they ultimately espouse may coincide. The disputed claim's
proponent may have to modify or reject it under pressure from more

[3] Contra Laurence BonJour, *The Structure of Empirical Knowledge* (Cambridge, Mass.:
Harvard University Press, 1985), 28–29.

compelling concerns. Or its opponent may find it or some variant integral to the system he finally endorses. Even if they differ over the initial tenability of

Gorillas are gentle,

they may come to agree that

Gorillas, though normally gentle, fight fiercely to protect their young

belongs to a tenable theory of primate behavior. This differs drastically from the foundationalist perspective. For claims capable of functioning as basic cannot acquire support from the structures they ground. If immediate experience doesn't justify

Red here now,

nothing ever will. For the foundationalist, disagreements over basics are eternally irresoluble.

GOING PUBLIC

Much of what I purport to know, I cannot personally justify. I am convinced, for example, that water is H_2O, that Tolstoy wrote *War and Peace*, that π is a nonrepeating decimal, that Nixon was implicated in Watergate. Yet I can say little to justify these claims. Nor can I validate many of the methods I confidently employ. I have no qualms about using litmus paper to test for acidity, a thermometer to measure temperature, the dates on a tombstone to mark the decedent's days. But I cannot certify that these methods are reliable. If I am solely responsible for the epistemic standing of my commitments, I am often on shaky ground. Nor am I peculiar in this regard. Other epistemic agents are no better able to fend for themselves.

The support I can rally looks feeble at best. This much I can say: some of these things I learned in school, others were widely reported in the press, yet others I gleaned from reliable informants. Some indeed are simply common knowledge—the sort of thing that normally goes without saying. The difficulty is that such defenses do not speak to specifics. They say nothing about water or π or litmus tests in particular. What they supply, evidently, is safety in numbers. But I have nothing else to offer. I am woefully ignorant of chemistry. So my belief that water is H_2O has little bearing on and derives little support from my other scientific beliefs. If the tenability of my cognitive commitments depends wholly on what is within my ken, my belief that water is H_2O and a host of other equally untendentious commitments come up surprisingly short. And a controversial thesis like

In the *Tractatus*, Wittgenstein espouses a form of nominalism

looks to be on epistemically better ground than

Water is H_2O,

for it is more tightly woven into a network of commitments I am personally in a position to defend.

My support for

Water is H_2O

and its ilk seems to consist mainly in the recognition that other people think
so too. Is that any justification? Oddly enough it is, although the level of
justification that intersubjective agreement supplies varies considerably.

We saw that a commitment's initial tenability derives at least in part
from its staying power—from the fact that thus far it has withstood pressures to abandon it. To be sure, it need not have been systematically or
sorely tested. What pressures it has been subject to are a function of its
place in a cognitive economy and the vicissitudes of fortune. Brute luck in
eluding serious challenge may account for its endurance. Nevertheless, its
having survived is a point in its favor.

People's commitments and experiences diverge. So a shared conviction
is apt to have withstood a wider range of challenges than an idiosyncratic
one. By pooling our resources, we can benefit from one another's experiences. My conviction that water is H_2O gains tenability when I learn that
others think so too. For their agreement is evidence that the belief survives
in a variety of cognitive environments. Still, mere agreement or disagreement in initially tenable commitments has but a marginal effect on overall
tenability. What we share (or what our detractors share) could just be a
common misconception. And its being widely held may shield it from
challenge. If nearly everyone agrees that bears hibernate, we might take
this commonplace for granted and lack incentive to explore the matter
further. Intersubjective agreement alone is too weak to convert initial tenability into full fledged tenability.

That similarly situated epistemic agents concur then avails me little. But
not all who share my conviction that water is H_2O are in my sorry epistemic state. Some of them have mastered chemistry. And because suitable
lines of communication link me to them, I can draw on their expertise.

Lines of communication vary in their capacity to transmit tenability.
Gossip, for example, is a poor conductor, being notoriously unreliable. A
journal like *Science*, on the other hand, is an excellent conductor. It is
known to be selective about what it reports and honest and careful about
how it reports. So a scientific commitment's tenability can be significantly
affected by the contents of *Science*. What makes the difference? Some sci-

entific journals are discriminating and designed to minimize distortion. Contributors are held responsible for the accuracy and adequacy of their reports. Gossip is indiscriminate, permitting promiscuous paraphrase, and frequently sacrificing accuracy for effect. Evidently, a line of communication can transmit tenability only to the extent that the medium is trustworthy and the message tenable.

A trustworthy medium inhibits distortion, dilution, exaggeration, and the like, and screens for untenable messages. No screen is perfect. Even the most scrupulous of journals occasionally publishes fraudulent results and honest mistakes. Still, some media screen well enough to create a presumption in favor of their messages. If a tenable message is conveyed by such a medium, a significant measure of its tenability is carried with it. A medium that is trustworthy for one sort of message need not be trustworthy for another. Broadcast news shows, for example, might provide trustworthy reports of political events but untrustworthy analyses of them. Trustworthiness involves a fit between medium and message.

My defense of the uncontroversial commitments mentioned above is that when it comes to such messages, education, journalism, suitably educated informants, and the like, are trustworthy media. I could of course be wrong. Perhaps education is a tool of ideology. Rather than transmitting tenable commitments, maybe it conveys subtle distortions designed to surreptitiously sustain the ruling class. In that case, the medium is untrustworthy, its messages suspect. Or perhaps chemistry is internally inconsistent, so the theses it promulgates, though widely accepted, are in fact untenable. Then even if education is trustworthy, it does not enmesh my belief that water is H_2O in a tenable system of thought. But if my scientific education constitutes a trustworthy connection to a tenable system of thought, and if no sufficiently tenable considerations contravene, my belief that water is H_2O is tenable. The same defense works for more recondite matters. My belief that Spinoza's philosophy was influenced by the Marrano culture of his forebears and my belief that $e^{\pi i} = -1$ owe their tenability to my having trustworthy ties to tenable systems that vindicate them. The epistemic status of commitments whose tenability is beyond my ken is then derivative and conditional on the trustworthiness of the medium and the tenability of the message.

The system that vindicates a commitment need be in no one person's ken. The scientists who collectively establish that the rain forests are being despoiled rely on one another's expertise in much the way the amateur relies on theirs. The various agronomists, hydrologists, botanists, and zoologists are not likely to be privy to the constellations of commitments that render one another's findings tenable. Nor are they apt to be able to validate the statistical techniques, calibrate the instruments, or vindicate the methods they use to establish their own findings. Together they do what none can do alone—construct a tenable ecological theory. There is then a division of cognitive labor. Rather than relying exclusively on considerations in my ken, I draw on the expertise of others, and they in turn draw on mine.

Why not hold each person individually responsible for supplying first-hand evidence to support her own cognitive commitments? In that case, much of what we purport to know is not in fact knowledge. I do not know that water is H_2O, that mountain gorillas are an endangered species, that flying is safer than driving. Moreover, many thoroughly established conclusions—that Venice is sinking, that the Sahara is spreading, that the universe is expanding—are known to no one, since the grounds for believing them are dispersed across an epistemic community. And seemingly excellent sources of information—almanacs, atlases, handbooks, and the like—are not repositories of knowledge, for they supply information without justification. To retain our commitment to rugged epistemic individualism, we would have to sacrifice a host of initially tenable commitments about what and how we know. Since many of these commitments are sustained if cognition is a community affair, and since their retention exacts no major cost, the method of reflective equilibrium favors an epistemology that recognizes the division of cognitive labor. A social epistemology accommodates our initially tenable commitments better than rugged epistemic individualism does.

Trustworthiness is just tenability of a chain of communication, so it is established in the way other cases of tenability are. Our views about media and messages may at the outset clash. We might, for instance, be initially inclined to credit government spokesmen, but find ourselves doubting much of what they say. To achieve accord, we could lower our estimates of the speakers' credibility, increase our confidence in their pronouncements, or devise a set of distinctions that more accurately reflects our assessments of when government spokesmen are to be trusted. In deciding among our options, we balance our initially tenable commitments about the medium, the information it draws on, the messages it transmits, the institutions that underwrite it, the ends it promotes, and so on. A valid measure of trustworthiness is thus a product of reflective equilibrium. Contra Coady, then, testimony is neither intrinsically reliable nor intrinsically suspect.[4]

The cause of a tenable commitment is not always what supplies its tenability. Woodward and Bernstein's masterful reporting did not cause me to believe that Nixon was implicated in Watergate. I jumped to that conclusion on my own, long before there was evidence for it. The news reports that came too late to cause my belief furnished its justification. They

---

[4] See C.A.J. Coady, *Testimony* (Oxford: Oxford University Press, 1992).

converted my originally unfounded conviction into a tenable one. More-over, multiple lines of communication may secure a commitment. Testi-mony of past and present smokers, reports in the popular press, articles in medical journals, and health education classes back my belief that tobacco is highly addictive. All lend support to my belief. But they cannot all have caused it. Epistemic standing is not a function of etiology. What matters is not a commitment's source, but its sustenance.

Obviously not every message conveyed by a sufficiently trustworthy medium will be tenable. An example of Harman's brings this out.

> A political leader is assassinated. His supporters, fearing a coup, announce that he survived. As a result, what is reported on television is an abortive assassination attempt. But before the announcement is made, and barely in time to meet his deadline, an enterprising newspaper reporter phones in the truth. His paper prints it. Having not heard the television reports, Jill believes what she reads in the paper.[5]

Her belief is true and her source trustworthy. But she does not know that the leader was assassinated. For even though she is unaware of the televi-sion reports, they undermine her belief's tenability. To be sure, Jill's belief is initially tenable. And its tenability is enhanced by the trustworthiness of her source. But her contemporaries have an initially tenable belief to the contrary backed by an equally trustworthy source. Trustworthy chains pull in opposite directions, resulting in a deadlock. Until one of the re-ports is discredited, Jill and her contemporaries do not know whether the leader was killed.

Considerations beyond one's ken can thus undermine a commitment's tenability. Can they also secure it? Suppose Jack believes that quantum events are inherently unpredictable on the grounds that in doing his phys-ics homework he never gets the same answer twice. The scientific commu-nity has excellent reasons for thinking quantum events unpredictable—reasons, needless to say, that have nothing to do with Jack's. It seems plain that Jack does not know that quantum events are unpredictable. His rea-sons are utterly untenable. And being oblivious to expert opinion on the matter, he cannot successfully defer justification. Less obtuse physics students can. Their scientific education constitutes a trustworthy chain linking their belief to a tenable theory. If information known to her peers undermines Jill's claim to knowledge, why doesn't such information sup-port Jack's?

An individual's grounds for a commitment consist of considerations he is in a position to adduce, including chains he trusts. If his grounds are

---

[5] Gilbert Harman, *Thought* (Princeton, N.J.: Princeton University Press, 1973), 143–144.

epistemically adequate, they give other members of the community sufficient reason to endorse his commitment. Neither Jack nor Jill has adequate grounds. Jack's are terrible. His incompetence affords no reason to
believe anything about physics, except that he has no future in it. Jill's are
better. They provide her compatriots with some reason to believe that the
leader was assassinated. But they are not good enough. People who have
heard the television reports ought not on reflection endorse her belief.

Epistemic interdependence involves more than calling on experts to
patch holes in our systems of thought. Even when a thinker backs her own
claims, community support is not far to seek. My tenable belief that trash
is collected on Tuesdays needs no support from the experts. My own experience bears it out. Still, to have that belief, and to have experiences
that count as evidence for or against it, requires knowing what trash is,
what trash collection is, what Tuesdays are. Such facts are socially constituted and are imparted through socialization. Without the resources the
community provides, I could neither formulate nor justify the belief in
question.

Perception is often held to supply direct epistemic access to its distinctive objects. Here if anywhere, it seems, I ought to be able to fend for
myself. I cannot. For on my own, I have no way to determine whether my
perceptions are reliable. I cannot, for example, tell directly by sight
whether I am color blind. Regularities I discern enable me to make and
sustain color ascriptions. If I am red-green color blind, however, they lead
me to ascribe the same color to ripe and unripe raspberries. There is no
incoherence in this, nothing in my visual experience to show me wrong.
Nor is there any a priori reason why ripe and unripe raspberries should not
be the same color. Only when I learn that other people draw distinctions
I cannot discern do I discover that my color ascriptions are untenable.
Nor could I discover on my own that I am tone deaf, astigmatic, or blind.
Standards of perceptual reliability are ineliminably intersubjective. Left to
my own devices, I do not know what I am missing.

That ripe and unripe raspberries differ in color, that trash is collected on
Tuesdays, that Venice is sinking, that water is H_2O—these beliefs are
tenable because they belong to tenable cognitive systems in reflective
equilibrium. The beliefs in question are mine, but the commitments that
sustain them need not be. The cognitive systems that underwrite my commitments are community property. Like a medieval tapestry, they are the
work of many hands. It follows that the locus of tenability is the community, not the individual. Understanding and knowledge are collective accomplishments.

If the community is the locus of tenability, it is also the source of initial
tenability. An acceptable cognitive system must answer not just to my
initially tenable commitments but to ours. What difference does this

make? Often the difference is negligible. Being a product of my culture, I am apt to credit much that my similarly situated compatriots do. So systems that answer to the individual's initially tenable commitments often answer equally well to the group's. But by broadening its base, a social epistemology controls for perspective and for eccentricity. A commitment whose plausibility derives from limited experience—as, for example, the belief that all swans are white does—is easily overridden when a wider range of experiences is brought to bear. And an idiosyncratic commitment that might survive in and skew a solipsistic system is unlikely to prevail when the initially tenable commitments of others are given their due. No matter how well it meshes with her other commitments, Ellen's suspicion that laboratory mice are peculiarly susceptible to cancer is unlikely to find a niche in a system that respects the initial tenability of her compatriots' views.

The requirement that we accord initial tenability to other people's opinions is not in the end very onerous. Not everyone's views on every subject need be taken into account. At the start of an inquiry we have initially tenable beliefs about whose views on the subject are worthy of consideration and about what makes them so. On the basis of these beliefs, we construct a system that delineates the epistemic community in question. The mere fact that someone agrees with me does not qualify her for admission, nor does the mere fact that she disagrees disqualify her. But interests, abilities, experience, and expertise are normally relevant in deciding whether an individual's commitments about a given matter deserve a hearing. An endocrinologist has reason to take the initially tenable commitments of other endocrinologists into account in attempting to accommodate an anomalous finding. About such matters, she normally has no reason to listen to her tennis pro. Here too feedback occurs. Advancement of understanding brings refinements in the delineation of the range of viewpoints that a given system need acknowledge.

Our intellectual heritage thus has a claim on our epistemic allegiance. For it constitutes a stock of initially tenable commitments. Still, respect for tradition might seem antithetical to advancement of understanding. The lore of our fathers is no doubt rife with errors. If we are required to ground our systems in it, how can we expect to progress?

That members of the community harbor a commitment makes that commitment initially tenable. But initial tenability is not full-fledged tenability. Neither is popularity. Contemporary psychology rightly repudiates the view that introspection affords immediate, infallible access to one's own mental states. For despite its widespread appeal, that commitment has no place in a tenable theory of mind. Tenability is not a function of the number of people who share a commitment or the strength of their confidence in it; tenability depends entirely on the commitment's place in a maximally tenable system in reflective equilibrium. Many widely shared commitments lack such a place.

We are not saddled with the time-honored errors of our ancestors then, but only with the obligation to treat our compatriots' commitments as we do our own. That obligation derives from the utility of drawing on the epistemic accomplishments of others. Acknowledging the social character of cognition and the initial tenability of our compatriots' commitments thus does not make consensus the criterion of acceptability. Advancement of understanding remains a matter of constructing, elaborating, and extending cognitive systems in reflective equilibrium. What social epistemology recognizes is that this is rarely a private enterprise.

One might wonder whether we are up to the task of generating an acceptable standard of justification. Stephen Stich argues that reflective equilibrium will not do.[6] Many people, he notes, commit the gambler's fallacy. Some of them are prepared on reflection to endorse a rule that permits the fallacious move—for example, 'The probability of throwing a seven in a game of craps increases with the number of times in succession that a number other than seven has been thrown'. The rules and particular inferences of such a gambler are, Stich says, in reflective equilibrium. Still, the gambler's fallacy is a mistake.

The equilibrium Stich objects to here is far too narrow. It is doubtful that the objectionable rule and the inferences it sanctions are even in reflective equilibrium with the full battery of relevant rules, inferences, and grounds that the gambler accepts. It is obvious that they are not in reflective equilibrium with the rules, inferences, and grounds we are prepared to endorse. The reflective equilibrium that underwrites tenability is both wide and social. If the gambler is a member of our epistemic community, the reflective equilibrium standard shows her inferences to be invalid. This is as it should be.

What if she is not? Suppose, Stich says, she belongs to a cult whose nutty but charismatic guru leads it to accept some bizarre rule. The inferences cult members make and the rules they endorse are in reflective equilibrium with each other. Even so, bizarre rules are untenable. It is noteworthy that at this point in his discussion Stich stops talking about the gambler's fallacy and starts talking about some unspecified bizarre rule. The gambler's fallacy is demonstrably untenable. In the long run, bettors whose behavior is guided by it lose, no matter what their gurus advise. Such a rule could not be in reflective equilibrium with a betting practice

---

[6] Stephen Stich, *The Fragmentation of Reason* (Cambridge, Mass.: MIT Press, 1990), 75–100. Stich takes reflective equilibrium to purport to be an *analysis* of the commonsense notion of justification. I contend that reflective equilibrium is an acceptable standard of justification. I do not consider it an analysis. Nor do I think an analysis is needed.

for games of pure chance. Still, Stich wants to argue, there must be—or at least might be—some bizarre rule endorsed by a nutty but charismatic guru that could be incorporated into a system in reflective equilibrium. That, he contends, is enough to disqualify reflective equilibrium within a community from serving as the standard for epistemic acceptability.

This leads him to consider reflective equilibrium with expert opinion. Experts presumably derive their authority from something more epistemically estimable than charisma. If our qualms about the previous case derive from distrust in the pronouncements of nutty but charismatic gurus, dependence on expert opinion should fare better. But according to Stich it does not. For there is no guarantee that the experts will not endorse a bizarre rule. A system of inferences that incorporates a bizarre rule is, Stich contends, untenable even if it is in reflective equilibrium.

I disagree. The mere fact that a rule or other commitment is bizarre does not demonstrate that either it or a system that includes it is untenable. Some systems we have no reservations about include counterintuitive components. A variety of familiar logical principles strike the uninitiated as bizarre. Novices regularly balk at the rule for the material conditional and the rule that blocks the inference from $(x)Fx$ to $(\exists x)Fx$. Experts, if they considered the matter, might well concede that the rules, although effective, are unintuitive. These concessions do not undermine the tenability of classical logic. For the utility of the aforementioned rules outweighs their peculiarity. The Heisenberg uncertainty principle boggles the mind. If bizarreness were grounds for exclusion, such a principle would have no chance of being accepted. But the principle fits into contemporary physical theory and enables us to make sense of otherwise baffling findings. So it qualifies as a tenable physical principle. Bizarre considerations are initially untenable. But initial untenability can be and sometimes is overridden through incorporation into a tenable system of thought.

There may be multiple, equally tenable systems, for reflective equilibrium can sometimes be achieved in a variety of ways. Stich regards this as a defect. He contends that only an epistemic chauvinist would have reason to consider a system intrinsically good if that system admits of alternatives. I do not see why. If I recognize that my system of thought is as good as yours and that at the moment there is none better, I am irrational to consider mine superior to yours, but I am not irrational to consider mine good. My reason for sticking with my own system rather than adopting your equally good one is practical. Converting to a new system takes time and effort. In the process mistakes are apt to be made. So I have good reason not to abandon my system until I find something better. You have equally good reason not to abandon yours. Neither of us is in an epistemically embarrassing position.

Bootstrapping

Inquiry is a matter of pulling ourselves up by our bootstraps. We interpolate, extrapolate, elaborate, and emend our initially tenable commitments; we mine them for analogies, disanalogies, insights, and strategies. We thereby generate additional candidates for our epistemic allegiance. If these candidates are unexceptionable, we provisionally endorse them and integrate them into a developing system. But if, on reflection, we cannot countenance the candidates we generate, we reject them and try again.

We profit from failures as well as successes. The realization that we cannot in good conscience countenance *p* typically engenders initially tenable commitments that conflict with *p*. For example, our initially tenable commitments about psychological states might accord with the thesis:

Mental content derives from linguistic content.

But confronted with the implications of this thesis we balk, unable to believe that a cat does not want the mouse she assiduously stalks. And because we cannot accept this consequence, we cannot endorse the thesis. Still, our efforts are not entirely in vain. They yield a new initially tenable commitment:

Cats (and presumably other nonlanguage-using animals) have contentful mental states.

We emerge from our investigation with an enriched body of commitments that serves as a basis for, and is tested in the context of, future inquiry. We know more than we did before about what we are prepared to count as a tenable theory of mind.

Descartes maintained that we should never fully trust a source that once deceived us. He therefore advocated totally *distrusting* such sources, excluding their deliverances from the corpus of knowledge.[7] He paid a heavy price. For such sources often afford our only access to epistemically distant realms. Memory, testimony, induction, and analogy, though less than entirely reliable, extend our cognitive range immeasurably. Still, Descartes had a point. To fully trust unreliable insights or information would be foolhardy. But to give some credence to considerations of doubtful provenance, to assign them some measure of initial tenability, is not obviously irresponsible.

---

[7] Descartes of course acknowledged the practical utility of memory, testimony, analogy, and induction. So he did not advocate eschewing them in practical deliberation. But he thought that their vulnerability to error debarred them from a role in philosophy and science. See René Descartes, "Principles of Philosophy," in *The Philosophical Writings of René Descartes*, vol. 1 (Cambridge: Cambridge University Press, 1985), part 4, Principles 204–205.

A solid diagnosis can hardly be grounded solely in the result of a test with a significant margin of error, or in a display of symptoms shared by several disparate diseases, or in a medical history that indicates a mild predisposition to a given condition, or in an off-the-cuff assessment by an astute diagnostician. But each of these factors confers some tenability on the diagnosis. Separately each is but a tenuous indication of the disease; collectively they may be decisive.

Recognizing that every commitment is vulnerable to revision or rejection, the constructionalist epistemology I favor incorporates self-monitoring, self-correcting mechanisms into its methodology. Equipped to root out error, it is prepared to take risks. It can adopt considerations too poorly supported for perfect procedural epistemologies to countenance, secure in the knowledge that unwise admissions can later be rescinded. Not that constructionalism advocates cavalier adoptions. It requires weak reasons to be more tightly woven into the fabric of commitments than strong ones. But it allows that this can be done, that collective action can compensate for individual shortcomings.

A constellation of weak reasons sometimes constitutes a strong case. So the capacity to credit such reasons is an asset. It affords access to epistemically remote realms, increases the range of data we can draw on, and deepens our understanding of both familiar and unfamiliar phenomena. Corrigibility compensates for fallibility, converting an apparent weakness into a source of strength.

Self-monitoring mechanisms provide a way to keep score—not only of current epistemic status but also of the fates of previous contenders. They record which initially tenable commitments have proven integrable into acceptable systems, how secure their tenure of adoption, what readjustments were required to secure a fit, what they contributed to the systems that emerged. They thus supply the resources for continual updating of epistemic standings.

Premonitions, for example, might once have been initially tenable. They are, after all, awfully compelling. But their claim on our epistemic allegiance is regularly overridden. My firm conviction that next week's X-rays will disclose a need for painful, expensive dental work withers in the face of our best theories of cognition and the track records of previous premonitions. As rejections mount, tenability wanes. When we no longer see any point in attempting to incorporate premonitions into our cognitive systems, when we lose all confidence in them, they cease to be even initially tenable. The fate of previous premonitions then tells against the initial tenability of current ones.

Tenability can be gained as well. Not long ago, ascriptions of unconscious motives were highly untenable, the term 'unconscious motive' being practically an oxymoron. With the advent of Freudian psychology, their status began to change. Ascriptions of unconscious drives acquired tenability through incorporation into tenable psychological explanations. With each success, their objectionability dwindled. Eventually their contribution to explanations of human behavior outweighed their implausibility. When our incentive to exclude them from psychology evaporated, they ceased to be initially untenable. Indeed, the tide seems to have turned. We now expect psychological theories to adduce unconscious forces and look slightly askance at accounts that do not.

Tracking yields grounds for refinement as well. We might once have considered all intimations of the past on a par and assigned them all a modest measure of initial tenability. But the record reveals that they cluster into classes with decidedly different prospects. Some are easily assimilated, others prove recalcitrant. This leads us to distinguish among them, classifying some as memories, others as feelings of déjà vu. We adjust assignments accordingly, increasing the initial tenability of memories, denying initial tenability to feelings of déjà vu. We need not stop there. We may find it fruitful to distinguish among memories so as to assign different levels of tenability to memories of different sorts.

Reconstruction is thus fueled by history, by an appreciation of the successes and failures, benefits and costs, engendered by previous attempts to accommodate commitments. Cognitive progress is no piecemeal accretion of separately established facts but a dynamic interplay of novel proposals and entrenched commitments. Integration of new material often requires reconfiguration of commitments already in place, revision or repudiation of earlier adoptions.

CHANGE IN FOCUS: FROM KNOWLEDGE TO UNDERSTANDING

To call the resulting epistemic achievement 'knowledge' would be unwise on several counts. First, the justification such a procedure produces is plainly conditional and provisional. What is tenable in today's epistemic circumstances may be untenable in tomorrow's. But by tradition, knowledge is a permanent achievement, its justification unconditional and insensitive to changes in epistemic clime. Second, justification within our procedure is of a piece. Values, rules, categories, and methods are justified along with and in the same way as judgments. If all satisfy the same standards, all merit the same status. But only judgments are supposed to be candidates for knowledge. A tenable system's nonpropositional elements are traditionally excluded from knowledge because of their logical form; at best, they are granted instrumental value in the epistemic quest. Third, knowledge by tradition implies truth. So a falsehood, however reasonable and illuminating, is never knowledge. But a falsehood might well be incorporated into a system in reflective equilibrium. And to good effect.

Objects in a vacuum fall toward the Earth at a rate of 32 ft/sec^2

is not strictly true since it neglects the gravitational attraction of everything except the Earth. Still, it provides genuine insight into the behavior of falling bodies, contributes to a general theory of terrestrial motion, connects observations and measurements with physical laws, and closely approximates the vastly more complicated truth. It is plainly epistemically valuable, even if its falsity disqualifies it as knowledge. We could, of course, simply redefine 'knowledge', excluding these objectionable features. Since knowledge as customarily construed is unrealizable, some revision seems mandatory anyway. But even after its reconception, 'knowledge' is apt to carry old associations. So continued use of the term may invite misunderstandings. Moreover, a tenable reconception should be reasonably faithful to antecedent usage. Under any such reconception, the aspirations of knowledge are too limited.

'Understanding' is a better term for the epistemic achievement that concerns us here. Not being restricted to facts, understanding is more comprehensive than knowledge ever hoped to be. We understand rules and reasons, actions and passions, objectives and obstacles, techniques and tools, forms, functions, and fictions, as well as facts. We also understand pictures, words, equations, and patterns. Ordinarily these are not isolated accomplishments; they coalesce into an understanding of a subject, discipline, or field of study.

Understanding need not be couched in sentences. It might equally be located in apt terminology, insightful questions, effective nonverbal symbols, intelligent behavior. A mechanic's understanding of carburetors or a composer's understanding of counterpoint is no less epistemically significant for being inarticulate. Even a physicist's understanding of her subject typically outstrips her words. It is realized in her framing of problems, her design and execution of experiments, her responses to research failures and successes, and so on. Physics involves a constellation of commitments that organize its objects and our access to them in ways that render those objects intelligible. Understanding physics is not merely or mainly a matter of knowing physical truths. It involves a feel for the subject, a capacity to operate successfully within the constraints the discipline dictates or to challenge those constraints effectively. And it involves an ability to profit from cognitive labors, to draw out the implications of findings, to integrate them into theory, to utilize them in practice. Understanding a particular fact or finding, concept or value, technique or law is largely a matter of knowing where it fits and how it functions in the matrix of commitments that constitute the science. But neither knowing where nor knowing how reduces to the *knowing that* that traditional epistemology explicates.

Knowledge is supposed to be an all-or-nothing affair. Either you know that p or you do not. But understanding admits of degrees. A rough approximation of the gravitational constant, being false, does not count as knowledge. In accepting it, however, we display an understanding of gravity. That understanding can be broadened and deepened, not just by adding to our stock of justified true beliefs about falling bodies but also by supplanting the approximation with a better one, relating it to our understanding of other natural forces, integrating it into physical theory, juxtaposing it with more primitive or more fanciful views, and so on.

Truth is a harsh master. An error in the fifth or the five-hundredth decimal place would compel traditional epistemology to deny that Newton knew the law of gravity. Epistemology as here reconceived can recognize that he understood gravity well. Not being in thrall to truth, a theory that takes understanding as epistemically central is in a position to validate cognitive achievements that classical theories of knowledge cannot.

These are not all lesser achievements. For truth does not always enhance understanding. An irrelevant truth is epistemically inert. Neither initially tenable nor part of a system we endorse, it is alien to our cognitive commitments. We have no reason to credit it; we can make nothing of it.

Even a relevant truth may be untenable. It might, for example, be so complicated that its assimilation into a tenable system would subvert other cognitive objectives. It might eclipse patterns and regularities an approximation reveals, drown theory in details, or require calculations so complex as to be impracticable. In such cases a reasonable approximation is cognitively preferable to truth. Understanding then involves realizing when increased accuracy ceases to compensate for the cognitive costs it exacts. Although strictly false, Boyle's law is not epistemically defective. It enhances our understanding of gases in ways the unmanageably complicated, unvarnished truth would not.

Tradition has it that truth is our overriding cognitive objective. Even if simplicity, sensitivity, fruitfulness, and the like are genuine goods, their value is supposed to be instrumental, residing in their capacity to promote the discovery of truth. On examination, however, the values in question display little sign of such capacity. Science no doubt favors simplicity. But the simplest theory compatible with the evidence typically has less chance of being true than some of its rivals. Suppose, for example, we examine many, widely distributed maple trees and find them all deciduous. Although none of the examined trees is in Eagleville, we should infer

All maple trees are deciduous

rather than

All maple trees, except perhaps those in Eagleville, are deciduous.[8]

But the latter would be preferable if truth were our goal. It is true if the former is; it may be true if the former is not. Sensitivity fares no better. The more sensitive our distinctions, the more vulnerable they are to error. So a cognitive endeavor whose overriding objective is truth should favor crude, widely spaced categories whose differences are easily marked. That cheetahs run fast is easily determined; that they reach a speed of 69.57 miles per hour is not. If we are bent on establishing truth then, we should eschew such precision. Examples can be multiplied, but the point is clear. The cognitive values that inform our inquiries do not always enhance their prospects of disclosing truth.

Perhaps those values are noninstrumental but subsidiary goods. Then science could exercise its penchant for simplicity, sensitivity, informativeness, and the like, while continuing its quest for truth. Indeed, on such a view, its other cognitive values might delineate the class of truths a discipline takes for its own. Still, truth would always trump. It would be epistemically irresponsible on such a view to forego truth to achieve other cognitive ends. The difficulty is that we regularly sacrifice truth. And to good effect. Science idealizes, approximates, smooths curves, and adduces undetected background noise or observational error to accommodate anomalous findings. It thereby makes order out of chaos, revealing patterns and regularities or startling discrepancies that the naked truth obscures. Other disciplines deploy similar devices to achieve their cognitive ends. This is not to say that science makes assertions it knows to be false. Proffering or putting forth a theory is not normally a matter of asserting it.[9] To assert that p is equivalent to asserting that p is true. To advocate believing that p is equivalent to advocating believing that p is true. But to proffer a theory, to recommend its adoption, is not ordinarily to claim, even implicitly, that it is true. In proffering a theory, a science contends that its acceptance is reasonable in the epistemic circumstances. Science regularly proffers theories containing claims that it knows are not strictly true—approximations, idealizations, simplifying assumptions, and the like. It is not epistemologically irresponsible to do so.

To be sure, we might construe such a stance as a tactical retreat, under-

---

[8] Nelson Goodman, "Safety, Strength, Simplicity," in *Problems and Projects*, 335.

[9] This view is akin to and influenced by Bas van Fraassen's. Unlike van Fraassen, though, I do not think there is a general principle for segregating the truth-stating elements of a scientific theory from those that make no pretense of being true. See Bas van Fraassen, *The Scientific Image* (Oxford: Clarendon, 1980).

taken to regroup forces for the long march to truth. But there is no evidence to support such a construal and much reason to doubt it. Knowing the pressure each gas molecule exerts on the walls of an enclosed volume is not in general cognitively preferable to knowing the approximation Boyle's law provides. So there is no justification for considering that law a temporary expedient accepted only in default of the truth it approximates.

Simplicity, sensitivity, explanatory power, and the rest are epistemically creditable not because they are conducive of truth or because they circumscribe a particular class of truths but because they belong with truth to a constellation of cognitive values whose realization promotes the sort of understanding science seeks.

I have focused on the values of science because science is widely regarded as our preeminent cognitive enterprise. If science tolerates falsity to achieve its ends, truth's claim to epistemic preeminence is overthrown.

Other disciplines, having different values and priorities, generate understanding of different kinds. Generality and scope, so central to science, are less important for biography and investigative journalism, where particular actions and events loom larger. But every field of inquiry has its constellation of cognitive values. And like any other element of such a constellation, truth may be waived in the interest of overall tenability.

Truth then does not always trump. Does anything else? Certainly no other element has higher epistemic priority than truth. But perhaps a global feature of a tenable system, rather than one of its elements, constitutes the end of inquiry. The best candidate seems to be permanent tenability—tenability that after some given time is never lost. Even more than truths, which may be irrelevant or inassimilable, permanently tenable systems would indemnify against epistemic misfortune. Surely this is an admirable epistemic goal.

Of course we cannot tell which (if any) currently tenable systems are permanently tenable. But we can evaluate the longevity and stability of the systems we hold. We might then define permanent tenability as the limit of a temporally bounded, epistemically accessible feature like enduring, unwavering tenability.[10] Permanent tenability would then function in our epistemology as a regulative ideal for whose realization or approximation other cognitive desiderata would justifiably be sacrificed.

But ends inform means. If permanent tenability is our paramount cognitive objective, our methods and standards should be designed to serve

[10] Such a view has been advocated by Nelson Goodman and by Hilary Putnam. See Nelson Goodman, *Ways of Worldmaking* (Indianapolis: Hackett, 1978), 123–125, and *Of Mind and Other Matters* (Cambridge, Mass.: Harvard University Press, 1985), 38; and Hilary Putnam, *Reason, Truth, and History* (Cambridge: Cambridge University Press, 1981), 55–56.

that end. In that case they should be highly risk averse. For the weaker our claims and the lower our standards, the less likely we are to ever have to give them up. The systems we endorse, though, are not so timorous. They brave error to enhance understanding. They seek a reasonable balance of safety and strength. To be sure, they do not always achieve such a balance. But setting our sights on permanent tenability would require major sacrifices. Cognitive values like informativeness, insightfulness, precision, and predictive power would be forfeit. A permanently tenable system may well sanction

Grasslike plants are often greenish.

Circumstances that would call it into doubt are difficult to envision. But it is hardly preferable to a statement like

Grass is green

or to an account of the way chlorophyll functions to produce color in plants of the family Gramineae. Indeed, the latter may be the best of the bunch even though the most likely to require revision as our understanding of botany grows. Concern with the verdict of history is but one of many considerations that inform the systems we construct. Different systems assign it different weights. Evidently, neither truth nor permanent tenability is our overriding cognitive objective. No better candidate waits in the wings. There is apparently no single end toward which all inquiry aims.

In repudiating the end of inquiry, we may seem to lose our last chance to construe epistemic procedures as imperfect. For imperfect procedures, like perfect ones, require an external standard to judge their products against. Realists take the world to set the standard, correctness consisting in truth by correspondence to mind-independent reality. For some nonrealists a different end of inquiry supplies epistemology's standard. Conclusions are right or wrong depending on whether they are empirically adequate or permanently tenable or fated to be believed in the ideal limit of unfettered inquiry or whatever. But if truths, methods, norms, and objectives are epistemic constructs, standards seem to be products of cognitive practices, not external checks on them. Constructionalism then looks like a pure procedural stance, vulnerable to the criticisms I marshaled against Wittgenstein, Rorty, and Kuhn.

In assimilating constructionalism to pure proceduralism, however, we go too fast. Although I view the standard against which a system is measured as a cognitive construct, I do not consider it constructed by the system it measures. Pure procedures can produce equilibrium. If the various components of a cognitive system need only be reasonable in light of one another, grounds for including or excluding particular considerations are strictly internal to the system involved. There is then justification *in* the system but no justification *of* the system. But epistemic success requires reflective equilibrium, and not every equilibrium is reflective. A mutually supportive network of largely implausible claims is not a system we can on reflection accept. To be in *reflective* equilibrium, a balanced system must be reasonable in light of what we already have reason to hold; that is, it must answer to our initially tenable commitments about the subject at hand. Such commitments, being independent of the system they tether, provide the standard we need. They supply the basis for justification of the system in question. There need be no single standard against which all inquiry is to be judged. For each inquiry, in acknowledging its responsibility to a range of initially tenable commitments, has its own standard.

Our criterion of tenability would be circular were it set by a system whose sole claim to our epistemic allegiance lay in its satisfying itself. But circularity is avoided, since only a tethered system can supply the requisite criterion. What qualifies such a system to set the standard of tenability is not its satisfying that standard but its answering to considerations we had antecedent reason to endorse. A tenable system then rests not on some Archimedean point but on a store of initially tenable commitments that serve as a rough test of our cognitive constructs.[11] Such a constructional-ism enables us to adopt a critical perspective without assuming a God's eye view. The considerations that tether a system are not taken as absolutes. Their epistemic authority derives from their status as our current best guesses about the subject at hand. They thus set a lower bound on acceptability of any successor system. Since a tenable system improves on the initially tenable commitments that tether it and serves as tether to its immediate successors, with the adoption of successive systems, the lower bound on acceptability is raised. With advancement of understanding come rising standards of tenability.

Constructionalist procedures remain imperfect. Despite the liberties allowed in devising systems, reflective equilibrium is not guaranteed. Confronted with a collection of initially tenable commitments, we may be unable to construct any system without rejecting commitments we consider beyond cavil or accepting ones we cannot in good conscience countenance. Such commitments then resist systematization. In other cases we may have good reason to believe we have achieved reflective equilibrium when in fact we have not. Perhaps our system treats as exceptionless generalizations that, unbeknownst to us, admit of exceptions or treats as reliable methods that in unforeseen circumstances break down. Or perhaps, although it improves on the tenability of its tether, a competitor

---

[11] Scheffler, "Justification and Commitment," 294.

does better. Then that competitor is more reasonable in light of our relevant initially tenable commitments. Although we devise heuristics to guard against such eventualities, we cannot preclude their occurrence. We can improve our cognitive practices, but we cannot perfect them.

THE GROWTH OF UNDERSTANDING

Reflective equilibrium plainly confers no immunity against epistemic misfortune. It shows rules, values, methods, and judgments to be reasonable in light of one another and the system they constitute to be reasonable in light of what we already accept. It thus justifies the system and its constituents by showing that, under the epistemic circumstances, endorsing them makes sense. Reflective equilibrium thereby qualifies the system and its constituents to serve as a background of reasonably settled convictions against which investigation may responsibly proceed.

Although it requires that a system answer to our antecedent commitments and that its components mesh with one another, reflective equilibrium does not require that the system be complete or comprehensive. A system designed to explain primate behavior is hardly to be faulted for its failure to accommodate antecedent beliefs about crop dusting or accepted methods for setting interest rates. Such matters are not its concern. Let us say that a system acknowledges a prior commitment just in case the system either incorporates that commitment or supplies suitable grounds for revising or rejecting it. Those it does not acknowledge, it ignores. Once we recognize that tenable systems need not acknowledge all our initially tenable commitments, we need a way to tell which such commitments a given system is answerable to.

It will not do simply to require that a noncomprehensive system acknowledge some initially tenable commitments and refrain from interfering with the rest. For a system is prima facie defective if it ignores commitments it ought to address. Our system's failure to acknowledge the currently well-founded belief that primates are social animals would not be exonerated by its lack of commitment to the contrary. How is the line to be drawn? How do we tell when a system's failure to acknowledge a prior commitment is a mark against it? Evidently such neglect is objectionable if the commitment in question is one the system ought to acknowledge, but unobjectionable if it lies outside the system's purview. But this is no help unless we know how to identify the commitments a system ought to acknowledge.

There is no delineating these a priori. At one time it may have been reasonable to study the behavior of gorillas in isolation from one another. If all gorillas are pretty much alike, then studying one should yield insight into all. But once we realize that gorilla communities have a complex social structure, we have to adopt a different methodology. A tenable system for explaining gorilla behavior now needs to acknowledge a variety of initially tenable commitments about social roles that were once considered irrelevant. The range of relevant considerations thus changes as inquiry proceeds, evolving with our understanding of a subject and the methods for investigating it.

Because a system in reflective equilibrium admits of elaboration, it serves as a springboard for further inquiry. Its network of commitments provides resources for framing problems that could not previously have been posed, and for motivating and structuring investigations that previously would have had neither rationale nor direction. A system suited to medicine, for example, might diverge from the initially tenable commitments that prompted it by classifying as cases of the same disease all and only ailments caused by the same etiological agent. Though largely agreeing with antecedent diagnoses, some reconfiguration of the domain would result. Meningitis, for instance, would no longer count as a single disease, since different cases have different causes. In elaborating the new system, we might explore relations between the agent that causes a disease, environments receptive to it, and signs and symptoms the disease presents. We might seek tests for the presence of etiological agents, medicines to combat them, vaccines to protect against them. In the process we may discover hitherto overlooked differences in the manifestations and prognoses of newly differentiated diseases. What seemed to be a spectrum of signs and symptoms characteristic of a single illness may cluster into separate, perhaps overlapping, clinical pictures. Before the new system's adoption, we had no reason to mark these particular differences, no reason to consider them significant. Moreover, the new system may enable us to explain differential responses to treatment. Why some meningitis patients respond to antibiotics and others do not ceases to be a mystery when we recognize that some suffer from a bacterial infection, others from a viral one. By exploiting the system's conceptual and methodological resources then, we can extend and refine the understanding it already affords.

In elaborating such a system, we apply methods it sanctions to generate additional insights. If these insights mesh with the system as it stands and do not clash with other commitments, the system readily incorporates them, thereby extending its range. The expanded system may in turn afford resources for refining methods the original system employed, and the newly honed methods can be applied to generate yet further insights. Our system for medicine, for example, enables us to formulate a germ theory of disease that yields an understanding of the production and function of antibodies. Armed with that understanding, we can develop more precise diagnostic tests, vaccines, and medications. The responses of patients to these tests, vaccines, and medications in turn provides additional insight into a disease and its course, insight that may lead to additional refinements in diagnosis and treatment and open the way to yet further elaboration of the system.

The growth of understanding is thus a matter of building on what we have already established. If things go smoothly, equilibrium is preserved as the system evolves. But each attempted elaboration is also a test, and test results have the potential to upset the balance.

As a system's range expands, its fabric of commitments may fray. Newtonian laws that work admirably at slow speeds and short distances turn out to be inaccurate at high speeds and vast distances. A system that takes them to be universal evidently cannot be sustained. Methods a system sanctions sometimes generate outcomes it cannot accept. Thus the Michelson-Morley experiment, designed and executed in conformity with the commitments of classical physics, yields a result that classical physics cannot accommodate. The system's theoretical and methodological commitments pull in different directions. A system may provide means and motivation to pose problems it lacks the resources to solve. The simple arithmetical system used by Meno's slave, for example, enabled him to ask, but not to answer, how to construct a square double the area of a given square. When well motivated, well-executed inquiries prove fruitless or yield ambiguous or conflicting results, it is a sign that a system cannot realize goals it sets for itself.

The elaboration of a system may bring it into conflict with other firm commitments. An otherwise tenable determinism, for example, may be stopped cold when it confronts the conviction that human beings have, and moral agency requires, free will. Such a clash does not, of course, directly impugn the system under development; the other party to the conflict might as easily be at fault. But the clash does reveal a tension among our various commitments. In showing that the deterministic system cannot respect our moral and metaphysical convictions, it calls the adequacy of that system into question.

A system's reflective equilibrium is thus challenged by the actual difficulties it confronts. But the mere recognition that it could somehow be wrong somewhere does not constitute an objection to it. Nor do imaginative 'counterexamples' we have no reason to credit tell against it. The recognition that a system would be untenable if pigs had wings does not discredit the system in the absence of reason to think that pigs have wings. Reflective equilibrium does not pretend to establish what is reasonable come what may, only what is reasonable in given epistemic circumstances.

But actual difficulties are not uncommon. When they arise, reflective equilibrium must be restored. The task may seem too simple to be epistemically creditable. By dismissing one or another of the competing considerations, a balance among the remainder can usually be struck. A variety of strategies are available for reestablishing equilibrium. We might restrict a system's range so that the conflict does not arise. We could, for example, retain most of our deterministic system, but limit its scope. If it does not purport to comprehend human action, it does not conflict with the claims of ethics. Alternatively, we might reinterpret commitments so that conflict between them dissolves. We could, for instance, adopt a compatibilist stance, denying that determinism is at odds with the sort of freedom morality requires. Then again, we might compromise, modifying a variety of commitments to bring them into accord. In that case we could espouse soft determinism and take 'free', morally evaluable actions to supervene on softly determined facts. Although each of these strategies is sometimes effective, they cannot be implemented arbitrarily. For the equilibrium we seek is a reflective one. Ad hoc modifications designed solely to eliminate conflicts are unlikely to yield a balance of considerations that we can on reflection accept.

Revisions reverberate. Ordinarily we cannot just repudiate an unwelcome result, leaving the rest of the system intact. For the difficulty would simply recur. To prevent recurrence, we need to alleviate the conditions that occasioned it. But these conditions typically have benign, even beneficial, effects as well as harmful ones. And we would like, as far as possible, to retain the desirable features. The tenability of proposed revisions thus turns on their consequences for the system as a whole. In some cases a fairly local and limited excision proves effective; in others a more global revision may be the treatment of choice. Either way, when reflective equilibrium is disrupted, construction begins anew. Both the components of the system we previously accepted and the commitments that blocked its way are accorded the status of initially tenable commitments. A tenable successor must be reasonable in light of them. Even when equilibrium is lost then, we proceed by bootstrapping. In treating our prior system as a source of initially tenable commitments, we build on the understanding of the domain that system supplied.

Forced to concede fallibility, imperfect procedural epistemology demands corrigibility. Rather than treating acceptability as irrevocable, it incorporates devices for reviewing accepted commitments and correcting or rejecting them should errors emerge. This seems entirely reasonable.

What may seem unreasonable is its propensity for looking for trouble. Instead of resting satisfied with reasonably extensive systems in reflective equilibrium, imperfect procedural epistemology encourages pushing a system's limits until rifts emerge. It seems bent on destroying any epistemic successes it manages to achieve. If reflective equilibrium is its standard of acceptability, shouldn't imperfect procedural epistemology recommend terminating inquiry when such an equilibrium is reached?

Since we can design other systems to address other interests, this strategy need not hobble our epistemic aspirations. Issues a given system did not address, another system might. But by taking the boundaries of a system in reflective equilibrium to be fixed, we could render its acceptability irrevocable.

Such a strategy, however, would be self-defeating. Systems in reflective equilibrium typically incorporate general commitments—rules, patterns, methods, norms whose application is in principle unbounded. Unless a system supplies a rationale for doing so, restricting the range of such commitments is ad hoc. Ordinarily our systems have no such rationale to supply. Newtonian physics, for example, purports to apply to all physical objects. It provides no reason to restrict the application of its laws to slowly moving bodies in the immediate celestial neighborhood. But a system is in reflective equilibrium only if its constituents are mutually supportive—only, that is, if none of its constituents is ad hoc. So the attempt to preclude anomalies by arbitrarily restricting a system's range would destroy the very equilibrium it sought to preserve. Nor would it be wise to incorporate border-closing devices into the systems we construct. Having forsaken foundationalism's reliance on self-justifying claims, we can enhance understanding only by drawing on what we have already established. A system in reflective equilibrium, we saw, creates opportunities for exploration that would not otherwise have been available. An antielaborationist stance would deprive us of them.

To be sure, other systems can be constructed, so such a stance does not automatically foreclose the growth of understanding. But sometimes the opportunities in question can only or best be realized against the background a specific system supplies. A scientific system that embeds the atomic theory of matter probably affords our best prospect of understanding radioactive decay. If so, to prohibit elaboration of that system would seriously diminish our chances of comprehending radioactivity.

Risks, moreover, often pay off. In elaborating a system, we frequently reinforce it. We incorporate new commitments that lend additional support to those already in place, and demonstrate that its tenability survives broader reflection. A system's capacity to sustain elaboration is evidence that its success is not a fluke—that its reflective equilibrium is not just a product of low standards or lucky guesses.

Epistemological constructionalism is thus a procedure for generating an unending series of increasingly tenable working hypotheses. The claim to increasing tenability is grounded in the procedure's continually testing accepted considerations, its using attempts to extend and deepen a system as a tool for rooting out received errors and other previously undetected inadequacies. Its claim to deliver nothing more than working hypotheses derives from the recognition that since its error-detection techniques are fallible, the results it sanctions remain provisional, subject to revision or rejection in the course of inquiry. A cognitive system is not a static framework of firmly established findings; it is a dynamic body of provisional commitments, continually being tested by its capacity to nurture understanding.

JUDGMENT CALLS

System building is informed by priorities—second-order commitments about the value of retaining various first-order commitments. Often these determine how conflicts are to be resolved. In empirical science, for example, evidence ordinarily overrides elegance. But our cognitive priorities are neither fine-grained nor regimented. They are unlikely to yield a well-ordered ranking of commitments. Competitors in some conflicts thus may have equal claims on our enduring epistemic allegiance. In that case, although different resolutions result in divergent systems, the systems that emerge are equally tenable. One system might sacrifice scope to achieve precision, another trade precision for scope.

We may find, for example, that a sociological account of gang warfare in San Francisco can be fleshed out with information about historical relations among Chinese tongs. But an account that draws on such information cannot explain patterns of rivalry in the South Bronx; for there is no reason to believe, and much reason to doubt, that multigenerational affiliations among Chinese-Americans affect the membership and behavior of Bronx gangs, whose members are not, for the most part, of Chinese origin. Two viable systems can then be developed: one applies to a restricted range of cases but affords a fairly detailed understanding of them; the other applies to a broader range of cases but supplies less detail. The first yields little (if any) insight into animosities in the Bronx but explains why particular rivalries in San Francisco endure; the second sheds light on the forces that generate and perpetuate gang warfare in both San Francisco and the Bronx but gives no insight into why particular gangs are rivals. Neither invalidates the other. Nor is there any reason to believe that a uniquely best system will emerge in the long run. The differences between the two systems are fairly minor. The systems overlap a good deal and agree where they overlap. They differ only in that each has something to say about issues on which the other is perforce silent.

Judgment calls can lead to far more drastic differences than these. Choices among equally tenable alternatives may affect the character of a system and the constitution of its domain. To accommodate the impossibility of ascertaining both the position and the momentum of an electron, for example, we must radically revise our views about physics. A number of modifications have been proposed. We might maintain that at every instant each electron has a determinate position and a determinate momentum but admit that only one of these magnitudes can be known. In that case science commits itself to the existence of things it cannot in principle discover. Or we might contend that measurement creates the magnitudes. Then an unmeasured particle has neither position nor momentum, and one that has position lacks momentum (since the one measurement precludes the other). Physical magnitudes are then knowable artifacts of our knowledge-gathering techniques. But from the behavior of particles in experimental situations, nothing directly follows about their behavior elsewhere. Yet a third option is to affirm that a particle has a position and affirm that it has a momentum but deny that it has both a position and a momentum. In that case we must so alter our logic that the conjunction of individually true sentences is not always true.

That science countenances nothing unverifiable, that experiments yield information about what occurs in nature, that logic is independent of matters of fact—the findings of quantum mechanics show such antecedently reasonable theses to be at odds. Substantial modifications are thus necessary to accommodate our theory of scientific knowledge to the phenomena it seeks to explain. Although there are several ways of describing and explaining quantum phenomena, none does everything we want. Different accommodations retain different scientific desiderata. Deciding which one to accept involves deciding which features of science we value most and which we are prepared, if reluctantly, to forego.

Pluralism results. The constraints on construction typically are multiply-satisfiable. Where competing considerations are about equal in weight, different trade-offs might reasonably be made, different balances struck. If any system satisfies our standards, several are apt to do so.

Even the constitution of a domain is subject to negotiation. Our initially tenable commitments often do not suffice to individuate the objects they concern. Our views about newspapers, for instance, may fail to determine whether samizdat or scandal sheets count as newspapers or whether today's tabloid-format, gossip-intensive rag is the same newspaper as the pinnacle of journalistic excellence that flourished in the 1960s. Our views about restaurants may fail to settle whether a restaurant retains its identity through changes in name, ownership, menu, or location. We may be hard put to decide whether to say

(A) This French restaurant used to serve Viennese food; before that, hamburgers.

or

(B) This French restaurant is located where there used to be a Viennese restaurant and before that, a hamburger joint.

(A) is committed to a single enduring restaurant that has undergone major changes in cuisine, (B) to three restaurants, each with a different cuisine. Our initially tenable commitments about restaurants and newspapers thus underdetermine their objects. To settle questions of identity and diversity, to determine how many restaurants or newspapers we have, and where one leaves off and another begins, the conceptions of their objects that our commitments mark out must be augmented and perhaps corrected.

Our goals and commitments in systematizing inform our choice of amendments. But these frequently admit of several realizations. So the constraints they impose are unlikely to mandate a particular scheme of individuation. Systems that count restaurants in the manner of (A) or in the manner of (B) are apt equally to suit our cognitive and practical ends.

To mold the conceptions our initially tenable commitments supply into serviceable concepts requires integrating them into a category scheme. Such a scheme sets criteria for the individuation of the items in its realm. It fixes conditions on the identity and diversity of the individuals and kinds it recognizes. Several acceptable schemes may do justice to the same constellation of commitments. All are acceptable if any is. Being elaborations of the same commitments, they are apt to employ much of the same vocabulary. But the individuals and kinds their shared terms designate may well be distinct. According to one tenable category scheme, *The Versailles* is (a later stage of) the same restaurant as *The Vienna Woods*, according to another, it is a different restaurant. According to one tenable scheme, an ermine is the same thing as a stoat; according to another, they are distinct. The category scheme they belong to thus determines the interpretation of our terms and the identities of their referents. And the scheme is an integral part of a cognitive system, designed to conform with the system's other commitments. Ontology is therefore relative to system. There is no saying, independently of all systems, what there is or whether two items are identical. Such questions can be answered only against the background of some acceptable system.[12] An affirmative answer relative to one such system is compatible with a negative answer relative to another.

Can truths then conflict? Truths belonging to a single tenable system cannot contradict each other. For the sentences of such a system can be conjoined, and a conjunction of truths is true. But what follows from a truth is true, and everything follows from a contradiction. So a system that admits contradictory truths counts every sentence true. Such a system

---

[12] W. V. Quine, "Ontological Relativity," in *Ontological Relativity and Other Essays* (New York: Columbia University Press, 1969), 26–68; Goodman, *Ways of Worldmaking*, 109–120.

clashes with our strongly held initially tenable belief that some sentences are false. So long as we retain that commitment, any system that countenances outright contradiction is untenable. The commitment is one we should be loathe to renounce, the ability to distinguish truth from falsehood being a valuable feature of any system that traffics in truth. A system that counted all sentences true would be unlikely to further our cognitive objectives.

Whether truths belonging to different systems can conflict is a trickier question. Two tenable systems may generate the same syntactical string and assign different truth values to it. A system that supports (A), for example, would count

(C) *The Versailles* used to serve hamburgers

true; one that supports (B) would count its denial true. We have here what seem to be mutually contradictory, equally tenable truths. The difficulty is that everything follows from a contradiction whether or not the contradictories belong to a single system. So if sentences from disparate tenable systems can conjoin to form a contradiction, anything goes. Hardly a welcome result.

We are not forced to embrace it. That sentences from divergent systems can conjoin to form a contradiction is not an unavoidable consequence of the position I have sketched. Terms tenable systems share may be ambiguous with respect to each other. And their occurrence in tenable, seemingly mutually contradictory judgments is evidence of ambiguity. If (C) is ambiguous, it bears one interpretation in (A)'s system, another in (B)'s. Moreover,

(D) *The Versailles* used to serve hamburgers & *The Versailles* never served hamburgers

is no contradiction if the first conjunct belongs to (A)'s system and the second to (B)'s. Since the systems the two conjuncts belong to individuate restaurants differently, the two occurrences of 'The Versailles' refer to distinct, though overlapping entities. Indeed, (D) is true. The entity recognized by (A)'s system used to serve hamburgers, the one recognized by (B)'s did not.

To escape contradiction through the introduction of ambiguity may seem ad hoc and illegitimate. It is not. We could have no better reason to construe a sentence as ambiguous than the fact that both its affirmation and its denial are tenable. I conclude then that the tenability of seemingly contradictory claims demonstrates that they are not in fact contradictory. They are mutually ambiguous.[13]

[13] See David Lewis, "Logic for Equivocators," *Noûs* 16 (1982): 431–441.

DEEPER CONFLICTS

Contradiction is not the only sort of conflict, though. Overpopulation threatens as well. Systems sharing a realm and answering to the same initially tenable commitments may differ in ontology. The restaurant that used to serve hamburgers is not the one that never did. But if

(E) *The Versailles* used to serve hamburgers

and

(F) *The Versailles* never served hamburgers

are true, then both referents of 'The Versailles' exist. (E), it seems, can secure a place for itself only by excluding (F). For there is room for only one restaurant at a time on the northeast corner of Beech and Elm. By endorsing the truth of (E) and (F), though, we seem to commit ourselves to the presence of at least two. Even if (E) and (F) do not contradict each other, they evidently conflict.

The solution to this difficulty is not far to seek. Although the systems in question differ over restaurant boundaries, neither contends that more than one restaurant occupies a given place at a given time. Each secures a spot for its restaurant by implicitly denying that the other's term 'The Versailles' denotes a restaurant. Still, the systems are not exclusionary. (A)'s system takes (B)'s term to denote a proper temporal part of a restaurant; (B)'s system takes (A)'s term to denote the fusion of several restaurants. Both systems recognize the reality of parts and fusions. And both agree that an object occupies the same location as its parts and occupies (at least part of) the same location as the fusions of which it is a part. So each concedes the reality of the object the other refers to. Since neither holds that every restaurant part or every restaurant fusion is itself a restaurant, the concession does not amount to locating more than one restaurant at a time on the corner of Beech and Elm. The reference of both occurrences of 'The Versailles' is thus secure. The disagreement between the two systems concerns which of the overlapping entities on the corner is properly called the restaurant. And that, as we saw, can be settled in favor of both parties by construing the word 'restaurant' as ambiguous.

We are not yet out of the woods, though. Reconciliation is possible because our contending systems agree on certain significant points. But such agreement is not always to be had. Consider two comprehensive physical theories: T_1 explains events by appeal solely to specks; T_2 explains the very same events by appeal solely to swells. Specks and swells may be thought of as analogous to the particles and waves of contemporary physics. The theories are implacably opposed. Swells neither constitute nor are constituted of specks; they neither supervene on nor are supervened on by specks; nor are swells and specks made up of common ur-elements. T_2's ontology has no room for specks; T_1's is equally inhospitable to swells. No mereological maneuvering will bring them into accord.

Both theories, we may suppose, are empirically and theoretically adequate. They answer to the evidence—past, present, and future. Being elaborations of the same initially tenable commitments, they accord equally with our antecedent understanding of physical reality and the methods for investigating it. They achieve an equal balance of simplicity, predictiveness, elegance, and explanatory power. Indeed, so well do they conform to our cognitive desiderata that we would not hesitate to accept either as true, were it not for the availability of the other. Together, however, they look like too much of a good thing. The empirical and theoretical adequacy of T_1 entitles us to believe that specks exist; T_2's adequacy gives us equal grounds for recognizing swells. Paradoxically, however, the adequacy of the two theories also gives us good reason to deny that *both* specks and swells exist. For if there are swells, physical events can be fully explained without reference to specks; if there are specks, physical events can be fully explained without reference to swells. Admitting either into our ontology makes the other superfluous. Admitting both would be multiplying entities beyond necessity—overcrowding the universe, populating it with entities we have no evidence for.

We cannot resolve the matter by appeal to ambiguity. For the problem is that we have too many objects, not too few words. We might conclude that at most one of the theories is true, even though we will never know which one. In that case we may accept their exclusive disjunction but must refuse to endorse either disjunct.

This way skepticism lies. For the problem I have posed is the ubiquitous problem of underdetermination. Unless our standards for theory choice are so exacting that no more than one of any pair of competing candidates meets them, the problem will arise. And our standards are nowhere near that exacting. Nor do we know how to make them so. But skepticism may well be correct. So the fact that a line of reasoning leads to a skeptical conclusion does not discredit it. Indeed, the skepticism we confront here is a sort that Bas van Fraassen endorses.[14] He maintains that we should suspend judgment on the truth of the nonobservational part of an acceptable scientific theory because there are bound to be empirically equivalent, theoretically adequate, but ontologically inequivalent alternatives to it.

Skepticism is not the worst of our problems, though. The main objection to concluding

Either T_1 or T_2 is true, but we will never know which

---

[14] van Fraassen, *The Scientific Image*.

is that we have no notion of truth capable of underwriting our claim. Truth is a property of interpreted sentences. And interpretation requires dividing a realm into entities, kinds, relations, and the like, and correlating terms with the constituents of the realm the division demarcates. Truth then is not independent of the systems we construct. For, as we have seen, it is those systems that individuate the objects and fix the referents of our terms. But multiple systems may share a realm and impose different orders on it. One system partitions the physical domain into specks; another partitions it into swells. Independent of both systems, there are neither specks nor swells. For the systems supply the criteria that individuate specks and swells, that mark off one speck or swell from another, that reidentify individual specks or swells across their various manifestations, that differentiate specks and swells from the complexes they enter into, that classify specks or swells into kinds. Relative to the system that sustains T_1, there are specks and truths about specks. Relative to the one that sustains T_2, there are swells and truths about swells. If T_1 and T_2 are as epistemically worthy as I have made them out to be, we have every reason to believe that they reveal significant truths about specks and swells, respectively. The existence of specks and swells is not of course conclusively verified. Nothing ever is. But a theory's statements about 'observables' and its statements about 'unobservables' are of a piece. We have as good reason to accept the one as the other. Global skepticism remains an option. But by recognizing that ontology is relative to system, we disarm van Fraassen's argument for limited skepticism.

Truth value varies with system. A sentence that is true under one tenable system may be false or truth valueless under another. Under one such system, '*The Versailles* used to serve Viennese food' is true; under another, it is not. Under one, 'Light consists of a series of specks' is true; under another, it is not. Only in the context of a system then is truth value determinate.

This might be doubted. We seem regularly to assess truth values successfully without invoking underlying systems. We do not ordinarily demand our interlocutor's criteria for individuating restaurants before accepting her statement that *The Versailles* used to serve Viennese food. We take her at her word. What this shows, though, is not that her utterance's truth value is independent of all systems but that the system(s) that decide an utterance's truth value need not always be explicitly specified. In taking our interlocutor at her word, we automatically embed her utterance in a system we consider appropriate.

Grice's cooperative principle helps to explain what we do.[15] According

---

[15] Paul Grice, "Logic and Conversation," in *Studies in the Way of Words* (Cambridge, Mass.: Harvard University Press, 1989), 26–31.

to Grice, it is a principle of conversation that interlocutors normally take one another to be speaking informative, relevant truths. So unless we have reason to suspect mendacity or mistake, when someone says that a French restaurant used to serve Viennese food, we interpret her utterance as part of a system that construes restaurants as enduring institutions that retain their identities through changes in cuisine.

My use of the cooperative principle threatens to deliver too much though. It suggests that we construe apparently system-neutral sentences as elements of systems in which those sentences are true. We can almost always contrive such a system. But to insist that all such sentences be interpreted as truths would surely be unwise. The cooperative principle, however, demands no such thing. It maintains that conversation proceeds smoothly when interlocutors can interpret one another's remarks as relevant, informative truths. It does not claim that conversation always proceeds smoothly or that relevance, informativeness, and truth never diverge. I do not then take Grice's principle to provide an exceptionless rule for locating each seemingly isolated utterance in a suitable system. I suggest, however, that it often applies. Where it does, it accounts for our ability to interpret utterances correctly even though no embedding system has been specified.

Truth, then, is not a matter of correspondence between sentences and a reality whose structure is independent of systematization. For any structure reality may have is imposed by a system that is informed by interests, objectives, and standards. Independent of our systems, there is no fact of the matter as to what constitutes a restaurant, a speck, or an electron; hence no fact of the matter as to whether

The Versailles once served Viennese food

is true or

Light consists of a series of specks

is true or

Unexamined electrons have no position

is true. Relative to appropriate tenable systems, these are matters of determinate fact. Truth is relative to system because interpretation is.

Correspondence theorists often deny the possibility of some range of truths—ethical truths, aesthetic truths, folk psychological truths, or whatever—on the ground that the world contains no corresponding facts. Nonvacuous truth, they maintain, consists in correspondence to the facts. Metaphysics, on such views, precedes and circumscribes semantics. But if truth is relative to system, what truths there are is a function of what systems we construct. This is no a priori matter. If we construct tenable systems that count such sentences true, then there are ethical, aesthetic, and folk psychological truths. As long as certain formal restrictions are observed, so that the semantic paradoxes do not arise, there is no a priori limit on what sorts of sentences can be true.

Despite their relativity to system, truths—and the facts that answer to them—are objective. For once a system is in effect, there is no room for negotiation. Events that are simultaneous relative to one frame of reference are successive relative to another. But it is determinate for each frame of reference whether given events are successive or simultaneous. Similarly, although some systems of psychology count neuroses as mental illnesses and others do not, once a system is chosen, there is a fact of the matter as to whether a compulsive hand washer is mentally ill.

Such objectivity might seem spurious if we can switch systems at will. What is true according to one tenable system may be false according to another. So can't we just pick our truths to fit our fancy? We cannot. Although truth values may vary from one tenable system to the next, it does not follow that every sentence is true under some tenable system. Indeed, the constraints initially tenable commitments place on tenability show that such is not the case. The initially tenable commitments that tether our systems include commitments from which it follows that some sentences are simply false. Unless we find compelling reasons to revise those commitments, tenability turns on their being respected. There is no reason to believe that grounds for radical revision are generally available. So the relativity of truth to system does not guarantee that, under some tenable system, 'The Holocaust never happened' or 'π is a rational number' is true. To adopt a system that held them true in current epistemic circumstances would be to adopt an untenable system.

Even though we construct the systems that fix the facts, we cannot construct whatever we want. If we take the notion of construction seriously, this comes as no surprise. Although we make all manner of inventions, we cannot make a nonfattening Sacher Torte, a solar-powered subway, or a perpetual motion machine. And although we design programs that endow computers with amazing abilities, we cannot program a computer to translate a natural language or consistently beat a grand master at chess or compute the last digit in the decimal expansion of π. Some of these incapacities are irremediable; others will eventually be overcome. My point in mentioning them is to emphasize that construction is something we do; we cannot do everything we want. Our capacities are limited; our aspirations often interfere with one another. So there is no reason to think we can convert any fantasy into fact by designing a suitable system. Plainly we cannot.

In constructing a political system, for example, we would like to maximize both personal liberty and public safety. We would like, that is, to arrange for as many actions as possible to fall under the predicate 'free to', and as many harms as possible to fall under the predicate 'safe from'. But we cannot maximize both at once. The cost of security is a loss of liberty; the cost of liberty, a risk of harm. With the freedom to carry a gun comes the danger of getting shot. So we have to trade off the values of liberty and safety against one another to arrive at a system that achieves an acceptable level of both. In constructing a physicalistic system, we would like all the magnitudes of elementary particles to be at once determinate and epistemically accessible. This is out of the question. Although we can measure either the position or the momentum of an electron, we cannot measure both at once.

Far from being primordial, facts are derivative of considerations of other kinds. Only in light of decisions taken, values espoused, options exercised, and methods applied do we have a framework that fixes facts. Still, once that framework is set, the facts it fixes are independent of, and may be contrary to, our beliefs and desires. Classical physics set the stage for the Michelson-Morley experiment by determining what makes for a physical fact and how such facts may be discovered. It did not thereby dictate the experiment's result. Indeed, the unanticipated outcome of the Michelson-Morley experiment contributed significantly to the downfall of the system that engendered it.

Here again, the parallel with more familiar cases of construction is helpful. We may build a chair by executing a well-laid plan that incorporates tenable views about what is wanted of a chair and about how the relevant objectives can be met. Still, whether the resulting chair wobbles and whether it will support a two-hundred-pound man are matters of fact, independent of our beliefs and desires about them and independent of the beliefs and desires that informed the chair's construction.

Constructionalism provides the resources for generating tenable cognitive systems satisfying a variety of epistemic desiderata. It does not, however, guarantee that all our epistemic objectives can be simultaneously met. Indeed, it forces us to recognize how often trade-offs are involved in achieving understanding of any kind.

RESTRICTIONS ON RELATIVISM

Several systems may acknowledge the same range of initially tenable commitments, the patterns of commitment inclusion, modification, and exclusion varying from one to the next. Typically, none delivers everything we want; many deliver something we want. Head-on collisions can be avoided by relativization or by the recognition of ambiguity. So the acceptance of one such system does not preclude the acceptance of others.

Have we any ground left for rejecting a coherent, tethered system? Its coherence insures that its components are reasonable in light of one another; its tether, that the system as a whole is reasonable in light of some of the things we antecedently had reason to endorse. If reflective equilibrium requires no more, constructionalist epistemology carries toleration too far. For surely some such systems are untenable. Even the wildest conspiracy theories about the assassination of President Kennedy, for example, incorporate the initially tenable belief that Kennedy is in fact dead. But a system that explains his demise by appeal to the intervention of space aliens would hardly be considered tenable. Nor does constructionalist epistemology contend that it is. Some hypotheses, including those in which space aliens prominently figure, are highly untenable. Adopting such a hypothesis is costly, since its inclusion diminishes the tenability of the system that results. Unless the advantages it provides compensate for the price it exacts, a system is better off without it. Although some initially untenable hypotheses prove sufficiently advantageous ('simultaneity is relative', for example), such is not normally the case. So there is in general no reason to expect a system that endorses an initially untenable hypothesis to be more tenable than one that does not.

What of less outré possibilities—say, an account that considers the assassination the result of a conspiracy between Fidel Castro, J. Edgar Hoover, and the southern Democrats? Such a system cannot be excluded out of hand, for the hypothesis in question, though farfetched, is not altogether implausible. Still, it is hardly a prime contender for our epistemic allegiance. Why not? Pretty plainly because competing accounts are much more tenable. They better accommodate our initially tenable commitments about the assassination and require the adoption of fewer or less onerous nontenable ones.

But we have the resources to evade competition. Why not use them? Even if the aforementioned conspiracy theory is substantially less tenable than the theory that Oswald acted alone or with a more congenial band of conspirators, it has something going for it; it incorporates initially tenable commitments that the more tenable theories do not. (Oswald had recently been to Cuba, Hoover hated Kennedy, Lyndon Johnson and his cronies benefited from Kennedy's death, and so forth.) We need only construe crucial common terms as ambiguous. Then we can accept all the theories that are even remotely plausible.

Like other commitments though, allegations of ambiguity require support. We need a reason to think that the terms in question are ambiguous. Sometimes our initially tenable commitments supply such a reason. In other cases the recognition that separately tenable systems would otherwise conflict serves as our ground. But the simple fact that we could have it both ways if key terms were ambiguous is by itself no reason to so construe them. For wanton allegations of ambiguity are untenable. Very often, apparent conflict is evidence of actual conflict. And in cases of actual conflict, the more tenable competitor wins.

Our goal is to maximize the tenability of the systems we endorse. And in order to decide whether a system maximizes tenability, we need to consider the competition. The pluralism I advocate recognizes that several coincident systems may be maximally tenable, hence simultaneously acceptable. It does not maintain that any less than maximally tenable ones are worthy of acceptance.

The relative standings of competitors can, of course, change. Currently nontenable, or even untenable, considerations may acquire initial tenability through, for example, the discovery of new evidence, the development of better methods, the defeat of their rivals or of considerations that tell against them. Their contribution to a system would then require recalculation. Tenability is determined by what is reasonable in the epistemic circumstances. It affords no guarantees that what is currently reasonable will remain so should circumstances change.

Chapter V

THE HEART HAS ITS REASONS

THAT REASON and passion are antithetical has long been an article of philosophical faith, less often argued than assumed. Emotive theories of ethics automatically construe themselves as noncognitive, and aesthetic theories that assign emotion a role in appreciation typically take themselves thereby to exclude art and its objects from the cognitive realm. Opposing stereotypes may account for complacency about the dichotomy. Stereotypical beliefs are cool, calm, settled convictions; stereotypical emotions are visceral, volatile, violent agitations. We would hardly put belief in the inverse square law in the same class as Othello's obsessive jealousy. Nor would we feel remiss about failing to justify the decision to assign them to disjoint classes. But actual beliefs and emotions diverge considerably from such simplistic stereotypes. Unwavering affection for a lifelong friend may be as stable, justifiable, and unperturbing as the belief that buffaloes once roamed the West; the momentary conviction that the home team is about to squander its commanding lead, as transient, unreasonable, and distressing as a stab of envy at a friend's good fortune. Emotions and beliefs can be enduring or ephemeral, calm or agitating, rational or irrational. Neither class of attitudes seems to possess any qualification for epistemic standing that the other lacks. That activation of passion involves abdication of reason is thus far from obvious. Even if Lear's rage is cognitively incapacitating, Huckleberry Finn's trepidation over Aunt Sally's plans to civilize him is not. If a response like Huck's can be at once cognitive and affective, epistemology's alienation of affections is unjustified.

Relatively recently, cognitivist theories of emotion have emerged to counter the traditional view.[1] They are ineffective though, because they construe the realm of the cognitive too narrowly. Typically they take an emotion to embed a belief, a belief to be an attitude toward a proposition, and the cognitive status of the emotion to derive from that of the belief it embeds.[2] Thus Fiona's fear of frogs is cognitive because it embeds her belief that frogs are dangerous. She would not—indeed could not—fear frogs, it is said, unless she harbored such a belief. This is just false. The

---

[1] See John Deigh, "Cognitivism in the Theory of Emotions," *Ethics* 104 (1994): 824–854.

[2] See, for example, Anthony Kenny, *Action, Emotion, and Will* (London: Routledge and Kegan Paul, 1963), 187–194.

shower scene in the movie *Psycho* regularly terrifies audiences who, well aware that the film is a work of fiction, do not believe that anyone is actually in danger. Beethoven's Ninth Symphony arouses in receptive listeners an objectless joy. Nor are the arts the sole sources of counterexamples to this position. Fiona might fear frogs even though careful study has convinced her that they pose no threat. Even if she cannot rid herself of the notion that frogs are dangerous, she does not for a moment believe it. A glorious sunrise, like a great symphony, can occasion objectless joy. And a baby can revel in his mother's love long before he develops the conceptual resources to entertain any attitude toward the proposition that she loves him.

These objections seem to tell decisively against the thesis that beliefs are essential to emotions. Still, one might urge that only such emotions as embed beliefs function cognitively. Thus objectless emotions, irrational emotions, and the emotions of infants and nonhuman animals are cognitively inert. I suggest, however, that emotions play a variety of cognitive roles, not all of them derived from or dependent on beliefs or propositions they embed. This is not to say that all emotions are epistemically estimable. Neither are all beliefs. But if the occurrence of wayward convictions does not justify banishing all beliefs from the epistemic realm, the occurrence of unruly passions ought not constitute grounds for the wholesale exclusion of emotions. Instead, I suggest, we should investigate the cognitive functions that emotions perform to see how they affect epistemic tenability. In this chapter, that is what I propose to do. I do not purport to provide anything remotely like a general theory of emotion, but only to identify some of the ways emotions advance understanding. My aim is not to anesthetize emotion but to sensitize cognition—to show that the understanding we achieve is not indifferent to emotion but that understanding is none the less objective for that.

FEELINGS

Emotions are often called feelings, but feeling alone does not emotion make. No matter how she feels, a toddler neither suffers from math anxiety nor hopes for eternal salvation, for she lacks the conceptual resources such emotions require. Queasiness does not qualify as fear unaccompanied by an intimation of danger nor does a twinge amount to remorse absent a sense of having transgressed. Neither does a feeling's mere occurrence in an appropriate context convert it into an emotion. Despite your awareness of impending danger, your queasiness could just be something you ate—particularly if you are inured to the threat or consider yourself suitably armed against it. But queasiness that registers an intimation of danger qualifies as a feeling of fear. Whether this is so is not always obvious. We are masters at hiding our emotions from ourselves. Still, the theoretical point is clear: absent any intimation of danger, a feeling does not qualify as fear.

This is not to say that emotions are peculiar to organisms who have concepts. For the cognitive realm is broader than the conceptual. The awareness of danger that the sight or sound or smell of a lion sparks in a springbok is the cognitive component of the springbok's fear. Granted, the springbok has no concept of fear. But fear and the concept of fear are two different things.

We might try to preserve the traditional cognitive/emotive dichotomy by factoring out cognitive elements and identifying emotions proper with the affects that remain. Even if it could be implemented, such a strategy would not be wise. For it would require factoring out features crucial to the individuation of emotions. Feelings that figure in distinct emotions are often phenomenologically of a piece. Pride and admiration, for example, can feel the same, their difference residing entirely in the fact that pride, unlike admiration, registers a sense that the excellence of its object reflects well on oneself. Remorse may differ from regret only by incorporating a belief that one is responsible for the misfortune it concerns. And a flutter of anticipation may feel the same whether it figures in hope or apprehension. In the one case it registers a favorable opinion of the event it forebodes; in the other, an unfavorable one. To identify emotions with feelings then would conflate attitudes and erase distinctions worth preserving. For emotions that feel alike do not always function alike. Nor do they always merit the same assessments. If I hope for a phone call from Fran, I may hover over the telephone; if I am apprehensive about the prospect, I may refuse to answer when it rings. If I admire Jane Austen's novels, I consider them excellent; if I take pride in them, I claim some credit for them. The former is reasonable; the latter is not. Unadulterated feelings then are not sufficiently sensitive to demarcate the distinctions we want to draw. We cannot, without significant loss, forego more robust, cognition-laden characterizations of emotions.

Perhaps a rush of anger or a surge of joy has a phenomenologically uniform feel. Usually emotions are more complex. Parental love, for example, is not just—or even mainly—a warm, fuzzy feeling that wells up whenever one's child happens to impinge on one's consciousness. It involves a concern for his well-being, an interest in his interests, happiness for his successes, sadness over his setbacks, pride in his achievements, hope for his future. These commingle freely with irritation at his failings, toleration of his foibles, amusement over his antics, exasperation over his excesses, and so on. Rather than identify parental love with a particular feeling then, we do better to characterize it as a frame of mind or pattern of attention that synchronizes feelings, attitudes, actions, and circumstances.

Nor is it only enduring, relatively stable emotions that constitute patterns of attention.[3] A momentary fright rearranges the landscape into a mosaic of hazards, vulnerabilities, escape routes, and defensive positions. Opportunities for fight or flight loom large. A cave in the woods ceases to be just a geological curiosity. Its capacity to serve as a lair for predators or as a haven from them suddenly stands out.

Feelings, moreover, do not always figure in emotions. Trust, for example, can be fully realized in the reliance I place on someone, in its not crossing my mind that she might fail me. This seems mainly a matter of (tacit) belief. No special feeling or complex of feelings need enter in. Courage can consist in the propensity to perform deeds one recognizes as dangerous, unimpeded by fear and unmotivated by self-destructiveness, whatever one's feelings may be. The fire fighter who rescues a child from a burning building is not without courage, even if she does not feel brave. Nor does she lack trust in her colleagues, even if her confident expectation of their support involves no particular affect. This is not to deny that feelings of trust and feelings of courage exist. But it is to suggest that the relation between having an emotion and feeling it is more complicated and less direct than it first appears.

FRAMES OF MIND

An emotion affects both the configuration and the constitution of a system of thought. It provides focus, highlighting some aspects of the domain, obscuring others, engendering relations of relevance and irrelevance. Free-floating anxiety, for example, brings alarming features to the fore and overshadows innocuous ones. It might point up the possibility and downplay the improbability of contracting rabies from a gerbil. On the other hand, it might latch onto and provide insight into something well worth worrying about. Should it light on the issue of global warming, for example, it might effect a realignment of information that constitutes a genuine contribution to the science of ecology.

What we notice is a function of our interests. Things we overlook in one frame of mind another renders salient. Emotions are sources of salience. Envy, for example, highlights available bases for invidious comparisons. Joan's envy over Felix's promotion to the Mugwump Chair of Metaphysics heightens her awareness of disparities in the reception of their respective views. It brings into focus the widespread practice of casting women's professional activities in a less favorable light than men's. Felix's manner is considered self-assured; Joan's is said to be aggressive. His first draft

[3] See Ronald de Sousa, "The Rationality of Emotions," in *Explaining Emotions*, ed. A. Rorty (Berkeley: University of California Press, 1980), 137.

shows promise; hers needs work. His criticisms are incisive; hers are carping. His work extends the insights of his predecessors; hers is derivative. The list seems endless. Considered separately, none of these descriptions is precisely inaccurate. But they coalesce into a pattern of usage that suggests that their juxtaposition would not afford a fair basis for comparison. For the pattern reveals that women tend to be characterized in more derogatory terms than men when both instantiate the same range of predicates. Women and men are not graded on the same scale.

That envy underlies Joan's insight does not discredit it. For Joan is not confabulating. The disparities her emotion exposes in fact obtain. Her reaction to Felix's promotion crystallizes seemingly diffuse material into determinate features and patterns whose further instances are easy to recognize. The raking light her envy casts reveals regularities hitherto camouflaged by the welter of details that surround them. In bringing the situation to exemplify those regularities, her emotion functions epistemically. Joan's envy then effects a shift in focus, drawing attention to aspects of usage she previously ignored. Her advance in understanding consists not in discovering new facts but in gaining insight into familiar ones. She was well aware that Felix's lectures were called learned. And she was well aware that hers were called pedantic. But until she saw the pattern connecting these and kindred characterizations, she did not realize how bias can infect choices about which applicable description to proffer.

That a contention is grounded in emotion then does not automatically discredit it. For emotion need not distort perception or derail reason. Emotions often heighten awareness, redirect attention, and sensitize their subjects to factors that had previously eluded them (and others). Absent specific reasons to distrust them, cognitive deliverances of emotion are initially tenable.

The emotion that occasions it does not, of course, secure the pattern Joan discerns a position in a tenable system of thought. Only by fostering reflective equilibrium does the insight earn itself a place. Emotion then confers initial tenability, not full tenability on its cognitive deliverances. Nor does the incorporation of the pattern into a tenable system show that her resentment of Felix is justified. The regularity she discovered provides reason to doubt that women candidates were given their due. This is not incompatible with Felix's meriting the chair. Thus the understanding an emotion engenders does not automatically justify the emotion that engenders it. So there is no circularity. If tenable, an insight like Joan's provides additional resources for investigating whether her envy was justified. But it does not prejudge the answer.

Emotions can be manipulated. This might lead us to look askance on the contention that they advance understanding. But I do not contend that they are wholly reliable sources of justified true beliefs. I claim only that they provide orientations that yield epistemic access to factors we might otherwise miss. Indeed, manipulation of emotions is a mechanism by which the arts effect valuable reorientations. By eliciting sympathy for a child molester, for example, Nabokov's novel *Lolita* sensitizes us to the sometimes tragic complexities of sexual desire. There is more to things than meets any particular eye. By reorienting ourselves to a domain, we gain access to unfamiliar facets of it.

Could an unjustified emotion then engender understanding? It seems so. Justified and unjustified emotions perform many of the same cognitive functions. Both fix mind sets that structure their domain, highlighting certain features and connecting them into patterns. Both have the capacity to draw attention to factors we might otherwise overlook. Moreover, both selectively heighten awareness, enabling us to detect subtleties, nuances, and intimations that ordinarily elude us. Rational and irrational optimism cast a rosy glow that focuses on and sensitizes their subjects to grounds for hope. Reasonable and unreasonable anxiety alike disclose grounds for concern.

This is not to say that they are equally estimable. Emotions function cognitively by orienting their subjects to their domains. Unjustified emotions provide potentially misleading orientations. They might, for example, effect inappropriate partitions. Thus excessive timidity could induce a subject to divide hopscotch players into those who have been injured in the game and those who have not. Noting the high rate of injury, she concludes that hopscotch is dangerous. Because her partition is too coarse to distinguish skinned knees from brain damage, she fails to appreciate how minor most hopscotch injuries are, and thus unreasonably includes the game along with sky diving in the extension of the predicate 'dangerous'.

Unjustified emotions can foster misinterpretation as well. Jealousy, for example, sensitizes its subjects to signs of infidelity. Irrational jealousy can oversensitize, prompting its subjects to treat as evidence of betrayal anything that could conceivably be so construed. It thus induces its subjects to ignore or discount available innocent alternatives. Evidence that admits of a given construal does not always demand that construal. A word or gesture or glance that *can* be taken as a sign of infidelity *need* not always be taken as such. The irrationality of Othello's jealousy lies in its prematurely blocking the claims of other construals. Because his orientation obscures their availability, it leads him to believe that the evidence of Desdemona's infidelity is unequivocal.

Justified emotions and their unjustified counterparts often differ only in emphasis. Under the sway of unreasonable emotions, a subject accords undue prominence to the factors they highlight. The grounds for hope that the cockeyed optimist identifies may genuinely exist. And conceivably the situation is so bleak that a more judicious assessment would occlude such encouraging signs as there are. An unreasonable emotion then might afford epistemic access to aspects of the situation that no reasonable stance would disclose. Still, it would be crazy to take much solace in the recognition that a dismal prognosis, however highly confirmed, does not amount to an entailment. This may be some reason for hope, but not much. What makes the optimism cockeyed is its failure to give the bad news its due. Highlighting some features and patterns involves overshadowing others. If, in accentuating the positive, cockeyed optimism ignores or underrates the negative, its contribution to understanding is skewed. For factors that the emotional stance obscures are significant.

To be sure, unjustified emotions *need* not undermine understanding. Deliverances of emotion, like other initially tenable commitments, are subject to compensation, revision, or rejection in the construction of a tenable system of thought. So a subject given to cockeyed optimism can use other cognitive devices to moderate its deliverances and control for its distortion, and thereby contrive a tenable assessment of her situation. Still, even though unjustified emotions do not have to mislead, they often do. Their deliverances, like those of other emotions, are in general psychologically compelling. Paranoids do not just *feel* persecuted, they typically think they *are* persecuted. Unless we have specific grounds for suspicion, we tend to consider our reactions justified. When, on the other hand, we consider an emotion unjustified, we are apt to discount its deliverances entirely. A self-aware hypochondriac is apt to construe all her symptoms as psychosomatic. Neither strategy recommends itself. The one leads us to accept what we should reject; the other, to reject what we should accept.

To mine unjustified emotions effectively, one must appreciate when one's reactions are inappropriate and then compensate for their skew. Even paranoids have enemies, so a paranoid's feelings of persecution ought not automatically be discounted. To give his reactions their epistemic due, a paranoid would need to develop a cognitive filter that sifts his irrational feelings of persecution from feelings that constitute evidence that he is actually being persecuted. Even hypochondriacs get sick. So to give her reactions their due, a hypochondriac requires a method for identifying the symptoms she ought to consider indications of illness. Developing and deploying the requisite compensation strategies is a labor-intensive process fraught with opportunities to go awry. Far better to obviate the need for them. Although the tenability of deliverances of justified emotions is not assured, their prospects are better. General and risky compensation strategies are not necessary to convert them into plausible candidates for incorporation into tenable systems. The reason is plain. Justified emotions are initially tenable sources of commitments.

Unjustified emotions are not. There is then a general presumption in favor of deliverances of justified emotions that deliverances of unjustified emotions do not share. Commitments engendered by either are themselves initially tenable. But the initial tenability of their source strengthens the epistemic of deliverances of justified emotions. Deliverances of unjustified emotions receive no such support. Each stands or falls on its own.

Emotions function cognitively, I have urged, by engendering patterns of attention or frames of mind. If, as I have intimated, beliefs are epistemically analogous, they do the same. Typically, in explicating belief and the other propositional attitudes, philosophers concentrate on the propositional aspect, construing each such attitude as a relation between a subject and a proposition. The cognitive function they focus on then is that of accepting a proposition. The analogy that interests me, however, derives from the attitudinal element. For an attitude is a complex, context-sensitive stance. Whether or not belief involves a relation to a propositional object, it supplies an orientation—a perspective that highlights some objects and aspects, some dimensions and characterizations, while obscuring or overshadowing or discrediting others. Expectations, states of perceptual readiness, patterns of salience, and dispositions to utter, accept, reject, and deliberate all figure in the attitude—each informed by the matrix of commitments it belongs to.

The belief that the dean acts dictatorially, for example, heightens the salience of certain aspects of her managerial style—her propensity to call meetings on short notice and schedule them at inconvenient times, her practice of setting agendas so that trivial issues receive undue attention, leaving little time for important matters, her willingness to act unilaterally and to appoint her cronies to committees, and so on. The belief also manifests itself in a propensity to look for, and an ability to discern, Machiavellian motives behind the dean's seemingly innocuous actions. The activation of this mind set does not require that the proposition 'The dean acts dictatorially' ever be expressly entertained. It is enough that the subject focuses on these particular aspects of her managerial style. Nor need the proposition be true. Conceivably, the features the pattern discloses stem from a combination of enthusiasm and administrative incompetence. Nevertheless, it is the belief that she acts dictatorially that brings them to the fore, enabling the subject to recognize them. I do not, of course, contend that delimiting a frame of mind is the sole cognitive function of belief. Nor is it the sole cognitive function of emotion. I mention it here because it is a function that is often overlooked and one that belief and emotion share.

By focusing attention, emotions even effect refinements in sensory discrimination. To the uninitiated, babies' cries sound pretty much alike. But parents who are dismayed over their infants' distress and concerned to alleviate it learn to discriminate among cries. They acquire the ability to differentiate the sounds of hunger, pain, frustration, and fear. What we hear depends on what we listen to and what we listen for. A person who is relatively indifferent to a child's distress—the denizen of a neighboring apartment, for instance—is apt to treat the child's cries as unpleasant background noise, an auditory intrusion to be blocked out as much as possible. Such an auditor is conscious only of the most obtrusive properties of the cries—volume and duration. But those who care about the child listen attentively to his cries and learn to focus on more subtle features that correlate with causes of distress. They learn to draw distinctions within what is for their neighbor and was once for them an undifferentiated din. Were it not for their concern for the child, they would have no reason to mark these distinctions and would never learn to hear them.

The parents react by providing different remedies in response to different cries. The child, on realizing this, comes to use what was originally just an expression of distress as a sign. He emits a cry of a particular kind to communicate a certain sort of distress. To do so, he begins to distinguish among his own feelings. He begins to differentiate feelings of frustration, fear, hunger, and pain. His parents' epistemic advance paves the way for his own.

Emotions can activate dormant systems of categories, reorienting us through deployment of classifications we would not ordinarily use. Compassion, for example, moves us to classify potential actions and utterances under such headings as 'considerate' and 'inconsiderate', 'tactful' and 'tactless'. Being outspoken, Clive normally says whatever comes to mind, heedless of his interlocutors' feelings. In a compassionate frame of mind, however, he realizes that 'Let's go out and get paralytic' is not the best way to invite a paraplegic buddy to go drinking. Compassion then sensitizes him to aspects of the invitation he would ordinarily overlook. These are not particularly recondite aspects. He need only raise the issue of tact to know how to resolve it. But unmoved by compassion, he would not raise the issue.

Emotions also underwrite reclassification. Remarks I originally count as friendly banter I reconstrue as ridicule when dislike for their utterer or sympathy for their target or discomfort over their tone awakens me to the teasing's nasty undercurrent. An action I initially consider optional—attending a reception or contributing to a charity, for example—I reconstrue as prima facie obligatory when gratitude moves me to appreciate that my participation would please or benefit my benefactor.

Both activation of dormant categories and reassignment across active categories can occur without discovery of new facts. Emotions often effect changes in emphasis, leading us to revise our assessments of features we were already—if dimly—aware of.

Emotions can of course provoke discovery. They incite us to investigate, motivate us to persevere, supply categories and standards of relevance to structure our searches. My curiosity about muskrats may impel me to study them assiduously. It may direct my attention, heighten my sensitivity, and extend my endurance, thereby enabling me to discover a multitude of hitherto unknown facts about the critters. My trust in Wilma may induce me to look for exculpatory evidence, when the case against her looks solid. And seeking such evidence, I may find it. To be sure, success is not guaranteed. My search may be fruitless. Or it may turn up the smoking gun that settles the case against Wilma, and thereby shows my trust to have been misplaced.

Even worse, emotions can inspire wishful thinking, leading us to misread evidence, to falsely believe we have found the facts we wanted to find. No more than other insights are deliverances of emotion certain. They are initially tenable but must promote reflective equilibrium to qualify as fully tenable. Indeed, the phenomenon of wishful thinking might seem inimical to the epistemology I advocate. The worry is that a fact I wanted to find and wrongly believe I have found threatens to mesh with my system of thought far better than an accurate assessment of the situation would. Being favorably disposed toward Wilma, I harbor a variety of commitments that accord with her innocence but are at odds with her guilt. Not wanting to believe her guilty of scientific fraud, I manage to find what I take to be her original data. These, I believe, constitute genuine experimental findings and vindicate her claim to have conducted the research she allegedly faked. My credulous construal of the data, being believed, is initially tenable. Since it meshes with my other beliefs about Wilma, it seems readily incorporable into my system of thought, hence fully tenable. But my construal is wrong. The data are fictitious, having been fabricated to cover up her fraud.

If wishful thinking so easily conduces to reflective equilibrium, my theory is in trouble. Credulousness is hardly an epistemic virtue. But in assuming that its accord with my beliefs about Wilma earns my construal a place in a tenable system, we go too fast. For a variety of other commitments weigh against its incorporation—commitments about scientific methodology, about evidence of scientific fraud, even about the dangers of wishful thinking. The irreproducibility of Wilma's results, the suspiciously convenient timing of my discovery, the damning alternative construal of the data, the fact that I would not normally take such data as sufficient for vindication—all tell against the tenability of my belief. Moreover, as we have seen, mine are not the only commitments relevant to the tenability of my views. That other members of the scientific community consider the data part of the fraud rather than evidence against it endows that construal with initial tenability as well. To earn my belief a place in a tenable system of thought then requires deflecting or discrediting a host of commitments like these. And it requires doing so in a way that we can on reflection accept. Integrating felicitous findings into a tenable system is far from easy. The cognitive costs of special pleading are in general higher than we can in good conscience pay. Since wishful thinking never confers more than initial tenability and, if recognized as such does not even confer that, it does not subvert the epistemic enterprise. For it provides no quick and easy route to acceptability.

TENABILITY

We would not and should not credit the outpourings of a deranged mind. Despite their initial tenability, we have ample reason to dismiss them as distortions. Nor should we credit deliverances of a deranged faculty of mind. So if, as tradition has it, passion disables reason, then despite their initial tenability, commitments that emotions embody ought to be dismissed. Even if emotions give rise to initially tenable commitments, it does not follow that they advance understanding. The challenge then is to show that emotions contribute to fully tenable systems of thought.

Few would deny that much that we fear is in fact dangerous; much that we cherish is actually valuable; much that repels us, genuinely repulsive. Nor is this a coincidence. Many emotions are sensitive to information, being elicited, modified, reinforced, and extinguished by findings of fact. The discovery that David has furthered my cause awakens my gratitude toward him. Awareness of the extenuating circumstances moderates my disappointment in Denise. Reports of Diane's continued success strengthen my confidence in her. News of Duncan's demise extinguishes my hope for his recovery. This is not to say that such emotions are wholly determined by findings of fact. Fiona may continue to fear frogs even after she learns that they pose no threat. Patterns of attention become habitual, and habits can be hard to break. Moreover, if Fiona's fear of frogs plays a central role in her psychology, the discovery that her fear is groundless may be insufficient to dislodge it. Still, to the extent that emotions are information-sensitive, the more accurate our relevant information, the better attuned our emotions will be to their surroundings. As Stephen comes to distinguish venomous from nonvenomous snakes, his indiscriminate fear of snakes is apt to evolve into a more discriminating detector of danger.

Putting the matter in this way may be somewhat misleading. It may suggest that emotions function as vehicles for views that are antecedently adopted and independently justified. Sometimes they do. Often though, the cognitive commitments emotions embody have no separate claim on the subject's epistemic allegiance. Attunement then occurs when feedback modifies the emotion itself. Seeing garter snakes handled without ill effect, Stephen ceases to fear them. And inasmuch as they no longer excite his fear, he no longer considers them dangerous.

Overpowering emotions like abject terror, blind rage, or rapt infatuation do not typically present themselves as opportunities to advance understanding. Ordinarily they call for action, not contemplation. No one in the grip of stark terror is likely to use her emotion as a scalpel for dissecting fear and its objects. She has more pressing matters to attend to. Does the violence with which the violent passions present themselves undermine my effort to integrate emotions into epistemology?

Undeniably, overwhelming emotions sometimes short-circuit reason. The question is what to make of this. We might take it to demonstrate that emotion as such is antithetical to the advancement of understanding. If emotion ever short-circuits reason, emotion is never to be trusted. Before drawing such a drastic conclusion, though, we should recall certain parallels with perception. Very bright light is blinding and often causes afterimages. Very loud noise is deafening and may occasion a variety of subsequent auditory distortions—echoes, a buzzing in the ear, and so on. But even though the visual and auditory systems can be overwhelmed, it would be unreasonable to expect epistemology to exclude all their deliverances. Rather, we need to learn when perceptual deliverances are not to be trusted. Likewise, I suggest, with emotions. Rather than exclude their deliverances entirely, epistemology should delineate the circumstances when they are untrustworthy.

We might then follow Hume and look askance at the violent passions, while remaining more sanguine about the epistemic prospects of the contributions of the calm passions. Terror would be disqualified, but trepidation would remain a source of initially tenable commitments. Clearly this is a preferable stance. But I think we can do better still. For it is not the case that even so violent a passion as terror is always cognitively incapacitating. Emotions excited by the arts typically are muted and displaced. So it is possible, and may be profitable, to use the terror a Hitchcock film inspires as a source of insight. We may find that modulations in our fear correlate with significant features of the film—features we would otherwise overlook. And we may learn to detect in ourselves subtle emotional nuances that we had previously lumped indiscriminately together under the label 'fear'. The insights we thus glean typically project beyond the aesthetic realm. We recognize the newfound nuances in our everyday emotional responses and use those responses as detectors of hitherto unrecognized aspects of the objects that occasion them.[4] This clearly is a cognitive advance.

[4] Nelson Goodman, *Languages of Art* (Indianapolis: Hackett, 1968), 245–255.

Refinement of the sensibilities increases emotion's epistemic yield. The undifferentiated category 'fear' engenders the initially tenable expectation that danger looms. Refinements such as alarm, consternation, trepidation, and dread register differences in magnitude, imminence, and likelihood of the dangers they portend. They thus engender initially tenable assessments of a danger's magnitude, proximity, and probability. When such emotions are reasonable, the assessments they register are apt to be sound. Reasonable emotions attune their subjects to their environments. Refinements amount to fine-tuning.

Emotions serve as distant early warning systems. Over time they can develop into acutely sensitive detectors of subliminal cues, often affording a measure of epistemic access before other, more obvious evidence is available. My growing anxiety about Arthur constitutes reason to consider his situation alarming, even before I can cite specific grounds for concern. My pity for Polly constitutes reason to think her unfortunate even before I can identify clear signs of misfortune. Emotions do not just provide early intimations, though. They attune their subjects and organize their domains so that further, surer evidence discloses itself. The pattern of attention my emotion engenders may be what enables me to recognize the evidence of Polly's unhappiness or Arthur's deterioration for what it is.

Emotions adapt to their environments. Early assessments of danger, for instance, may be quite wide of the mark. We start out fearing things we should not and failing to fear things that we should. Over time, however, feedback reinforces some fears and discredits others. Gradually fear converges on danger. It comes to serve as an indicator of actual, not just apparent, danger. This is not to say that either actual or apparent danger is easy to identify. Emotions occur not in isolation but in intricate networks of interanimating attitudes. What is untroubling in one psychological setting may be deeply disturbing in another. An atheist and a fundamentalist are apt, for example, to feel differently about the perils of blasphemy. Where the fundamentalist fears divine retribution, the atheist may fear social censure. If either has internalized the relevant religious values, he may reasonably fear the psychological cost of violating its taboos. To complicate matters further, actions and objects are sometimes endowed with idiosyncratic symbolic significance. In such cases they occasion reactions because of what they symbolize to a given subject. Thus the atheist might be afraid to blaspheme, not out of religious conviction but because to him blasphemy signifies the total rejection of parental authority. A subject's fear of blasphemy thus may embody the (perhaps inarticulate) view that blasphemy poses a spiritual threat, a social threat, or a direct or indirect psychological threat. Although they may be hard to distinguish, these are different attitudes. They constitute frames of mind that orient their subjects to different real or apparent dangers.

Experience is limited. So fear should never be considered a failsafe test of danger. Coincidences confuse, leading us to fear innocuous concomitants of genuine perils. Dangers we escape unscathed often fail to leave their mark. Dangers we have yet to encounter may have little influence on our mind sets. A sensibility finely attuned to the perils of urban living may be woefully insensitive to dangers in the wild. My purpose though is not to show that emotions always embody tenable commitments, but only that the initial tenability of the commitments emotions embody is not in general gratuitous. Their being embodied is a nonnegligible, albeit imperfect indication of tenability.

Even better than generally crediting or discrediting emotions as sources of understanding would be to distinguish those that are creditable from those that are not. For emotions are not epistemically of a piece. Those we retain purely out of habit or irrational need are unlikely to serve as conduits of tenable commitments. Those that are duly sensitive to information fare better. Refined sensibilities are apt to be better conduits than crude ones. That a novice is afraid to ride a horse is some reason, but perhaps not much, to consider the horse dangerous. That expert equestrians are afraid is a strong indication that the horse is not safe to ride.

Emotions are subject to public evaluation. We regularly criticize one another for being unjustifiably angry, overly optimistic, or needlessly concerned. We credit one another with being rightly resentful, justifiably proud, or entitled to grieve. And we often achieve consensus about such matters.

The possibility of assessing emotions presupposes the existence of (perhaps tacit) standards of assessment. The fact that independent assessors so often agree indicates that the standards are shared. The possibility of challenging and defending assessments by argument indicates that the standards are more than the coincidence of converging idiosyncrasies. And the fact that resolution of such arguments often turns on correct characterization of relevant circumstances indicates that our standards measure the appropriateness of emotions to contexts.

EMOTIONAL HONESTY

Emotions need not be acknowledged in order to function epistemically. Like self-avowed emotions, suppressed rage and unacknowledged anxiety structure experience and orient us toward objects. We do not have to know what our emotions are to have our world structured by them. This is not to say that a suppressed emotion and its confessed counterpart provide the same orientation. Repression clearly gives rise to orientations of its own. Other modes of denial or self-deception probably do so as well. Nor is it to say that unacknowledged emotions advance understanding as much or as well as confessed ones do. But initial tenability attaches to the deliverances of unacknowledged emotions just as to those of their confessed counterparts. For initial tenability derives from a commitment's being held, not from its adherent's knowing that it is held. Nor does our inability to avow the emotion that embodies it prevent a commitment from entering into a tenable system. Indeed, if Freud is right, humanity's greatest epistemic advances have been fueled by emotions too awful to acknowledge. Insofar as emotions define patterns of attention then, they can advance understanding whether or not they are avowed.

Still, emotional honesty pays epistemic dividends. In knowing how she feels about something, a subject knows what she thinks of it. Self-awareness then affords epistemic access to the cognitive commitments emotions embody. These may be commitments the subject never expressly entertained, even ones she would be loathe to acknowledge as her own. So her emotions may disclose convictions she has no other way to discover. In appreciating that she is afraid of frogs, for example, Fiona recognizes that she thinks frogs are dangerous. In appreciating that her emotion embarrasses her, she recognizes that she considers frogs unworthy of fear. Had she been unable to own up to her emotions, Fiona would be unaware both of her attitude toward frogs and of her attitude toward her attitude toward frogs.

Revelations reverberate. Roger's recognition that he was relieved to learn that he had lost the election discloses to him that he had been ambivalent about winning, that he feared the loss of privacy that accompanies public office, and that despite his public persona, he is in fact quite shy. Since many attitudes have attitudes as their objects, emotional honesty can be a fecund source of self-knowledge, disclosing a variety of emotions and cognitions nested one within another.

Moreover, because emotions are sensitive to circumstances, their occurrence constitutes evidence that circumstances of a given kind obtain. In recognizing an emotion then, we gain access to that evidence. Friendly and malicious teasing, for example, evoke distinct—though not always easily distinguishable—feelings. By learning to tell those feelings apart and honestly assessing her own responses, the teaser's target gains insight into her interlocutor's attitudes—attitudes he is apt to mask, sometimes even from himself. To be sure, self-ascriptions are not self-certifying. They acquire epistemic credentials in the same way other commitments do—through incorporation into tenable systems of thought. So Fiona's confession that she fears frogs is tenable only if it figures in an appropriate tenable system. That she believes she fears frogs does not make it so. Nor does Flora's contention that she feels victimized by Fred's banter insure that that is how she feels. Perhaps she is just uncomfortable about being the object of his attention at all.

Self-deception is a cognitive handicap then because it cuts off avenues of epistemic access. Unable to acknowledge her feelings of victimization, Flora lacks access to the evidence of hostility that Fred's teasing presents. Were she attuned to her emotions, she would be better able to understand Fred. Insensitivity similarly incapacitates. Because he cannot empathize with the recipients of his largesse, the philanthropist is mystified when they consider his gift patronizing, and bewildered by their evident lack of gratitude. His lack of empathy prevents him from understanding his beneficiaries' perspective and undermines his prospects of doing the good he is trying to do.

Earlier I urged that emotions need not be felt. Still, they often are. And where felt, emotions present themselves to their subjects as they do to no one else. If repudiating privileged access requires disqualifying feelings as sources of insight into our own emotions, it goes too far. Surely feeling delighted is not evidentially unrelated to being delighted. The issue is not whether feelings afford a distinctive mode of access to emotions but whether that mode of access confers epistemic privilege. It does not. A person can feel angry without being angry. So her feeling is not self-certifying. And there may be ample reason to deny that she is angry even though she feels angry. So her feeling does not override the other considerations that bear on the characterization of her state. We may realize—and she may agree—that despite her feeling, she is not really angry, just tired, discouraged, frustrated, and sorry about the way things turned out. Feelings yield initially tenable self-ascriptions. But such self-ascriptions are not self-certifying any more than other initially tenable commitments are.

CLASSIFICATION

Feelings do not characterize themselves. We have to learn how delight, dismay, compunction, and the like, feel before our agitations and composures afford grounds for self-ascription. Nor is this merely acquiring an ability to attach labels to homogeneous, antecedently individuated affects. For in different contexts the same feeling can register different emotions, and the same emotion manifest itself in different feelings. A feeling of reluctance registers compunction or misgivings depending on whether one's reservations are morally or prudentially based. Loathing may be felt as dismay or delight depending on whether the object of one's disaffection fares well or badly. Feelings then do not fix the character of the emotional realm. Unless we already recognize the various emotions, we cannot tell what or how feelings bear on them.

If, as I have suggested, an emotion involves a pattern of attention, then identifying an emotion involves recognizing such a pattern. And taking a feeling or behavior or salience as a manifestation of an emotion involves construing it as part of such a pattern. It is not distress *simpliciter* but distress as an element of a particular matrix that qualifies as a feeling of dismay. So learning to recognize feelings of dismay requires learning to locate distress in the appropriate matrix.

This is a public enterprise. It proceeds initially in settings where suitable elicitors and responses are, and are known to be, relatively unequivocal and intersubjectively accessible. Seeing her pupils observe a playmate laugh spontaneously upon catching the ball he plainly wanted to catch, a teacher might describe him to them as delighted. Her pupils—including the child who caught the ball—begin to associate delight with satisfaction of desires and with laughter. Over time, as they encounter a variety of examples, the children become aware of delight's characteristic features. They note that its subjects tend to seek out occasions of delight, that they focus on pleasurable aspects of situations that delight them, that they are apt to overlook or minimize difficulties such situations present, and so forth. They learn to identify delight's more subtle manifestations and to recognize it in a variety of settings. As they come to identify in themselves the pattern of attention that characterizes delight, the children discover that certain feelings are elements of it. They learn then to recognize feelings of their own as feelings of delight and to take those feelings as revelatory of a complex attitudinal structure. They thus acquire the ability to use their feelings as a basis for self-ascription.

Patterns of attention interweave. And much of our learning to identify emotions involves learning to recognize the various patterns in the intricate tapestries that constitute our emotional lives. As the children mature then, they learn how the pattern for delight intertwines with other patterns. They learn to recognize it as, for instance, an elaboration of a general schema for enjoyment or as occurring, among other places, where the patterns for enthusiasm and a sense of accomplishment merge. Eventually the children come to appreciate the ways other attitudes affect the pattern and its manifestations. They thus discover that delight can be muted, exaggerated, feigned, or masked. And they learn to recognize indications that such is the case.

Context influences emotion. Feelings that qualify as love against one background amount to infatuation against another. So accurate ascription of emotions requires appreciating their psychological milieu. A callow adolescent's inability to distinguish love from infatuation may stem from his failure to recognize or appreciate the significance of the matrix of attitudes within which his affection occurs. He may, for example, have no idea whether his attitude is primarily self- or other-regarding—that is, whether he mainly values his beloved for herself or for the way his affection (requited or not) reflects on him. Because he cannot tell how it figures in his psychology, he is ill-equipped to identify his emotion. Nor is this problem peculiar to self-ascription. His buddies might be equally oblivious to the network of attitudes that inform his emotion.

As we become more discriminating, our bases for ascription increase in complexity, sophistication, and interrelation. We come to appreciate the myriad ways emotions and other attitudes inform one another and influence behavior. We recognize, for example, that the desire to be considered cool often reverses fear's polarity, causing it to manifest itself as bravado. We discover that Sarah's civility so constrains her conduct that her suppressed rage betrays itself only in the punctilious politeness she shows to her adversaries. We realize that Jon's faith in his daughter's abilities both moderates his worry and exacerbates his irritation over her mediocre grades.

Learning to identify emotions thus involves learning what sorts of situations typically elicit a particular emotion, what saliencies it gives rise to, what range of verbal and nonverbal behaviors generally manifest it, and what sorts of defeaters undermine the foregoing generalizations. Part of what we learn is how complicated emotions are, how deeply and intricately interwoven into our fabric of commitments.

A single situation can elicit any of a fairly broad range of nondeviant emotions. For example, suffering might evoke pity, outrage, contempt, or fear. A single emotion, moreover, can manifest itself in a wide variety of behaviors. Fear may reveal itself in blenching, bravado, whimpering, or whistling in the dark. Ascribing emotions involves construing behavior in context, in tailoring our general knowledge to the particulars of a situation. Knowing how nervousness normally affects Nina, and realizing that the prospect of public speaking is apt to unsettle her, we readily recognize her cough as a sign of anxiety, even though we would consider a similarly situated stranger's cough evidence of catarrh. Aware of the Masai custom of inuring themselves to pain, we take the wince of a Masai as a sign of agony, even though we would treat the wince of a similarly afflicted American as evidence of mild discomfort.

Individual feelings and behaviors arise from and belong to patterns of attention that characterize emotions. Thus reactions that are highly ambiguous in isolation are often unequivocal as parts of such patterns. Both joy and sorrow can reduce a person to tears. Brimming eyes alone then do not afford enough evidence to safely ascribe either emotion. But we rarely encounter brimming eyes alone. Minimally we have access to other aspects of the subject's demeanor. Often we know a lot more—about her behavior and attitudes prior and subsequent to her weeping, her character and commitments, the nature of the events that occasion her tears, and so on. Tears accompanied by a wide grin, evoked by the news that the subject has just been awarded the Nobel Prize, are difficult to construe as signs of sorrow. Likewise, a feeling that is ambiguous in isolation is often unequivocal in context. An agitation that belongs to a pattern of attention highlighting dangers and risks may unequivocally announce itself as foreboding, even if the same feeling in different surroundings would qualify as anticipation. Moreover, within a single pattern there may be a multiplicity of feelings that, *as part of the pattern*, qualify and can be recognized as a single emotion. My dislike of Fred may manifest itself as enjoyment at his discomfiture, resentment over his success, distress on encountering him, and so on. Distinct feelings then instantiate a single emotion.

Behaviors are indicative of patterns of salience. Frequently we can tell what someone is focusing on by the way she reacts, and identify her emotional state by the features she focuses on. That Pat is relentlessly raising practical objections shows that she is attending to the project's downside risks, hence that she has misgivings about it. Pam's ethical objections reveal that she is focusing on the morally dubious aspects of the plan. She has compunctions. Paul's cavalier dismissal of his colleagues' concerns, his failure to see the patterns they discern, shows that he is sanguine about the project. By attending to such behaviors, we learn what it is to have misgivings, compunctions, or to be sanguine, and we learn to recognize such states in ourselves as well as in others.

Emotions that take objects realize dispositions to respond differentially to particular classes. Fear, for example, is a differential response to dangers, and pity a differential response to misfortunes. The classes in question are often ones we cannot identify without recourse to emotions. Perhaps there are emotively neutral criteria for dangers and misfortunes. But we would be hard put to say what repulsive things have in common beyond their propensity to repel or what amusing things have in common aside from their tendency to amuse. Conceivably we will someday uncover such commonalities. But as things stand, emotions afford epistemic access to otherwise undemarcated and therefore inaccessible classes.

To say we have access to such classes only via emotions is not to say that each of us can appeal only to her own emotions. We appeal to the emotions of others as well. A pathologist can recognize that an excised tumor is repulsive, without being personally repelled. All she need know is that it is the sort of thing that generally repels. To be sure, not everything that repels anyone belongs to the class of the repulsive. Emotions can be misplaced. When they are, a frame of mind is activated in the absence of a suitable target. Thus, for example, a system of saliencies and a network of attitudes called for by repulsive objects may be activated even though no such object is present. Although Peter is repelled when he catches a glimpse of it, a wet dish cloth is not genuinely repulsive.

Perception provides an illuminating parallel. Even if hearing affords our only access to the vocal realm, that a voice sounds strident to me does not make it so. Sometimes circumstances conspire to make a melodious voice sound harsh. So a voice's membership in the class of the strident is not settled by an individual's perception of it. Nor in deciding how to classify a sound are we restricted to our own occurrent sensations. We appeal to the ways it appears to others and to the ways it would appear to us in suitably different circumstances. We know of conditions that distort or mislead and can often tell whether they obtain. We recognize, for example, that amplification frequently makes melodious voices sound strident. On the basis of such considerations, we start to develop standards of evidence that specify when and to what extent perceptual assessments of stridency are to be trusted. Over time, as we gain experience and accumulate evidence, our standards improve.

To characterize our revisions as improvements does not require independent access to the class of the strident. For refinement here is not a matter of adjusting our aim at an already known target. Rather, we modify our standards to integrate our ascriptions and grounds for ascription into increasingly detailed, increasingly comprehensive tenable systems. When we realize that amplification makes normally melodious voices sound strident, we conclude that amplification distorts, and dismiss or discount assessments of stridency that fail to compensate for its effects. When we recognize that a medication induces hearing loss in the lower registers, we distrust the judgments of stridency made under the influence of the drug. When we notice that sexists are prone to characterize women's demands as strident on the basis of content rather than tone, we discredit their characterizations of female voices. Although we have no reason to think that our current standards are perfect, and no independent check on their reliability, we justifiably take them to afford epistemic access to the class of strident sounds. They function as fallible indicators of membership in a class whose extension is not wholly known.

Similarly we develop standards that specify when and to what extent emotional reactions afford evidence of membership in their correlative classes. Not all do. A sufficiently besotted swain might delight in his beloved's laundry list. But that would hardly qualify it for inclusion in the class of the delightful. And a sufficiently censorious critic may fail to delight in anything. But that would not show the class to be null. Setting tenable standards of evidence here is not easy. For the route from individual response to correlative class is circuitous. Emotional reactions are often idiosyncratic, being heavily influenced by the matrix of attitudes that embed them, the circumstances that give rise to them, and the sequences of events they belong to. Still, over time we learn to control for historical accident and personal idiosyncrasy, as well as for variability and volatility in individual responses. We learn, that is, how to use our own and one another's delight as evidence of membership in the class of the delightful.

Our evolving standards of evidence are, of course, fallible. Still, as they are integrated into increasingly tenable systems of thought, they afford an increasingly tenable presumption that the reactions they credit are indicative of membership in the class of the delightful. Nevertheless, we cannot responsibly claim that they are accurate enough to demarcate the boundaries of that class exactly.

Refinement of the sensibilities affords epistemic access to less populous, more homogeneous classes. Where regret supplies access to the class of misfortunes, remorse targets the subclass consisting of the misfortunes the subject is responsible for. So in developing a capacity for remorse, the subject gains access to that subclass. To be sure, access is neither immediate nor direct. Suppose Meagan's recognition that she considers herself responsible for particular misfortunes is accompanied by a distinctive feeling of regret. Although that reaction does not arise in response to every misfortune she regrets, it does arise in response to some misfortunes she had not previously considered herself responsible for. On realizing this, she has reason to suspect that she subliminally holds herself responsible for the latter misfortunes as well. This in turn gives her grounds for suspecting that she is in fact responsible for them. Such a suspicion is, of course, defeasible. Meagan might easily feel remorse when she ought not to. Or the pangs she has been experiencing might be something other than remorse. But just as taking something to be blue is reason to think that it is blue, taking oneself to be responsible is reason to think that one is responsible. Remorse about a situation embeds the initially tenable belief that one is responsible for it. Like other emotions, it can be misplaced. But once we have remorse in our emotional repertoire, we are in a position to fashion and hone standards that tell when a subject's remorse reflects real responsibility for the misfortune it concerns.

Our interests, practices, objectives, and institutions influence the course that refinement of the sensibilities takes. Because morality provides an incentive to identify the misfortunes we are responsible for, it gives us reason to focus on the regrets those particular misfortunes occasion. It thus puts us in a position to notice their distinctive features. Our concern with responsibility then provides a perspective from which we can distinguish remorse from mere regret. Having no particular incentive to distinguish misfortunes that occur on Mondays, I have no reason to attend especially to the regrets that Monday's misfortunes occasion. As a result I do not put myself in a position to notice features peculiar to misfortunes occurring on Mondays. Unless there is a more salient or significant characterization of those misfortunes, I am unlikely to develop an emotion that targets them.

The members of any collection are alike in some respects and different in others. So by itself the principle that like cases should be treated alike avails us little. Before that principle can do any work, it needs to be supplemented by standards that specify appropriate likenesses and differences. Emotional reactions often figure in the assessments of such standards. They make fine discriminations that can cut across, and thereby cast doubt on, the adequacy of accepted categories. When we feel differently about cases that are currently classified as alike or feel the same about cases currently classified as different, our emotions afford grounds for reevaluating a classificatory scheme.

If, for example, we find ourselves as outraged over being intentionally misled as we are over being lied to, the line conventional morality draws between truth telling and lying looks to be misplaced. Our reaction suggests that imparting misleading truths is as objectionable as imparting falsehoods. If so, moral categories need to be reconfigured and moral rules reframed. Evidently the moral standing of an utterance depends on the truth value the speaker ascribes to the belief she seeks to convey, not the truth values of the vehicles used to convey it. If drug dependence in victims of painful medical conditions does not excite the same distress as drug dependence in otherwise healthy subjects, a legal or moral system that considers all narcotics addiction on a par appears too pat. Our reactions lead us to wonder whether drug dependence as such is always a bad thing. They remind us that there are other places where lines might plausibly be drawn, and prompt us to investigate whether a partition that better reflects our emotional responses would be more tenable.

There is, of course, no assurance that it would. Emotions can be manipulated, so reactions to particular cases might mislead. And even if they do not mislead, a system that reflected the difference they discern might violate other, more tenable commitments. Moreover, an emotional reaction that convinces us that a new line needs to be drawn typically does not determine where to draw it. Even if compassion for the suffering undermines the wholesale condemnation of narcotics addiction, it does not specify the conditions under which addiction is tolerable. Emotions alone do not effect a realignment of moral categories. But by detecting unacknowledged kinships and differences, they supply motives and resources for realignment. They perform the second-order epistemic function in assessing the adequacy of first-order systems of classification.

EMOTION AND THE RANGE OF EPISTEMOLOGY

In crediting emotion and its equally dubious confederates—metaphor, fiction, and exemplification—with epistemic standing, I might seem to extend epistemology's scope unduly. Traditional theories of knowledge, after all, construe their range more narrowly. From within my theory, the response is clear. Epistemology must comprehend such matters because they affect the tenability of systems of thought. But, one might charge, that just shows what is wrong with the theory. It admits within epistemology's purview matters that do not belong. How can this challenge be met?

I shall defer to the next chapter my defense of the inclusion of fiction, metaphor, and exemplification within the realm of epistemology. In concluding this chapter I want to argue that the cognitive functions emotions perform are ones epistemology cannot responsibly ignore. I have shown that emotions orient their subjects, focus attention, and supply grounds for classifying objects as like or unlike. So if I can demonstrate that epistemology must address matters of orientation, focus, and categorization, I will have made my case.

Such matters do not admit of support by empirical evidence. So a theory that takes its task to be identifying the conditions under which evidence supports a hypothesis might try to bracket them, to construe them as lying at a distance from epistemology's proper concerns. Such a theory might, for example, determine whether available evidence warrants accepting the sentence 'All vegetables are nutritious' under some interpretation of the predicates 'vegetable' and 'nutritious'. But it will not afford the resources for evaluating the classification that that interpretation reflects. This might seem unobjectionable, even reasonable. So long as we know where the lines are drawn, we know what accepting the sentence amounts to. There may be pragmatic grounds for favoring one partition of the domain over others, but the impracticality of a scheme that includes pine cones in or excludes artichokes from the class of vegetables is hardly epistemology's concern.

The difficulty is that the grounds for rejecting a hypothesis sometimes derive from the categories in terms of which it is framed. In evaluating 'All emeralds are grue', for example, the issue is not whether the evidence at hand supports the hypothesis but whether the hypothesis admits of evidential support. To decide that requires assessing the suitability of the category 'grue' for induction. Epistemology cannot evade the problem of induction, hence cannot ignore the challenge the grue paradox poses. To address that challenge requires recognizing that the partition of the domain that a category scheme supplies is a proper object of epistemic scrutiny.

Nor can epistemology distance itself from matters of orientation. The Copernican hypothesis was originally proposed as a factual claim. As such, it was clearly within epistemology's purview. With the repudiation of absolute space, however, its status becomes trickier. Neither the Earth nor the sun is absolutely in motion or absolutely at rest. For all motion is relative to a frame of reference. Because nature favors no one frame of reference over the others, there is no saying absolutely whether the Earth moves. Still, the denial of absolute space does not exempt the Copernican hypothesis from epistemological scrutiny. It just shifts the grounds for assessment. Even if there is no saying absolutely what is in motion and what is at rest, there is something *to be said for* taking some things to be in motion and others at rest. What is to be said for the Copernican hypothesis is that when the sun is treated as fixed and the Earth as moving, the solar system displays an order that makes sense of astronomical observations and fits planetary astronomy into a more comprehensive physical theory. The heliocentric perspective thus affords epistemic access to regularities in celestial motion that the geocentric perspective obscures. The elaboration and evaluation of such a defense is the business of epistemology. What is at issue is the acceptability not of a law or a factual claim but of an orientation. If the defense succeeds, it demonstrates the tenability of adopting a particular frame of reference.

Even salience is subject to assessment. In arguing for punctuated equilibrium, evolutionary biologists focus on, rather than glossing over, gaps in the fossil record. Such gaps have long been recognized. The theory of punctuated equilibrium highlights them, insisting that evidence for the course of evolution consists not just in the forms we find but also in the fact that we fail to find 'intermediate' forms. An epistemological assessment of the theory of punctuated equilibrium must decide whether the lacunae deserve the status of evidence.

Orientation, categorization, and focus are then already within the scope of any epistemology that accommodates science. Rather than extending epistemology's range, I have shown that epistemology's acknowledged range comprehends the functions emotions perform.

Chapter VI

SHIFTING FOCUS

NOTHING is sacred. Even truth and literal denotation can be sacrificed to achieve a suitable balance of cognitive goals. So there is in principle no objection to integrating into our systems statements and other symbols that are not literally true. Still, what is unobjectionable in principle is not always rewarding in practice. The epistemic tenability of such symbols turns on their contribution. If they serve to maximize the tenability of the systems that accommodate them, they are tenable; otherwise, they are not. Sometimes they do. In this chapter I explore several devices that enhance understanding even when they do not augment our stock of literal truths. These devices are common to the arts and the sciences and perform similar functions in each. Science is plainly a cognitive enterprise. An epistemology that cannot accommodate it is too anemic to serve. But an epistemology robust enough to account for its cognitive contributions cannot, I suggest, avoid accommodating the arts. For they make many of the same contributions. If I am right, the issue is not whether but how the arts function cognitively.

Attempts to assimilate aesthetics to epistemology are often dismissed out of hand. "In such a light," Mary Mothersill writes, "the arts make a poor showing: as a means of acquiring new truths about the world or the soul, they are in competition with the sciences and with philosophy."[1] She is right. If our overarching epistemic objective is the acquisition of new truths, we would be ill-advised to turn to art. We would also be ill-advised to turn to science or to philosophy. The abundance of anomalies and outstanding problems confronting any science is reason to doubt that currently available scientific theories are true. And since science faces the tribunal of experience as a corporate body,[2] we cannot hope to separate a science's constituent truths from its falsehoods. Philosophy is no more reliable. Outside formal logic, few if any philosophical theses have been firmly established. Some may be true, but none supplies the level of justification needed for knowledge.

If our goal is simply to augment our stock of justified true beliefs, we should stick to the more pedestrian claims of common sense. That there have been black dogs, though hardly illuminating, readily admits of con-

---

[1] Mary Mothersill, *Beauty Restored* (Oxford: Clarendon, 1984), 8.
[2] W. V. Quine, "Two Dogmas of Empiricism," 41.

firmation. If, however, it is understanding we seek, such a strategy loses its appeal. For in shifting its focus from knowledge to understanding, epistemology devalues truth. No longer our paramount cognitive objective, truth is but one of a number of desiderata and may lose out to the rest. Science is rife with approximations, idealizations, simplifying assumptions, and other falsifications that contribute to our understanding of phenomena. Indifference to particular truths evidently is not always an epistemic failing. But once we acknowledge that our interest in particular truths can be overridden, we have no ground for disallowing the wholesale disregard of truth. There is, in principle, no reason why a maximally tenable system couldn't trade off truth entirely, compensating for its loss by other cognitive gains. So disciplines indifferent to truth—for example, those whose deliverances are nonpropositional—may yet be repositories of understanding. If they are, their study falls within the scope of epistemology.

TELLING INSTANCES

The Michelson-Morley experiment demonstrates that the speed of light is constant. Jackson Pollock's *Number One* highlights the viscosity of paint.[3] Neither states a truth. Neither needs to. Each makes its case effectively without saying a word.

The experiment affords instances of light's unvarying speed. There is nothing remarkable about that, though. Every working flashlight does the same. But by measuring the time it takes light to travel equal distances in different directions, the experiment underscores the invariance of the speed of light. *Number One* supplies instances of paint's viscosity. So does every other painting. But through its clots and streaks, dribbles and spatters, *Number One* makes a point of viscosity. Most paintings do not. They use or tolerate viscosity but make no comment on it.

To highlight, underscore, display, or convey involves reference as well as instantiation. An item that at once refers to and instantiates a feature may be said to *exemplify* that feature.[4] I shall call such an item an *exemplar*, and its referent a *feature*. Under this usage, substances, attributes, relations, patterns, and so forth, qualify as features.

Exemplification is a mode of reference, so anything that exemplifies is a symbol. Not only do experiments exemplify theoretically significant fea-

---

[3] The works of art and science I cite serve as examples. Nothing in my account hangs on the correctness of my choices. The reader who disputes them may readily provide alternatives.

[4] Goodman, *Languages of Art*, 52–56. See also Catherine Z. Elgin, *With Reference to Reference* (Indianapolis: Hackett, 1983) 71–95. It should be obvious that I am enormously indebted to Goodman's work.

tures, and works of art formally significant features, ordinary samples and examples exemplify the features they display. A fabric swatch exemplifies its pattern, color, texture, and weave. A sample problem worked out in a textbook exemplifies reasoning strategies to be used in the course. Examples, samples, experiments, and abstract paintings then all serve as symbols. Though they denote nothing and state nothing, they refer by means of exemplification.

Since exemplification requires instantiation, a symbol can exemplify only features it instantiates. *Number One* can exemplify neither the constancy of the speed of light nor the pattern of a herringbone tweed, for it instantiates neither feature. Nor can it exemplify *all* the properties it instantiates. For exemplification is selective. *Number One* exemplifies paint's capacity to drip, spatter, blot, and clot, but not its capacity to depict, portray, record, and illustrate. Other paintings about painting—seventeenth-century gallery pictures, for example—make the opposite selection, exemplifying paint's capacities as a medium while merely instantiating its material capacities.

Exemplification is selective. But nothing in the nature of things makes some features inherently more worthy of selection than others. Reselection advances understanding by bringing things to exemplify features that had previously only been instantiated. Rather than using volumes and shapes as means for depicting scenes, Cézanne uses the depiction of scenes as a vehicle for the exemplification of volumes and shapes. By, as it were, shifting figure and ground, he makes us mindful of the composition of a painting, of the elements and combinations that make it up. And rather than taking the lives and material conditions of the common folk as the inarticulate backdrop against which major—that is, political and military—historical events transpire, Annales historians construe the lives and conditions of the common folk as the stuff of history. If we want to understand Victorian England, they maintain, knowing who said what to whom in Parliament is less important than knowing how industrialization affected the structure of communities and the dynamics of family life. Conditions that traditional historians take eras merely to instantiate, Annales historians take them to exemplify. We understand the past and our relations to it differently as a result.

Although a symbol must instantiate the properties it exemplifies, its instantiation need not be literal. Thus an experiment can metaphorically exemplify properties like power, elegance, panache, and promise; a painting, properties like electricity, balance, movement, and depth.

The features an object exemplifies are a function of the categories that subsume it. So opportunities for exemplification expand as new categories are contrived. Some are the benefits of hindsight. When Cézanne's works were first exhibited, it was, for obvious reasons, impossible to see him as a harbinger of cubism. Now his paintings practically cry out for such a reading, so plainly do they exemplify the shapes of things to come. When it was first performed, the Michelson-Morley experiment was not recognized as the death knell of classical mechanics. But through its stubborn resistance to Newtonian interpretation, it came to exemplify the inadequacies of the Newtonian world picture. We rightly read it in retrospect as the beginning of the end of classical physics.

New categories often reconfigure a domain, connecting previously isolated features to form patterns, focusing on factors hitherto unworthy of attention. Not long ago, weak joints, curved spines, and blurred vision were just additional afflictions befalling certain tall, thin heart patients. But with the identification of Marfan's syndrome, they coalesced into a clinical picture, their exemplification affording a basis for diagnosis and treatment. Similarly the introduction of feminist categories in literary criticism discloses new contours in fictional works, exemplifying long overlooked patterns and relationships. And the introduction of Freudian categories gives both life and art a new look. Once we recognize the possibility of unconscious drives, we have to go beyond sincere avowals to discover motivation. Dreams, jokes, oversights, and slips of the tongue become salient, often exemplifying desires the (real or fictional) agent can neither acknowledge nor control.

Exemplification of unsuspected features may, moreover, induce reconception. When *The Rite of Spring* exemplifies tonal patterns classical music cannot accommodate, or the Michelson-Morley experiment exemplifies electromagnetic phenomena classical physics cannot coherently describe, the inadequacies of available conceptions are manifest. Such revolutionary works both attest to the need for and supply constraints on a reconfiguration of their domains. They serve as exemplary instances of categories whose extensions and interrelations remain to be developed.

An exemplar affords epistemic access to the features it exemplifies. From a fabric swatch one can discover the look and feel of a herringbone tweed; from *Guernica*, the horrors of war; from a blood test, the presence of antibodies. An exemplar then is a telling instance of the features it exemplifies. It presents those features in a context contrived to render them salient. This may involve unraveling common concomitants, filtering out impurities, clearing away unwanted clutter, presenting in unusual settings. If motives are ordinarily mixed, it may be hard to find among our fellows a clear example of unmitigated malevolence. But in Iago the feature shines forth. If ores ordinarily contain impurities, we may be unable to extract a sample of pure copper from the mine. But we can readily refine one in the lab. Stage setting can also involve introduction of additional factors. Thus a biologist stains a slide to bring out a contrast, and a composer elaborates a theme to disclose hidden harmonies.

It might seem that instantiation is all that matters—that for epistemological purposes, at least, reference is otiose. Not so. For not all instances
are telling. A flashlight beam affords an instance of, but no epistemic access to, light's constant speed; Botticelli's *Birth of Venus* affords an instance of, but no access to, paint's viscosity. Perhaps what is wanted then
is a conspicuous instance, one that makes the feature all but impossible to
overlook. This will not do either. Conspicuous instances of a feature frequently fail to exemplify it. A can of house paint spilled on the rug presents
an all too vivid instance of paint's viscosity. But it is unlikely to exemplify
viscosity or anything else. Moreover, exemplars often convey obscure or
elusive features while glossing over glaring ones. The most obvious feature of an experiment may be the complexity of its apparatus, and of an
opera the implausibility of its plot. Yet neither is apt to be exemplified.
The experiment may exemplify all but undetectable differences among
allotropes of sulfur, and the opera nearly indiscernible distinctions among
types of love. Even a fabric swatch can exemplify a less than obvious feature, like the difference in drape a bias cut makes. Works of art and science
often exemplify inordinately inconspicuous features—subtle nuances, almost indistinguishable difference, abstruse kinships, patterns and regularities that elude all but the most attentive gaze.

It is, moreover, possible to agree about what is instantiated while dis-
agreeing intensely about what is exemplified. Evolutionary theorists all
acknowledge enormous gaps in the fossil record. By and large, transitional
forms are not to be found. Gradualists, following Darwin, regard this as
an unfortunate paleontological fact. Sedimentation is sporadic, so much
evidence is bound to be lost. They thus smooth over the gaps, interpo-
lating the many missing links necessary to complete the incremental evolutionary chain. Adherents of punctuated equilibrium, on the other hand,
construe the gaps in the fossil record not as a lack of evidence of transitional forms but as evidence of a lack of transitional forms. The reason
there are no fossils of intermediate stages, they contend, is that there were
no intermediate stages. Evolution, they believe, proceeds largely by
leaps—long periods of stasis being punctuated by short intervals of rapid
speciation. Successor species then differ significantly from even their closest ancestors.[5] I am not remotely qualified to take a stand on this debate.
I mention it to illustrate how a shift in emphasis can alter the intellectual
landscape. Adherents of punctuated equilibrium adduce no new information. To frame their alternative, they just highlight acknowledged gaps in
the fossil record and elevate them to the status of evidence; that is, they
bring the fossil record to exemplify the gaps it previously only instantiated.

[5] Stephen Jay Gould, "The Episodic Nature of Evolutionary Change," in *The Panda's
Thumb* (New York: Norton, 1980), 179–185.

An effective exemplar can also revivify the obvious. *Number One* does not exemplify unfamiliar or recondite properties. Quite the opposite. It exemplifies features so obvious that we routinely look right past them. The painting forces us to focus on aspects of paint we have overlooked since early childhood. And a significant psychological study may tell us something we have never thought to doubt—for example, that early deprivation leads to lifelong difficulties. What is wanted then is not just an instance or an obvious instance but a telling instance—one that reveals, discloses, conveys aspects of itself. It is by referring to those aspects that an exemplar points them up, singles them out, focuses on them. It thereby presents them for our scrutiny.

Exemplars, being symbols, require interpretation. To understand a drawing, an experiment, even a paint sample, requires recognizing which of its aspects exemplify and what features they refer to. If we take commercial paint samples as our paradigm, interpretation seems straightforward. For the system such samples belong to is regimented, its application routine. Exemplars operative in the arts and sciences are generally not so well behaved. The features a symbol exemplifies depend on its function. And a single symbol often performs a variety of functions. A painting that exemplifies viscosity in a gallery might exemplify volatility in an investment seminar. A chemical reaction that exemplifies acidity in the lab might exemplify economy in a manufacturing process. Function, moreover, varies with context. A picture that does not normally exemplify the heavy-handedness of its imagery may be brought to do so through juxtaposition with works with a surer, more delicate touch. And the acidity exemplified in one experiment may be mere by-product in another, even though the same chemical reaction occurs in both.

The intention of its producer does not determine an exemplar's interpretation. For its producer has neither privileged access to nor a monopoly on the symbol's function. He may just be wrong. Van Gogh intended *Vincent's Room* to exemplify comfort, security, and repose. What it actually exemplifies is a restless, feverish agitation. Michelson and Morley intended their experiment to exemplify the presence and magnitude of ether drift. Through its failure to oblige, it exemplified not only the nonexistence of luminiferous ether but also the incapacity of classical categories to accommodate electromagnetic phenomena—something Michelson and Morley found inconceivable. Even commercial samples can decline to exemplify what their makers intend. A swatch that promptly begins to unravel may exemplify a fabric's shoddiness rather than the understated elegance the manufacturer intends it to convey.

Moreover, many symbols admit of multiple right interpretations. Theorems common to classical and intuitionistic mathematics exemplify different logical forms in each. And under different, equally correct interpretations, Shakespeare's *Henry V* exemplifies positive and negative attitudes toward war. Whether such multiplicity was originally intended makes no difference.[6]

Exemplars operate against a constellation of background assumptions. An interpreter ignorant of those assumptions may be incapable of interpreting or even recognizing the symbols. An experiment in superconductivity involves assumptions about electricity and temperature, about what has been shown or suggested or left open by earlier investigations, about the capacities and limitations of the experimental apparatus, and so on. A nativity scene is grounded in assumptions about theology, iconology, religious and artistic tradition, as well as assumptions about the representational and expressive range of the medium, style, and subject. These assumptions need not be articulate. Nor need the works presuppose their truth or adequacy. Like an indirect proof, a work of art or science may undermine its grounding assumptions. But without an appreciation of what those assumptions are, an interpreter is ill-equipped to tell which features the work exemplifies, ill-equipped therefore to understand the work.

Not all background assumptions are propositional. We assume stances, perspectives, frames of reference, and the like, when we take them for granted in our constructs. Our doing so need not involve, and on pain of infinite regress cannot always involve, assuming *that* something or other is the case. Syntactic and semantic assumptions are embedded in the symbol systems we deploy. These delimit the forms of symbols and the categories in terms of which they are to be construed. The periodic table of the elements supplies categories for the interpretation of chemical samples, and plane geometry categories for the interpretation of cubist works. The forms of classical music and classical mathematics dictate the significant structures of symphony and proof. Vocabulary and grammar need not, of course, be verbal. Properties and patterns exemplified in the arts and sciences frequently have no exact verbal formulation. What we cannot quite put into words is often captured in equations or harmonies or diagrams or designs.

With a change in background assumptions, a symbol can come to exemplify new features. The advent of relativity theory caused the Michelson-Morley experiment to exemplify features that were unrecognized by, hence unavailable for, exemplification under the Newtonian framework. New categories of mass, energy, space, time, and acceleration came into play. Later classical music provides a new framework for understanding Haydn. Harmonies, textures, tonal patterns, and dynamics clearly exem-

---

[6] Nelson Goodman and Catherine Z. Elgin, *Reconceptions* (Indianapolis: Hackett, 1988), 49–65.

plified, sharply articulated, and fully developed by Mozart are found exemplified in the works of his predecessors. An attentive ear attuned to Mozart listens for and hears in Haydn's work patterns Mozart prepared it to find. Nor is it only explicitly artistic development that affects the background for interpreting art. After the Vietnam War, the lighthearted lunacy of Joseph Heller's *Catch-22* took on a darker, more sardonic tone.

I have urged that exemplification depends on and varies with context, function, and background assumptions. Although examples from art and science back my claim, commercial samples seem to belie it. The system of conventions governing the interpretation of commercial paint samples apparently treats them as neutral, invariable, and unambiguous. I demur. Rather than denying the relevance of context, function, and background assumptions, the system privileges a particular set. It can do so because it presupposes that its audience shares a limited but well-defined interest in house paint. The normal function of paint samples is to aid in the selection of house paint. We are presumably concerned about the color of the paint we select and are interested only in available alternatives. So the system is designed to supply easy epistemic access to these. That is all it does. In view of what we use the samples for, it is enough.

The very same samples might, of course, exemplify other features as well: the contemporary preference for rich colors, the unavailability of a warm brown, or the muddiness of one manufacturer's colors as compared with the vibrancy of another's. They may even exemplify features having nothing to do with color—for example, sloppy workmanship and inattention to detail exemplified by paint chips that promptly peel off the sample cards. But to see the samples as exemplifying such features requires overstepping the boundaries the conventional rules define. And outside those boundaries interpretation proceeds without rules.

Commercial paint samples, as normally interpreted, are thus atypical. Interpretation is rarely a matter of routine application of fixed rules. For exemplars are highly sensitive to context, function, and background assumptions, and these admit of enormous variation. Nevertheless, interpretation is neither arbitrary nor hopelessly difficult. Traditions, rules of thumb, accepted interpretive practices and precedents guide, though they provide no recipes. And despite their unruliness, context, function, and background assumptions often suffice to determine or narrowly circumscribe interpretation of particular exemplars. We do not need an algorithm for interpreting experiments to infer that, whatever else it may exemplify, an experiment consisting of an apparatus hooked up to a volt meter exemplifies voltage.

Interpretation of denoting symbols, it is worth recalling, also proceeds without rules. As the census bureau recognizes to its regret, we have no nonvacuous rule for determining the extension of the term 'household'. We go by practice and precedent, drawing on available contextual cues, precedents, conversational implicatures and functional roles, resorting to guesswork and stipulation where necessary to assign referents to our terms. Indeed, exemplars may give us an easier time. For they are subject to a constraint that denoting symbols are not. An exemplar can exemplify only features it instantiates. But a denoting term can refer to anything or to nothing at all. There are of course no guarantees. What a symbol exemplifies or denotes may permanently elude us or remain forever in dispute. Perhaps we will never know exactly what Schrödinger's cat or Giorgione's *Tempest* exemplifies or who, if anyone, 'Shakespeare's dark lady' denotes.

Learning from Examples

If we focus exclusively on illustrative or pedagogical cases, exemplars may seem mere heuristics. We provide examples in class to enliven our subject. But if students truly understand the material, we are apt to think, examples are not really necessary. A student has all she needs to do the problem sets when she has mastered chemistry and all she needs to analyze the *Eroica* when she has mastered music theory. I doubt it. Every theory admits of multiple models in a given universe.[7] So a student could grasp a theory without knowing how it applies. One role of examples is to select among admissible models. To be sure, an example will not fix interpretation uniquely. Models that diverge elsewhere may agree about a particular case. Still, an example grounds a theory in its domain and gives the student a purchase on applications.

In any case, not all exemplars function primarily as heuristics. Experiments do not. Their main function is to test—to disclose whether phenomena have the features a theory attributes to them. Anyone who contended that experiments are superfluous once we master chemistry would profoundly misunderstand empirical science. Without experiments there would be no chemistry. Experiments do not just convey what is already understood, they engender further understanding. Nor is art primarily heuristic. Like science, it provides telling instances that show that, how, and to what effect particular features are instantiated. No more than in science is this always a matter of illustrating what is already known. *A Doll's House* exemplifies what, many years later, *The Feminine Mystique* describes—the stifling limitations on women's lives that conventional middle-class marriages enforce. When *The Feminine Mystique* appeared, critics doubted that the predicament is as painful as Friedan makes it out

[7] Hilary Putnam, "Models and Reality," in *Realism and Reason* (Cambridge: Cambridge University Press, 1983), 1–25.

to be. They did not realize that Ibsen had already answered their doubts. Nora's predicament demonstrates that a gilded cage is still a cage and that the denizens thereof, however pampered, are still trapped. It took nearly twenty years and a scientific revolution to produce a framework that accommodates the phenomena exemplified in the Michelson-Morley experiment, more than eighty years and a social revolution to produce one that accommodates the predicament exemplified in *A Doll's House*.

Works of art often bring out hitherto unnoticed or poorly differentiated features. We might think, for example, that there is no difference (except perhaps in degree) between sorrow and grief. We need only compare Michelangelo's *Pietà* with the figure at the left in Picasso's *Guernica* to learn otherwise. Each portrays a woman holding her dead child. The Michelangelo expresses incalculable sorrow, the Picasso unmitigated grief. Sorrow evidently can be as profound as grief. There need be no difference in degree. But grief, we discover, is grittier; it is tinged with anger. Sorrow is smooth. The comparison effects a refinement of the sensibilities, leaving us unlikely again to conflate or confuse the two emotions.

Science functions similarly, bringing overlooked features to the fore and drawing distinctions among them. With the articulation of a clinical picture, for example, characteristics that were once considered medically insignificant acquire the status of symptoms. A patient comes to exemplify qualities he previously just instantiated. And as the clinical picture is refined, conditions that had been conflated come to be differentiated.

In my haste to recognize parallels between the arts and the sciences, I may seem to neglect a significant difference. Science purports to concern matters of fact. Art does not. Indeed, fiction makes a fetish of indifference to fact. This suggests two difficulties—one semantic, the other epistemic.

The semantic problem is this: an item cannot exemplify features it does not instantiate. Works of art are inanimate. Therefore, it would appear, they are constitutionally unable to instantiate emotions, feelings, or other states of mind. If so, they are incapable of exemplifying such features. *A Doll's House* then cannot exemplify Nora's discontent nor can the *Guernica* figure exemplify grief. Such works can, of course, exemplify features having to do with style, genre, technique, and the like. For they evidently instantiate such features. But their exemplification of properties like these hardly suits them for the major epistemic role I have cast them in.

It is quite true that inanimate objects cannot literally instantiate states of mind. But they can and often do instantiate mental states metaphorically. I shall have more to say about metaphor below. For now it is enough to note that metaphorical instantiation, though it is not literal instantiation, is nonetheless real instantiation. The semantic difficulty dissolves. For works of art can and often do exemplify features they metaphorically instantiate. *A Doll's House* metaphorically exemplifies discontent, the *Guernica* figure grief.

This leads directly to the epistemic difficulty. It is not at all clear how— or even that—a fiction's metaphorical exemplification can advance understanding of anything beyond the fiction. We cannot infer that the blind obsession metaphorically exemplified by Ahab is anywhere literally instantiated. So what, if anything, could an understanding of Ahab's obsession reveal about the world?

Rather than tackle that question directly, let us turn again to science. For science has fictions of its own—for example, thought experiments. These are imaginative exercises designed to disclose what would happen if certain conditions were met. Thought experiments may be purely cerebral, as Einstein's were. Or they may be mathematical models or computer simulations. But they are not actual experiments. So they do not literally instantiate the phenomena they concern. Still, they are obviously informative. Einstein was able to draw out startling implications of the theory of relativity by imagining what someone riding on a light wave would see. And scientists studying superconductivity discover from computer simulations how electric currents would behave in metals cooled to absolute zero.

Like other fictions, thought experiments instantiate phenomena they concern not literally but metaphorically. The computer simulation will not run unless the computer is warm. Still, what occurs can be metaphorically described as at a temperature of absolute zero. In the context of inquiry into superconductivity, the simulation exemplifies this description of itself. That the simulation occurs in something metaphorically cold is scientifically significant. That it occurs in something literally warm is not. The simulation discloses that at absolute zero, electrical resistance disappears. It does not, of course, demonstrate that absolute zero ever in fact is reached or that resistance ever in fact disappears. But by revealing what would happen in the limit, it enhances our understanding of the connection between resistance and temperature, and suggests avenues for further investigation.

The success of a thought experiment turns on the accuracy and adequacy of its background assumptions. If our computer simulation omits factors that affect resistance or assigns them incorrect functions or weights, its output is not to be trusted. In this regard, thought experiments are no different from other experiments. Unless we are right to assume that only acid turns litmus paper pink, litmus tests for acidity are unreliable. Both literal and metaphorical experiments can, of course, disclose that their background assumptions are faulty. The failure of the Michelson-Morley experiment to detect ether drift undermined the assumption that ether is there to be detected. And the failure of a simulation of radioactive decay to reach equilibrium demonstrates the inadequacy of the assumptions on which it is based.

Just as thought experiments are fictions in science, works of fiction are thought experiments in art. Both are vehicles for exploration and discovery, providing contexts in which features may be demarcated, their interplay examined, their implications drawn out. Freed from the demands of factuality, fictions can separate constant companions and commingle traditional rivals. By doing so, they may transform our understanding of features and the conditions of their realization.

To anyone of even a mildly behaviorist bent, it might seem obvious that a person could not sincerely resolve to reform yet continue to behave as badly as ever. Indeed, lack of improvement seems a sure sign that the resolution was not sincere. But through his characterization of Pierre Bezukhov, Tolstoy convinces us otherwise. Pierre truly means to reform his indolent ways. He just never gets around to it. Pierre exemplifies the capacity of inertia to override resolution. The bond between resolution and action is broken. And how resolution relates to action again becomes an open question.

Love and hate, one would think, are natural enemies. Vacillation between them is surely possible. But it seems obvious that one cannot both love and hate the same person at the same time—obvious, that is, until one encounters a work like *Who's Afraid of Virginia Woolf?*, where the possibility and pain of such a mix are clearly exemplified. The play forces us to recognize that antagonistic attitudes are not mutually exclusive and opens our eyes to configurations of emotions we once would have excluded a priori. In so doing, it deepens and enriches our understanding of emotional life.

Like other thought experiments, literary fictions often go to extremes. Ahab's obsession is not a mind set one encounters every day. But by seeing how it plays itself out, how it comes to dominate not just Ahab's mind but also the lives and destiny of his crew, we gain insights that may be applicable to more moderate, more familiar cases of psychopathology. Features that are salient in extreme situations are often realized without being obvious elsewhere. By going to extremes, fictions bring these features to the fore, delineating their characteristics, demarcating their boundaries, disclosing patterns of concurrence and independence. Fiction feeds back on fact. Once we have learned to recognize such features and the possibilities open to them, we often can locate them and their kin in their natural habitats.

An exemplar, I said, is a telling instance—an instance that discloses the features it refers to. Its embodiment of those features shows something of what they are and something of how they are realized. An exemplar thus facilitates recognition of further instances of the features it exemplifies.

Features often belong to families of alternatives. And the exemplification of one member provides indirect access to others. We acquire the ability to recognize additional instances not only of the exemplified feature but also of its kin. From a leaden cadence that exemplifies sadness, we readily infer the spritely sound of joy. Exemplars thus equip us to go on—to apply the categories they highlight to new cases. This is not always easy or automatic. To follow where innovative exemplars lead often requires radical reorientation and reorganization. The stranglehold of habit can be difficult to break.

The insights exemplars afford are tested by further applications. Experimental results are acceptable only if repeatable. But mere repetition is not enough. That would control for dishonesty and negligence but not for misleading results. By holding exemplified features fixed and varying unexemplified ones, we perform a more stringent test. A result that recurs under such circumstances is one we have greater reason to trust.

Something similar occurs in the arts. The adequacy of an aesthetic 'experiment' is tested not by trying to produce exactly the same effect in exactly the same way but by trying to project the exemplified feature or family beyond the work that first exemplifies it. Constable did not continually paint the same cloud configuration. He projected his vision of clouds through a variety of configurations. And the viewer confirms that vision by coming to see actual clouds and other cloud pictures as having the forms Constable's works exemplify.

Not all exemplars afford a valid basis for projection. But even those that do not may enlighten. When we realize that the moral absolutes exemplified in cowboy films do not extend beyond the fictive realm, we learn something about the moral ambiguities and complexities of human life and about the simplifying assumptions of the genre. And when we realize that the fuel economies exemplified in test situations are not matched by cars on the road, we come to appreciate both the effects of driving conditions and techniques on fuel consumption and the deceptiveness of advertising.

Exemplification's epistemic contribution has little to do with justified true belief. Justification in the sense of argument from accepted premises is out of place. An exemplar is vindicated not by what backs it up but by what it brings forward. If it illuminates features that are worthy of attention (a contextual matter, to be sure), humble origins are no handicap. If not, the most patrician pedigree is no help. Nor is truth crucial. Experiments and pictures, paint samples and fabric swatches, inform by means of exemplification. Being nonverbal, such symbols are neither true nor false. Their success in advancing understanding thus does not turn on their truth. Nor need epistemically effective verbal exemplars be true. Effectiveness sometimes depends on nonsemantic features such as syntax, style, inflection, or emphasis. And even where semantics is involved, a telling falsehood may be as revealing as a truth. If no one ever said, 'Give me liberty or give me death!', someone surely should have. An illuminating exemplar need not even affect belief. Its cognitive contribution may consist in augmenting one's conceptual repertoire, refining one's discrimination, honing one's ability to recognize, synthesize, reorganize, and so on. Even if extant beliefs remain in place and no new ones immediately form, it is hard to maintain that exemplars that perform such functions are epistemically inert.

Fiction in Fact

Fictions, as we have seen, abound. And not just in the arts. Science is rife with idealizations, approximations, thought experiments, and other falsifying assumptions. Philosophy too takes liberties with truth. Political theorists ground civic duty in social contracts no one ever signed. Philosophers of science contrive rational reconstructions of reasoning processes no one ever performed. Epistemologists worry about malevolent demons. Metaphysicians brood over brains in a vat.

Were they committed to the reality of their referents, theories deploying such devices would be in sorry shape. But such devices are fictions. So failure of reference does not discredit them. To assess their tenability, we need to determine whether despite—or even because of—their falsity, they enhance understanding. Sometimes they do. Even if literal, factual truth is an initially tenable commitment of inquiry, fiction often compensates for falsity by displaying relevance, sensitivity, fecundity, and/or other cognitive virtues the unvarnished truth cannot match. Like any other initially tenable commitment, truth can be sacrificed to achieve a suitable balance of epistemic ends. The profusion of fictions in philosophy, science, and other manifestly cognitive enterprises attests to the fruitfulness of the sacrifice.

That there exists no ideal gas does not discredit the ideal gas law. But that there exists no phlogiston decisively discredits the laws of phlogiston theory. The difference is plain. The ideal gas law is a fiction. So its falsity does not tell against it. Since phlogistic laws purport to be factual, their falsity is their undoing.

The ideal gas law configures the domain, locating actual thermodynamic processes by reference to a fictive ideal. That ideal is selective. It specifies only thermodynamically significant features and restricts itself to thermodynamically relevant characterizations of them. It does not, for example, determine how the ideal gas is supposed to smell, even though odors of actual gases are often overpowering. The ideal is designed to fit the demands of the discipline—to supply the sort of understanding thermodynamics seeks within the constraints the science sets for itself. The concept of an ideal gas involves sweeping simplifications. It construes its molecules as perfectly elastic spheres and characterizes their behavior only under idealized conditions. The concept of an ideal gas is not, and does not purport to generate, a complete gas description.

Ignoring complexities does not of course eradicate them. We cannot responsibly treat argon or neon as though it were an ideal gas. Calculating thermodynamic properties of actual gases involves recognizing and accommodating divergences from the ideal. Still, the fictive ideal provides focus. Patterns and properties it exemplifies remain salient when complicating factors reenter. And the statistical stance the law adopts yields insight into nonideal gases as well.

A driving assumption of thermodynamics is that characteristics and behaviors of actual gases can be understood as deviations from the ideal. The science's success attests to the utility of this assumption. Intractable direct comparisons give way to streamlined indirect ones, the (fictive) ideal serving as common denominator. Irrelevancies wash out. For the law serves as a filter, disclosing regularities hidden among the myriad complexities of actual molecular interactions. By paring away inessentials, the ideal gas law presents a fiction that cleanly exemplifies thermodynamically significant features. By characterizing actual gases as deviations from the ideal, thermodynamics brings them to exemplify the same features. Not despite but because of its limitations, simplifications, and idealizations, the ideal gas law furthers the ends of the science.

Literary fictions function similarly. A fictive character like Don Quixote or a fictive action like tilting at windmills serves as a polestar, enabling us to orient acts and aims by reference to it. The domain of human behavior reconfigures around the fiction of the Don. Devices for description become available; aspects of behavior and circumstance stand out. The amateur who devotes herself to regimenting English grammar, despite years of frustration and the active discouragement of professional grammarians, is no longer just a crackpot, even if her prospects of success remain dim. As *Don Quixote* exemplifies, courses of action like hers are at once noble, preposterous, hopeless, and eminently worth pursuing—they are, in a word, quixotic. Seen in the light of Cervantes' great work, what once looked like profitless, idiosyncratic endeavors take on a different, more admirable cast.

Advancement of understanding often requires projecting or extrapolating from a limited class of cases. Any class admits of infinitely many divergent descriptions. Not all afford a sound basis for extrapolation. What favors those that do? If our data points conform to both a straight line and an intricate, irregular curve, why extrapolate along the former rather than the latter? If our survey polls individuals who are both Democrats and non-giraffes, why take their opinions to be representative of the one group rather than the other? The problem is not so intractable as it might appear. For an evidence class exemplifies only some of its descriptions. And only under descriptions it exemplifies does a class provide grounds for generalization. The data points exemplify their linear, not some curvilinear description; the opinions voiced exemplify the political, not some zoological classification of the respondents. Just what descriptions an evidence class exemplifies is not always obvious. Considerations of purpose, practice, and precedent, as well as simplicity, context, and relevance, come into play. I am not concerned here, however, to rehearse the general problem.[8] Rather, I want to take up extrapolation from fiction.

There the evidence class is null. For fictive terms lack denotation. It might then seem either that no extrapolation is possible or that every extrapolation is permissible, since no evidence constrains inference. Neither is the case. For as we have seen, constraints on extrapolation derive not just from the contents of the evidence class but also from the descriptions the evidence exemplifies.

Different fictions bring the extension of the null class to exemplify divergent descriptions. Descriptions that purport to denote Don Quixote, for example, denote actual individuals who are not in the extension of descriptions that purport to denote Oliver Twist. By exemplifying such descriptions, a fiction affords a basis for generalization. If we understand the characterization Cervantes supplies and correctly extrapolate from it, we may gain insight into a distinctive class of people, conceivably a class we had not previously marked out. Our reasoning is ampliative but not strictly inductive since we have no positive instances. As in induction, there are no guarantees. Despite its persuasiveness in fiction, a description may fail to generalize. It may have no instances in fact.

Like the ideal gas law, a literary fiction is selective. It does not detail all its protagonists' characteristics or deeds but restricts itself to significant attributes and episodes. In relating them, it deploys a particular vocabulary, perspective, stance, and style. To the extent that it advances understanding, it vindicates its selection. To illuminate telling features, fictions focus, organize, omit, and elaborate. They may exemplify complex constellations, subtle nuances, bizarre patterns, or ordinary occurrences whose very familiarity provides their camouflage. They present matters in context—not necessarily in contexts where they typically occur, but in contexts designed to bring particular features to the fore.

Shakespeare's *Coriolanus* highlights the irreconcilable demands we regularly make on our heroes. We insist that they be both larger than life and

---

[8] For a fuller discussion, see Goodman, *Fact, Fiction, and Forecast*, and Elgin, *With Reference to Reference*, 88–90.

no different from the next guy. Rock idols, movie stars, professional ath-
letes, and political figures no doubt chafe under such discordant demands.
By deviating from literal truth, Shakespeare could arrange events and calibrate tensions to reveal their tragic potential. The arrogance, self-reliance,
and sense of superiority that enabled Coriolanus to prevail in battle caused
his downfall afterward. He had neither the humility nor the hypocrisy to
pass himself off as a man of the people. And the hoi polloi would permit
him no other role. Having saved their homes for them, he had no home
among them.

Fictions can transmute virtues into vices, vices into virtues. What we
would ordinarily condemn as intransigence, *High Noon* portrays as integrity. What we might easily consider industriousness, Uriah Heep embodies as obsequiousness. By exemplifying features that tell against our off-
the-cuff assessments, fictions sensitize us to delicate differences in degree,
demeanor, and detail that affect moral standing. If they thereby make
moral deliberation more demanding, they also make moral judgment
more acute.

By transposing events into an alien medium or milieu, fictions can distance us, disengaging emotions that block understanding. An epidemiol-
ogist who would be incapacitated by their suffering were she to study
AIDS patients directly, can dispassionately investigate the disease's pro-
gression via a simulation—a schematic, fictional portrayal of the course of
the disease. Citizens caught up in the fervor of a political movement or
moment can discover the dangers of enthusiasm through a work like *The
Crucible*. And anyone contemplating an extended lawsuit would do well
to read *Bleak House* before engaging counsel.

By the same token, fictions sometimes activate emotions that advance
understanding. After lulling his audience into a stereotypical conception
of Shylock as a grasping, usurious Jew, Shakespeare confounds us, evok-
ing compassion through the soliloquy, 'Hath not a Jew eyes?'. As a result,
The Merchant of Venice ends on a more troubling note than the early com-
edies do. We have been forced to recognize that villains suffer, too—indeed, that their villainy may stem from the suffering ostensibly virtuous
people inflict.

FICTION'S FEEDBACK

 Works of fiction provide new resources for thinking about ourselves and
our situations. They contrive categories and illustrate their utility. In Toni
Morrison's *Beloved*, for example, 'whitewoman' is a single, unbreakable
predicate. It partitions the population in such a way that black women and
white women belong to disparate kinds. The predicate is a vehicle of es-
trangement, distancing the women who use it from those to whom it

applies. The abyss that divides the races need not be described. It is presupposed in the language the characters speak.

Fiction's influence on language runs deeper still. Most people probably believe that a term's meaning precedes and circumscribes its applications. Nelson Goodman argues the opposite: the facts and fictions it figures in delimit the meaning of a term. Both dogs and dog stories then affect the meaning of the word 'dog'. According to Goodman, a term's meaning is a function of its primary and secondary extensions—of the things the term denotes and the things compound terms containing it denote.[9] Its applications to matters of fact fix its primary extension. Its occurrences in fiction contribute to its secondary extension. Neither determines the other. Some dogs answer to no dog-descriptions; some dog-descriptions describe no dogs. But even fictive dog-descriptions and dog-depictions belong to secondary extensions of, hence figure in the meaning of, the word 'dog'. If Goodman is right, then the stories we tell and the pictures we paint affect the meanings of the words we use.

This is not so implausible as it first appears. Rarely do necessary and sufficient conditions for its application accompany a term's introduction into the language. Typically we are offered a few putatively paradigm cases and some more or less vague intimations about the rest. Thus poodles and spaniels and the like fall under the heading 'dog', and Mars and Venus and the like fall under the heading 'planet'. We are expected to extrapolate from clear cases to less obvious ones. Extrapolation is not wanton augmentation of a term's previously accepted extension. Considerations of purpose and context normally come into play, as do prior decisions about applications of kindred terms. But such factors typically fail to fully determine the basis or extent of a term's extrapolation. They do not tell us just what lines to draw or exactly where to draw them. They do not, for example, tell us whether to include coyotes in the extension of the term 'dog'.

Both primary and secondary applications afford avenues of extrapolation. From accepted instances, we extrapolate to further instances, thus augmenting primary extension. And from accepted instance-portrayals— descriptions, pictures, and the like—we extrapolate to augment secondary extension. Thus, on the basis of the pictures and descriptions we have already classified as dog-portrayals, we generalize to further pictures and descriptions we are prepared to count as such. Each new application alters the precedent class against which further candidates will be judged. Even if our original paradigms provided little incentive to classify Newfoundlands as dogs, once we have so classified St. Bernards, leaving Newfound-

[9] Goodman, "On Likeness of Meaning" and "On Some Differences about Meaning," in *Problems and Projects*, 221–238.

lands out would seem arbitrary. And even if our paradigm depictions provided little incentive to classify the cartoon figure Snoopy as a dog-picture, once we have so characterized Goofy, we have no grounds for excluding Snoopy. So things we were initially indifferent about may come to be naturally included or naturally excluded as precedent evolves.

Goodman's discussions of likeness of meaning emphasize the logical independence of primary and secondary extensions. But, I believe, much of their cognitive significance derives from their interanimation. New factual applications provide fodder for fiction. And new fictional applications influence further findings of fact. That what we count as a dog influences what we count as a dog-description is hardly a surprise. But the converse is unexpected. What we proffer as dog-descriptions and dog-pictures influences what we count as dogs.

The primary extension of 'dog' provides no rationale for drawing boundaries where we do. Coyotes, for example, differ little from some of the canines we keep as pets. But fictional dog-stories portray their subjects as thoroughly domesticated—as loyal, loving companions and/or devoted servants. Even stories about vicious dogs construe their subjects as exceptions to the norm. Familiar fictions thus disincline us to extend the term 'dog' to coyotes, jackals, and other notably nasty members of the canine family. No one raised on stories like *Lassie* would feel comfortable calling such animals dogs. If I am right, animals that do not in fact differ much from dogs are excluded from the term's extension because they do not conform to the dog-descriptions favored by our fictions.

Primary extension dominates the meaning and extrapolation of the word 'dog'; fictive uses play a supporting role. But secondary extensions are not always so retiring. Sometimes they take the lead. Tending sheep and tending cattle are, I suppose, quite similar occupations. Extensive retraining probably would not be required to switch from one line of work to the other. Yet 'cowboy' and 'shepherd' have practically opposite connotations. The difference derives from our fictions. Cowboy tales typically portray their protagonists as rough, tough tamers of the old West, ever ready to engage in gunplay to fend off the bad guys. Any connection with cattle is purely coincidental. Stories of shepherds, on the other hand, have a biblical ring, their protagonists being gentle, kindly guardians whose selfless concern for their flocks provides their raison d'être. It is hard to imagine John Wayne in the role of a shepherd. One could, to be sure, write a story about a compassionate tender of cows or a gunslinging keeper of sheep. But the use of the terms 'cowboy' and 'shepherd' in such a context would sound strained, if not ironic.

Such divergences in secondary extension affect metaphorical usage. An independent-minded, trend-bucking investor might be called a cowboy; a prudent protector of capital, a shepherd of her investments; a flamboyant trial lawyer might qualify as a legal cowboy; and a meticulous estate-planner, a legal shepherd.

The residues of fiction thus infuse findings of fact. For the literal extrapolations and figurative applications that augment our fact-stating repertoire are sensitive to secondary extension. Meaning is not a fixed feature of terminology, given once and for all with the mastery of our words. It is a dynamic interplay, evolving over time in response to the facts we discover and the fictions we contrive. Fiction's contributions to cognition are not incidental. They pervade the language we speak.

WHAT WE LEARN ABOUT WHAT WE KNOW

To advance understanding, we need not discover anything new. We already have a vast store of information at our disposal. But a jumble of disorderly data has little cognitive value. Our problem, often enough, is what to make of what we've got. Advancement of understanding then involves finding order in or imposing order on the information at hand. Fiction helps. It highlights patterns, spells out implications, draws distinctions, and identifies possibilities we had not recognized in the welter of information before us.

Fictions, as we have seen, function as thought experiments. They explore commitments and test their tenability. Hilary Putnam's Twin Earth fantasy, for example, debunks the once routine assumption that intention determines extension. The fiction describes Twin Earth as a planet exactly like Earth but for the absence of H_2O and the presence of XYZ, a chemical with H_2O's phenomenal properties and ecological functions. Our counterparts on Twin Earth even call XYZ *water*. Many inhabitants of the two planets, knowing no chemistry, cannot tell H_2O from XYZ. That being so, nothing in their conceptions of (what they call) water, or in their dispositions to use the term 'water', need differ from ours. Indeed, denizens of the two planets could be in exactly the same psychological state and in phenomenologically indistinguishable circumstances whenever they use the term. Still, their referents differ. The Earthling's 'water' refers to H_2O, the Twin Earthling's to XYZ. To think otherwise would be to deny that the term's reference figures in the explanation of its successful usage.[10]

Because the situation Putnam imagines does not obtain in fact, a fiction was necessary to bring out the possibility the story embodies. But a possibility suffices to show that a correlation is contingent. So Putnam's fantasy discredits a longstanding assumption of philosophical semantics. It shows that what a speaker intends may fail to fix a unique extension for each of her terms.

[10] Putnam, "The Meaning of 'Meaning,'" 215–271.

Fictions refract, enabling us to see what we might otherwise overlook. Shakespeare's tragedies, as Stanley Cavell reads them,[11] are studies in the problem of other minds. For Othello, nothing could demonstrate that Desdemona loved him alone. Lear both craved and had to settle for hyperbolic protestations of filial devotion, being unable in the nature of things to be sure they were sincere. The *real* problem of other minds, Cavell maintains, is not that we cannot know whether other people have minds but that we cannot know—even when it matters most—what is on their minds. This problem philosophy is powerless to dispel. Shakespeare's plays exemplify the immense cost of our mutual inscrutability.

Plot is not the only refractive lens. Evidently any aspect of a work can serve. Flaubert's flat, emotively neutral description of Emma Bovary's attempt to gain solace from her priest exemplifies the banality that envelops her more powerfully than any emotion-laden outpouring could. Terminology and tone reveal the reality of Emma's situation.

Traditional philosophy's ambition to adopt a God's eye view owes much of its plausibility, I believe, to the omniscient narrator's stance. If a fictive narrator can know everything that occurs in her world and can accurately assess its significance, why shouldn't we aspire to do likewise? Our actual epistemic situation, fraught with obstacles and opportunities, has its fictive counterpart in the (woefully nonomniscient) participant observer's stance. Sometimes bewildered, sometimes falsely confident, occasionally right on target, such a narrator reports on events from a limited perspective, often on the basis of incomplete or misleading information, striving to make what sense she can of events as they transpire. Our dissatisfaction with the quality of her reports echoes our frustration with our own.

Every entity admits of infinitely many descriptions, few of which leap immediately to mind. If we restrict ourselves to the familiar few, we settle for parochial, pedestrian conceptions of things. If we branch randomly out, we find many accurate descriptions cognitively inert. We can contrive a category consisting of integers, insufflators, and insurance agents. And we can easily identify its instances. But an item's inclusion in or exclusion from that category is unlikely to prove illuminating. Fictions bridge the gap. They at once deploy atypical modes of description and illustrate their utility. Even if the vocabulary is familiar, the function it performs in a fiction often is not.

When Virginia Woolf contrasts contented, connected Clarissa Dalloway with the isolated, shell-shocked suicide, Septimus Smith, responsiveness to sensory stimulation is the measure of emotional well-being.

---

[11] Stanley Cavell, *Disowning Knowledge* (Cambridge: Cambridge University Press, 1987).

Clarissa's world vibrates with color and light. For Septimus Smith, every-thing has gone gray. "The world of the happy is a different one from the world of the unhappy," Wittgenstein remarks.[12] As Woolf describes it, the difference is palpable.

Rawls's original position is a fictive stance from which to negotiate the social contract. A veil of ignorance screens out potentially prejudicial in-formation. So long as that information is excluded, negotiators may ad-duce any considerations they like. Fairness results from what is left out.[13] By revealing the importance of appropriate omissions, Rawls shows that incorporating irrelevant information can be more than a stylistic gaffe. It can, on occasion, scuttle a cognitive project.

Thermodynamics makes no attempt to locate individual ideal gas molecules, being concerned solely with statistical aggregates. Its success vindicates its statistical stance by demonstrating that further specificity is unnecessary—indeed, that beyond a certain point, additional precision inhibits understanding. Its perspective yields the sort of insight into the behavior of a gas that the science seeks. That the 'gas' in question is a fiction does not diminish the achievement.

We already know how to garner the relevant statistics, how to describe things in terms of their apparent colors, how to disregard the particulars of our own situations. What we learn from the fictions is how to bring this knowledge on line, how to implement it in areas where we would not ordinarily call it into play. The fictions advance understanding here, not by conveying new information but by more fully deploying resources at hand.

By exemplifying particular patterns, a fiction may, moreover, prompt us to form hypotheses about matters of fact—hypotheses we have ample evi-dence for but might, without the fiction, never have thought to frame.[14] Certain facts about slavery in the United States are well known. Slave fam-ilies were often sundered—parents, spouses, and children were separately sold. None ever saw the others again or learned their fates. Many slave women were forbidden to nurture their own children and were forced to nurture the children of their masters. Slaves' highest achievements were transformed into instruments to further their oppression. Sex was used by the oppressors as a means of humiliation and degradation, not an expres-sion of love. We need no fiction to tell us this. Still, Morrison's *Beloved* draws out an implication we might otherwise overlook. Where such facts obtain, the self-protective strategy

[12] Ludwig Wittgenstein, *Tractatus Logico-Philosophicus* (London: Routledge and Kegan Paul, 1961), 6.43.

[13] Rawls, *A Theory of Justice*, 118–161, and passim.

[14] David Lewis, "Truth in Fiction, Postscript," in *Philosophical Papers* (Oxford: Oxford University Press, 1983), vol. 1, 279.

   Don't love anything

is rational. When a person is powerless, love is an invitation to soul-shat-
tering grief. The novel shows how the institution of slavery corrupts the
most intimate human relationships—parent and child, husband and wife,
artist and work—by making love a luxury that slaves can ill afford. Morrison makes us realize that the tragedy of slavery consists not only in what
was done to the slaves but also in what slaves had to make of themselves
in order to survive. Familiar facts supply the evidence; the novel shows
what follows from them.

   By the same token, of course, fictions may mislead. A fictional work can
chart a course through our commitments that makes a persuasive case for
an untenable conclusion. Works that play off invidious stereotypes often
have this effect, as does science fiction. In some cases, the commitments
invoked are untenable. Thus science fiction's dependence on common-
sensical, quasi-Newtonian assumptions about velocity may convince read-
ers that intergalactic travel is theoretically unproblematic. In others,
fiction plots an untenable course through tenable commitments by, for
example, omitting or underrating contravening considerations. By ne-
glecting to mention that their homeland had been invaded, once popular
Westerns were able to foster the view that American Plains Indians were
murderous savages. In yet other cases, fictions may encourage untenable
extrapolations. Horatio Alger stories fuel the widespread propensity to
ignore crippling obstacles and believe that the disadvantaged can succeed
if only they try. I do not, then, contend that a work of fiction can *demonstrate* a factual truth, only that it can exemplify a constellation of commitments that supports a factual claim. It may then lead to the discovery of an
unsuspected truth, but it need not. The capacity of data to support untenable hypotheses is a regrettable but unavoidable fact of epistemic life.

                        GETTING PERSPECTIVE

There is more to things than meets any particular eye. What one perspective discloses, another may obscure. A gesture that looks generous from
one vantage point looks self-serving from another, cowardly from a
third. By adopting a variety of viewpoints, then, we discern more than any
single stance reveals. Understanding how things look from an alien point
of view is itself an epistemic achievement. To appreciate why, for instance,
a policy motivated by benevolence will be construed as patronizing is to
gain insight into the policy and the environment in which it aims to operate. Understanding an event typically requires more than correctly plotting the trajectories of the relevant matter in motion. We also need to
know what other people make of it, how they receive it, characterize it,

work with it, and incorporate it into or exclude it from their systems of thought. Cognition would be crippled were other perspectives epistemically inaccessible.

Not every viewpoint is valid, of course. Prejudice and emotional blindness distort some, inexperience and ignorance limit others. To appraise the insights a perspective affords requires assessing the perspective itself. That there are many legitimate ways of looking at things does not mean that every perspective is to be trusted. Still, the appearance that a thing presents to an inaccurate perspective can itself be a telling feature. Given that gorillas construe eye contact as a sign of aggression, it behooves me to avoid locking eyes with gorillas in the wild, even though they would be wrong to read malevolent motives into my gaze. My well-being depends on how I appear from their viewpoint, whether or not that viewpoint is accurate. And my understanding of my own situation depends on my appreciation of their construal of my stance.

That we *should* look at things from a variety of vantage points we learn early. What we need continuously to discover is how to identify different vantage points and the insights they afford. Works of fiction teach us. By imparting the ways things look and feel to others, they liberate us from our egocentric and ethnocentric predicaments. Fictions filter events through alien sensibilities. One need not have a romantic temperament to understand how Emma Bovary feels. Nor need one have been charged with an unknown crime to identify with Kafka's Josef K. Works of fiction enable us to try characters, commitments, and circumstances on for size, to see how the world looks and feels through them. We thereby learn about those to whom the perspective comes naturally and about the world as seen from that point of view. We do not just see the events of their stories through the protagonists' eyes. Having adopted their perspectives, we can shift our gaze. We can look with Puck's bemusement at foibles he never surveyed, react with Lear's rage to indignities he did not suffer. New perils and prospects, options and obstacles, emerge under the influence of perspectives fictions afford.

These days even science contrives fictions to delineate alien points of view. No human being ever surveyed the galaxy from Alpha Centauri. Yet a computer simulation can show how things would look from there. Although the data consist entirely of information acquired on or near the Earth, the relationships the fictive perspective discloses may be undetectable until we adopt a suitable extraterrestrial stance. We can then gain genuine astronomical insight by, as it were, viewing our solar system from the outside.

Is the detour through fiction really necessary? Couldn't we gain access to diverse points of view through sufficiently broad acquaintance with facts? What we would need is not access to a denatured characterization of

'objective facts' as viewed from nowhere but rather access to facts as sub-
jectively construed. We need to know not just the appalling fact that slave
children were forcibly abducted from their parents but also how the fact
and prospect of abduction affected parent and child. Memoirs, diaries,
letters, and the like, might yield the necessary insights. But perhaps not.
The requisite documents may fail to exist. Even widely shared perspectives
need leave no factual trace. And legitimate, telling stances may be ones no
one can actually adopt. The view from Alpha Centauri is a case in point.
That of a Connecticut Yankee in King Arthur's court is another.

Fictions manipulate character, commitments, and circumstances to
generate combinations not to be found in fact. Such combinations can
be particularly revealing. In *Middlemarch* Dorothea Brooke exemplifies
"spiritual grandeur ill-matched with . . . meanness of opportunity."[15] Not
being beholden to fact, George Eliot could fine-tune Dorothea's assumptions, aspirations, and situation, casting into bold relief their failure to
mesh. She thereby called into question the value of spiritual grandeur in
a world that lacks suitable outlets for it. Conceivably no actual person's
experiences would make the point so well.

Rawls's original position is plainly a fictive stance. No one is actually so
oblivious to the particulars of her situation as deliberators behind the veil
of ignorance are supposed to be. Still, the fictional perspective is effective.
By filtering out factors that make actual negotiations inequitable, it insures that deliberators negotiate as equals. Critics sometimes purport to
be unable to feign the ignorance of their own circumstances that the original position requires. They do themselves an injustice. Any reader of fiction can do what Rawls demands—that is, take up a fictive stance. If we
can imagine our way into Rip Van Winkle's muddle, having slept through
a revolution, or into Billy Pilgrim's plight, having come unstuck in time,
or into Faust's bargaining position as he dickered with the devil over the
price of his soul, we have no trouble suspending knowledge of our own
situation and reasoning within the constraints a fiction dictates. That is all
it takes to enter the original position.

Thoughts and actions depend not only on what transpires but also on
how things are construed. To understand others then requires knowing
not just what happens to and around them but also what they make of it.
Attitudes color events. Fictions lay the process plain. Shakespeare shows
how Othello's obsessive jealousy transmutes innocent acts and utterances
into seemingly sure signs of infidelity. Twain shows how Huckleberry
Finn's affection for a runaway slave overrides his conviction that he is
morally obliged to return the man to captivity.[16] By providing access to

---

[15] George Eliot, *Middlemarch* (New York: New American Library, 1964), vii.

[16] See Jonathan Bennett, "The Conscience of Huckleberry Finn," *Philosophy* 49 (1974):
123–134.

personalities and thoughts, works of fiction show why people view things as they do and why their doing so bears the fruits it does. We could not understand our world or our place in it if we did not understand what others make of it.

TENABLE FICTIONS

If the insights a fiction embodies are integrable into an epistemically acceptable system of thought, they are epistemically tenable. Not all are. Neither are all those drawn from facts. Opportunities for error abound. We might mistake a fictive statement for a statement of fact, thereby holding it answerable to inappropriate epistemic standards. We miss the point of creation myths, for example, when we dismiss them as primitive attempts at empirical science.[17] Or we might misconstrue a work's tone—perhaps by treating an ironic work like *Sense and Sensibility* as though it were sincere.

Difficulties also arise in moving from work to the world. John Updike's Rabbit Angstrom, for example, is often taken as a fictional everyman—an exemplar of the universal human predicament. On such a reading, the epistemic contribution of Updike's trilogy is slight. Beyond familiar platitudes, it discloses little that extends to human beings generally. Under a different interpretation, however, the work fares better. It affords genuine insight into the trials and tribulations of contemporary, middle-class American men.

A fiction's epistemic effect depends, of course, on the background it operates against. Some fictions are sources of continual illumination. Others fade with time. Because it admits of multiple, increasingly sophisticated interpretations, *Madam Bovary* continues to enlighten. As our understanding evolves, we develop the capacity to glean new insights from it. Because the development of thermodynamics provides additional, increasingly complex opportunities for its application, the ideal gas law remains fruitful. Our maximally tenable cognitive systems still benefit from fictions like these. But a fiction that is effective in one milieu may be inert in another. Today *Uncle Tom's Cabin* is of little more than historical interest. When it first appeared, though, despite its soppy sentimentality, superficial characterizations, and racist stereotypes, it conveyed the horrors of slavery to an audience insufficiently aware of them. In its time it made a genuine cognitive contribution, even if that contribution was later eclipsed by a more accurate understanding of the lives of American slaves.

Much that I have said about fiction pertains to factual discourse as

[17] Israel Scheffler, "Symbolic Aspects of Ritual I," in *Inquiries*, 41–51.

well. Mere falsity does not epistemically incapacitate a fiction nor truth alone activate a statement of fact. A motley collection of truths ordinarily conveys little more than a motley collection of falsehoods. But an orderly arrangement of carefully culled, carefully worded statements of fact, like a carefully contrived fiction, may encapsulate insights that advance understanding considerably. And selection, vocabulary, emphasis, and order may be as crucial to the cognitive efficacy of factual works as to works of fiction.

FIGURATIVE FUNCTIONS

Epistemically effective statements of fact or fiction need not be literal. During the Watergate scandal, several prominent and reasonably honorable politicians swore that they would not consider President Nixon culpable until they saw the smoking gun. None, when queried, could say precisely what would qualify as a smoking gun. Yet when the evidence was discovered, the verdict was unanimous: the tape on which Nixon is heard ordering the cover-up is the smoking gun.

'Smoking gun' is a metaphor. As such it is apt to be dismissed as a mere literary conceit—suggestive and decorative perhaps, but too imprecise and subjective to be genuinely informative.[18] I have argued elsewhere against such a position.[19] Anyway, Nixon's smoking gun belies it.

Drawing on popular crime stories where the villain is found over the victim, freshly fired murder weapon in hand, a metaphorical smoking gun is compelling evidence that closely links a culprit to a crime. If we cannot say literally how close the link or how compelling the evidence must be, it is not because the metaphor is imprecise but because our literal vocabulary is wanting. The metaphor precisely delineates a standard of evidence that no literal locution captures. Nor is the dearth of literal equivalents a surprise. Since we rarely invoke the standard in question, we have little need for, hence little incentive to invent, a lasting literal label. Metaphors are ad hoc expedients introduced to take up the slack that literal language inevitably leaves. Not that they are question begging or arbitrary. On the contrary, they are tailor-made to fit their contexts. But they make no claims to versatility. Their merits are to be judged entirely by their effectiveness in the contexts for which they are contrived.

They are, moreover, insusceptible to precise paraphrase. No more than Nixon's colleagues can we say exactly what makes for a metaphorical smoking gun. Nevertheless it is widely agreed both that the incriminating

[18] See Donald Davidson, "What Metaphors Mean," in *Inquiries into Truth and Interpretation*, 245–264.
[19] Elgin, *With Reference to Reference*, 59–70.

tape is a smoking gun and that the culpability of Nixon's cronies is not. Metaphors thus admit of consensus. And argument can affect consensus. A tenable innocent—or merely less damning—interpretation of Nixon's instructions would disqualify the tape as a smoking gun. Because no such interpretation was forthcoming, even Nixon's erstwhile defenders conceded that the standard had been met.

Amenability to intersubjective accord engendered by evidence and argument is a hallmark of objectivity. So metaphorical assertions are objective. 'The incriminating tape was Nixon's smoking gun' has earned its place in the political history of our time.

Metaphors evidently perform the same functions as literal symbols, and others besides. They denote. 'The smoking gun' denotes the incriminating tape. They figure in true sentences. 'Nixon was powerless to distance himself from the cover-up once the smoking gun was found' is true. They inform. The headline, 'Smoking Gun Found', imparted the news that overwhelming evidence of Nixon's complicity in the cover-up had been discovered. They explain. 'Despite evidence that George Bush engaged in similar chicanery, there was no smoking gun so he was not forced to resign' explains why Bush, unlike Nixon, served out his term. They can be supported and adduced as support. Evidence that Nixon had reviewed the tape and then lied about it buttressed the contention that it was a smoking gun. And its status as a smoking gun is evidence of the inadvisability of recording incriminating conversations.

Any object belongs to myriad classes. Some have literal labels associated with them. Most do not. Metaphor is a device for recognizing membership in normally neglected classes. A metaphor reorganizes the items in a realm, grouping together things more familiar categories keep apart, distinguishing among things familiar categories group together. Since class membership is determinate, there are facts of the matter as to what belongs to the classes metaphors mark out. Metaphorical denotation and truth then are semantically unproblematic. A term construed metaphorically denotes the members of its metaphorical extension, just as a term construed literally denotes the members of its literal extension. And metaphorical truth, like literal truth, is delimited by Convention (T).

'S is p' is true ≡ S is p.

Nontautologous sentences are true only under an interpretation. Whether that interpretation is literal or metaphorical makes no difference. Literal truths are sentences that satisfy Convention (T) when interpreted literally; metaphorical truths are sentences that satisfy it when interpreted metaphorically.[20]

---

[20] Ibid., 65–68.

Nor are metaphors inherently vague. They admit of as much precision as literal locutions do. 'Smoking gun' specifies a standard at least as precise as 'beyond reasonable doubt'. But because the classification a metaphor effects is atypical, we may be hard put to tell whether a given item belongs to the extension of a metaphorical predicate or whether a sentence containing such a predicate is true. Still, such epistemic difficulties do not undermine metaphor's semantic status. For they plague all unfamiliar classifications. Unless we understand psychiatric jargon, the literal classification of mental disorders is apt to give us pause. Uncertainty about applications no more impugns the denotation and truth of metaphorical locutions than it does the denotation and truth of locutions cast in unfamiliar literal language.

Whether an item belongs to a particular class is open to argument. Evidence can be brought to bear. And an item's membership in a given class can be evidence of some further fact. This is so whether the classes are typical or atypical, whether the labels associated with them are literal or metaphorical. Just as the smell of cordite affords evidence that a revolver belongs to the class of literal smoking guns, the tape's apparently inescapable, damning implications afford evidence that it belongs to the class of metaphorical smoking guns. Just as the revolver's membership in the class of literal smoking guns affords evidence that the butler committed the murder, the tape's membership in the class of metaphorical smoking guns affords evidence that the president was party to the cover-up.

For all that I have said so far, 'smoking gun' could just be ambiguous—denoting recently discharged firearms under one interpretation, highly incriminating evidence under another. This is no accident. For in matters of truth and evidence, metaphor and ambiguity function alike. The difference is this: merely ambiguous terms are semantically independent, their several interpretations mutually indifferent. A term's metaphorical interpretation recalls and is guided by its literal interpretation. It is because 'smoking gun' literally denotes recently fired murder weapons that it metaphorically denotes direct and damning evidence.

In a metaphorical usage, a term likens the objects in its metaphorical extension to those in its literal extension by effecting the joint exemplification of a constellation of telling features. Often the constellation in question is semantically unmarked. Then our language lacks the resources to say precisely what shared features underwrite the metaphor.[21] Despite their obvious differences, certain murder weapons and the incriminating tape are alike in directly and damningly implicating the culprit in the

---

[21] Sam Glucksberg and Boaz Keyser. "Understanding Metaphorical Comparisons: Beyond Similarity," *Psychological Review* 97 (1990): 3–18.

crime. When we label the tape a smoking gun, we highlight such similarities. The metaphor thus forges a chain of reference, linking literal and metaphorical referents of the term.

This might seem to undermine the contention that metaphors elude literal paraphrase. If the tape qualifies as a smoking gun because, like literal smoking guns, it directly and damningly implicates a culprit in a crime, why isn't 'evidence that directly and damningly implicates a culprit in a crime' the literal paraphrase of the metaphor 'smoking gun'? In fact, of course, it is *a* paraphrase—but an inadequate one. For it is neither exact nor exhaustive.

Feathers in his whiskers are the smoking gun that convicts the cat of swallowing the canary, the empty commercial broth container the smoking gun that convicts the self-styled gourmet chef of cutting corners. Evidently smoking guns can incriminate perpetrators in noncriminal as well as criminal offenses. Still, we cannot just substitute 'offense' for 'crime' in our paraphrase. For not all offenses seem to admit of smoking guns. The configuration of cutlery remaining on the table might provide pretty conclusive evidence that a diner failed to use the proper fork. But it hardly constitutes a smoking gun. For such a breach of etiquette is too minor to merit a smoking gun. Apparently only sufficiently serious offenses admit of smoking guns.

Nor does highly incriminating evidence of sufficiently serious offenses always amount to a smoking gun. Demonstrative evidence does not. Proof that the perpetrator did the deed would not be a smoking gun. It would obviate the need for one. Smoking guns afford circumstantial, albeit highly incriminating evidence. I could go on trying to triangulate, but by now the point is clear. Even so pedestrian a metaphor as 'the smoking gun' outruns our efforts to paraphrase.

The reason is not just the dearth of literal labels. Metaphor's resistance to paraphrase stems from the complexity and interdependence of its multiple referential functions. A sufficiently long-winded explication could conceivably enumerate the bases and degrees of likeness of literal and metaphorical smoking guns. But in likening the two referents, the metaphor does more. It exemplifies a shared constellation of interanimating features. An enumeration does not ordinarily exemplify the features it lists. Nor does it coalesce them into a constellation. The enumeration does not then exhibit the ways the features it lists bear on one another or the ways their doing so connects the two classes of objects that instantiate them. A fully adequate paraphrase preserves reference. But a literal paraphrase can preserve some of a metaphor's referential functions only by ignoring others. Inevitably something is lost in translation.

One of the things that is apt to be lost is epistemic access. Even if a statistician could state precisely and literally just how strongly the tape implicated Nixon in the cover-up, many of us would not know what to make of the statistic until we were told that it is equivalent to the weight of evidence a smoking gun affords. Nonstatisticians need the metaphor to make sense of the literal claim.

RECONFIGURATION

Literal, entrenched taxonomies tend to rigidify thought, guiding it along well-worn channels toward clearly demarcated goals. Metaphor reconfigures the domain, drawing boundaries that cut across familiar distinctions, disclosing features of the terrain that hitherto had eluded our gaze. To call a philosophy program *demanding* is to class it with other difficult endeavors, under a literal and not especially illuminating label. To call it *boot camp* is to do more. It is to class the program among enterprises whose arduous demands are expressly designed to inculcate vital professional skills. The metaphorical classification equips us to see how the program is like other brutal training regimens, such as medical internship or preparing to run a marathon, and how it differs both from more nurturing, supportive educational environments and from grueling ordeals like prison camp, whose hardships and indignities are not contrived to benefit those who suffer them. The metaphor brings to light the fact that the program's demands, harsh though they be, are not in general gratuitous. They are backed by a conception of what professional survival requires.

A metaphor points up affinities within and across domains. It likens its referent both to other members of the metaphorical extension and to their literal counterparts. It coalesces features into patterns, affording epistemic access to features and regularities we might otherwise overlook. The inflexible faculty, the inhospitable setting, the relentless criticism, the construal of philosophy as a series of attacks and defenses no longer seem independent objectionable aspects of graduate student life. The boot camp metaphor effects a realignment that enables us to see them as integral to a practice designed to transform raw recruits into philosopher warriors. It also equips us to ask whether this is what we want to do. For realignment provides resources for raising new questions. Once we recognize the constellation of factors a metaphor exemplifies, we can investigate whether the conception that underlies them is sound. Are the virtues and values boot camp inculcates ones we think philosophers need? Are the attributes it extinguishes ones philosophers should lack? Are important aspects of the subject slighted by the sort of training boot camp provides or the vision of the subject it engenders? And so forth.

Questions that could neither be framed nor motivated given just a literal description of the program press for answers when the program is construed metaphorically.

Like other symbols, metaphors often bear interpretations their authors fail to appreciate and fail to sustain interpretations their authors ascribe to them. In calling the program boot camp, for example, a speaker might intend only to underscore its difficulty, being oblivious or indifferent to the myriad other affinities with military training that the metaphor brings to light. She might even invoke the metaphor to point up a connection that does not in fact obtain, perhaps believing that the program has onerous physical demands. Still, despite the superficiality or wrong-headedness of her interpretation, her description is apt. The program is a metaphorical boot camp. And many of its more alienating features become intelligible when we construe it as such. The inadequacy of its author's interpretation then does not automatically impoverish a metaphor. There can be more to a symbol than meets its author's eye.

Indeed, a subject can proffer a metaphor without having anything much in mind. This hardly sounds like an epistemic virtue. But it is. For it means that metaphors can be ventured hypothetically. For the flimsiest of reasons, a thinker might suggest that perhaps the universe began in an immense explosion or maybe the principal scientist is the lab's silverback or possibly a paint brush is a pump.[22] Then she and others can investigate whether the metaphorical ascription can be sustained and whether the reorganization it effects is cognitively fruitful. Such initially underinterpreted metaphors frequently advance understanding considerably.

At the cutting edge of inquiry, available conceptual resources often are inadequate. We find ourselves lacking a literal taxonomy suited to our theoretical needs. We could of course invent one. The difficulty lies in deciding where to draw the lines. We do not yet know which distinctions are worth marking. Since any partition we propose looks suspiciously arbitrary, none is initially tenable.

A more promising tack is to import a partition that has already proven effective elsewhere. Even if we do not quite know what we are getting at in calling a mind a computer or a burned-out star a black hole, in deploying the terms metaphorically we bring our understanding of literal computers and literal black holes on line. Such a metaphor points up affinities between the literal and the metaphorical referents of the term. And these affinities guide research.

---

[22] I owe this last example to Donald Schon, "Generative Metaphor: A Perspective on Problem-Setting in Social Policy," *Metaphor and Thought*, ed. A. Ortony (Cambridge: Cambridge University Press, 1979), 257.

To treat a metaphor as a scientific hypothesis is to entertain the assumption that the order it imports will organize the domain in a way that furthers inquiry. Then the kinds it demarcates figure in lawlike statements and the entities it delimits display regularities the science seeks. The hypothesis that the mind is a computer, for example, configures the mental realm into a system of individuals, kinds, operations, and the like, that mirrors the functional organization of a digital computer.[23] Thinking, on such a model, is identified with data processing, assimilating new information with updating files. If the hypothesis fulfills its promise, its construal of the mental will afford epistemic access to psychological laws.

Still, words are cheap. Why should we credit the extravagant promise implicit in an as yet woefully underinterpreted metaphor? We shouldn't. Not immediately anyway. But if the affinities the metaphor highlights are psychologically significant, if the features it exemplifies are ones psychology has reason to focus on, the conception of mind that the computer metaphor advances merits further study. It is initially tenable.

We have at the outset no nonmetaphorical way to individuate the processes the metaphor marks out. Such understanding of those objects as we have is couched in irreducibly metaphorical terms. The metaphor then is no mere decorative device. It affords our sole route of epistemic access to the things we would study. The metaphor is constitutive of our conception of the objects of inquiry.

A metaphorical hypothesis functions like other scientific hypotheses. It is subject to elaboration and investigation and is susceptible to confirmation or disconfirmation on the basis of empirical evidence. It is, moreover, public property. Regardless of who proposed it or what he had in mind, any qualified scientist can investigate it, explore its implications, assess its tenability.

Constitutive metaphors typically come into play early in inquiry. If their promise is borne out, the research programs they give rise to render them obsolete. As we acquire ever more detailed information about their objects, we develop the resources to characterize them literally. The open-endedness that originally enabled the metaphor to spark a research program is devalued once a sufficient stock of stable truths is in store. For susceptibility to multiple interpretations is taken to threaten the stability of established findings and the prospects of intersubjective agreement as to what those findings are. Even if it retains the terminology, as the science matures, that terminology loses its metaphorical functions. Cosmology's understanding of the origin of the universe no longer draws on affinities that the big bang shares with more down-to-earth explosions.

---

[23] My discussion of the computer model of the mind draws heavily on Richard Boyd's "Metaphor and Theory Change," in *Metaphor and Theory*, 359–364.

As a science develops, its reliance on constitutive metaphors wanes. The metaphors turn literal, or a literal technical vocabulary supplants them to mark the distinctions the science needs. Still, metaphors remain important. Although the creation of technical vocabularies promotes the advancement of science, specialized terminology makes scientific understanding increasingly difficult to convey. Outsiders find it hard to tell just what the scientists are talking about. Metaphors bridge the gap. By describing the unfamiliar in terms of the familiar, they afford an entrée into the scientific realm. Contemporary economists could presumably conduct their inquiries and state their findings without recourse to the invisible hand. Its omission would jeopardize neither rigor nor warrant. But to explain themselves, not just to laymen but also to students, to other social scientists, even to one another, the metaphor is invaluable. A science's employment of heuristic and pedagogical metaphors reflects the recognition that a ladder that can be kicked away once we have climbed it ought not be jettisoned before we have made the ascent. A characterization like 'the invisible hand' that is unnecessary once we have fully grasped the science's conception of the phenomena may nonetheless constitute our best hope of coming to understand it.

Of course not all metaphorical descriptions of objects of scientific scrutiny function as scientific hypotheses. Cognitive psychology is unlikely to embrace 'The mind is a mollusk', even though it is true and occasionally apt. For the metaphor does not engage its interests. A discipline's initially tenable commitments constrain the considerations it has reason to entertain. A description—literal or metaphorical—that shows no prospect of increasing the understanding captured in its stock of initially tenable commitments has little to contribute to a science. Even if true, as things stand it is irrelevant. Psychology rightly ignores the mollusk metaphor and looks for its hypotheses elsewhere.

Such selectivity is not peculiar to science. Literature, politics, sportscasting, and religion likewise eschew metaphors that do not serve their ends. Every object admits of a host of metaphorical descriptions, many of them irrelevant, uninformative, or unproductive. A system of thought has no more reason to incorporate these than it does to incorporate irrelevant, uninformative, or unfruitful literal descriptions. For their assimilation would not increase its tenability. Truth alone is not enough. If our epistemic objective is to advance understanding and our method is the construction of increasingly tenable systems of thought, there will be any number of truths—literal and metaphorical—that do not merit consideration.

This is not to say that a system of thought can afford to ignore metaphors that threaten its stability. Clearly it cannot. 'The mind is a computer' threatens any number of complacent assumptions about human cognition—the conviction that emotions figure in cognition, for example, and the conviction that the felt quality of sensory experiences contributes to their cognitive function. Still, because it points up features of cognition that are obviously relevant to the commitments psychology already holds, the computer metaphor deserves a hearing.

SUMMING UP

The deliverances of emotion, exemplification, metaphor, and fiction are rarely literal, descriptive truths. Often their causal antecedents are less than refined. Their reliability tends to be suspect. They are sometimes unamenable to evidential support. As a result they are not the sorts of things traditional epistemology is prepared to countenance. Nevertheless they perform a variety of functions epistemology cannot afford to ignore. Because orientation, organization, salience, and focus figure in our construing things as we do, they are cognitive matters. But they are not all literal, descriptive matters. Emotion, metaphor, exemplification, and fiction affect the constitution and adoption of orientations, the construction and application of category schemes, the generation and extinction of saliencies, the fixing and blurring of focus. They therefore function cognitively. That being so, they fall within the province of epistemology. Their contributions to cognition are subject to epistemic assessment.

Often the assessment is positive. Whether or not they deliver literal, descriptive truths, they frequently advance understanding considerably through the arts, the sciences, and other systems of thought. Nor should we suppose that the list of contributors is complete. Other symbolic devices and psychological mechanisms may be expected to function similarly.[24] Symbols other than literal truths and faculties other than ratiocination engender insights that prove tenable. By counting their deliverances initially tenable, constructionalist epistemology acknowledges a defeasible presumption in their favor. Other things being equal, we have reason to incorporate them into our systems of thought.

[24] See Jill Sigman's unpublished "It Came from Tolerating Ambiguity" for an excellent discussion of the ways ambiguity in the arts advances understanding.

Chapter VII

EPISTEMIC INTERDEPENDENCE

LOTS OF ANIMALS learn from experience. Human beings learn from one another's experiences. We do not need to mount our own military campaign to discover the folly of invading Russia in winter. The fate of Napoleon's army affords evidence enough. To learn from one another's experiences requires understanding what other people undergo *as* experiences. This is not done by plotting trajectories of protoplasmic matter in motion. Nor do the findings of ethology suffice. "When we quote a man's utterance directly," Quine contends, "we report it almost as we might a bird call."[1] If so, direct quotation yields little insight into what the man is saying or why. Conceivably ethologists could correlate some human vocalizations with salient features of the environment. But our languages are so rich and our responses so variable that the fruits of such labor are bound to be sparse. Unlike crows, who have a common, distinctive warning cry, humans—even those who speak the same language—have a vast array of alternative responses to perceived danger. We differ considerably over whether, how, to whom, and in what circumstances we voice alarm. If we are to learn from one another's experiences then it is not enough to report one another's words as we do a birdcall. We need to construe other people's behavior as intentional—movements as actions and reactions, vocalizations and scribbles as utterances and inscriptions, neurological activity as thinking, planning, feeling, and so on. But what is the basis for such a construal?

VERSTEHEN

Some think it is supplied by *verstehen*—empathetic identification with the people we study.[2] If we can identify with Napoleon's retreating soldiers, we are in a position to do more than reckon the body count. We can understand (at least something of) the turmoil, trauma, tedium, and terror they felt. Verstehen's epistemological credentials are suspect, though. So before countenancing its deliverances, we should weigh the charges against it.

---

[1] W. V. Quine, *Word and Object* (Cambridge, Mass.: MIT Press, 1960), 219.

[2] Max Weber, "The Interpretive Understanding of Social Action," in *Readings in the Philosophy of the Social Sciences*, ed. M. Brodbeck (New York: Macmillan, 1968), 19–33.

One objection is that empathy is an emotion. And by tradition, deliverances of emotion are epistemologically inert. If so, any construal that depends on an emotion is also inert. But that tradition is one we have found reason to repudiate. Far from inhibiting understanding, emotion often advances it. The mere fact that verstehen involves empathy does not then discredit it.

Another worry is this. To identify with what someone else is going through requires imagination. And imagination, one might argue, is a creative, not a cognitive, faculty. Imagining that pigs have wings hardly constitutes evidence that they do. This in the end is Quine's objection, not only to verstehen but to any characterization of human behavior in terms of attitudes and actions. We cannot, he maintains, make the requisite ascriptions without imaginatively projecting ourselves into the agent's situation. But, Quine contends, imaginative projection, being an essentially dramatic act, is unscientific, hence noncognitive.[3]

Granted, unfettered imagination provides fodder for fiction more directly than for judgments of fact. Still, the bearing of this on the epistemic viability of verstehen or other ascriptions of propositional attitude is not altogether clear. Fiction, as we have seen, often advances understanding. So even if we find that the deliverances of verstehen are fictions, it does not follow that they are epistemically vacuous. Nor should we be too quick to consign those deliverances to the fictive realm. Not all imaginative projection produces fictions. Although continuing a series and plotting a curve require imagination to go beyond the data at hand, we do not ordinarily consider such processes exercises in fiction. The reason is obvious. In operations like interpolation and extrapolation, imagination is severely constrained. Even if unfettered imagination generates fiction, deliverances of a sufficiently fettered imagination remain squarely within the realm of fact. They may of course be false. But they are to be assessed as true or false *as* statements of fact.

Verstehen, arguably, is sufficiently fettered. Our understanding of the physical, social, and psychological milieu provides the requisite constraints. If, for example, we know that Napoleon's soldiers were poorly shod, ill-educated Christians, we must factor that information into our imaginative projection. We cannot claim to enter into their mind-sets by adopting the attitudes of well-dressed Buddhist intellectuals. The more relevant contextual detail our construals accommodate, the richer and more reasonable the deliverances of verstehen are apt to be. The tenability of such a projection plainly depends on the accuracy and adequacy of its background assumptions. So deliverances of verstehen are vulnerable. In this they do not differ from the results of other nondeductive reasoning.

[3] Quine, *Word and Object*, 219.

Dependence on background assumptions and the consequent vulnerability of conclusions are familiar facts of epistemic life. It is not obvious that they weigh more heavily on verstehen than on other modes of reasoning.

A more serious worry looms. Experience is subjective. It depends not just on what events impinge on the sensory surfaces of an organism but also on the fine-grained texture they acquire when filtered through a particular historically and culturally conditioned sensibility. It is, one might argue, sheer hubris to claim to understand what someone else experiences. The evidence at hand, however plentiful, is always woefully inadequate. This concern is legitimate. Verstehen cannot plausibly purport to replicate a person's subjective state exactly. So if empathetic identification requires exact replication, verstehen is doomed. But verstehen's ambitions may be more modest. Even if I cannot know precisely how any one of Napoleon's retreating soldiers felt, I can identify with them closely enough to recognize that their feelings fell well within the scope of the predicate 'miserable'. So long as verstehen does not pretend to provide greater precision than available grounds for empathetic identification warrant, it remains viable.

The real worry is not with the possibility of reproducing other people's subjective states but with the point of doing so. Understanding is our goal. But being in a subjective state is not the same as, and does not insure, understanding it. All too often we are befuddled by the states we find ourselves in. Verstehen, as I have construed it, evidently cannot do what it sets out to do. Not because we cannot enter into one another's subjective states but because doing so is not sufficient for objective insight into those states or the perspectives they afford. If Pierre is oblivious to his state of mind, bewildered by it, or mistaken about it, then by adopting his mind-set, I come to share his confusions. This hardly constitutes an epistemic advance.

The theory of verstehen derives plausibility from the once widespread assumption that the first-person perspective possesses unquestionable epistemic authority. Roughly, the story goes, if I feel p, I know that I feel p. So if someone empathetically identifies with me, she both feels my p and knows that she feels my p. But the root assumption is untenable. My feeling p guarantees neither me nor those who identify with me knowledge that I feel p. The gap between subjective and objective is not so easily bridged.

This is not to say that verstehen is epistemologically valueless. That remains to be seen. Rather, it is to set a requirement. If verstehen's deliverances are to be epistemically estimable, they cannot be merely subjective. Verstehen must do more than enable us to get inside one another's heads. It must engender an objective understanding of what we find there. This requires incorporating the deliverances of verstehen into a broader, more comprehensive system of tenable claims.

LANGUAGE

Despite the alleged subjectivity of personal experience, we often know what is on other people's minds. The explanation is not far to seek. Humans are a garrulous lot. We relentlessly recount, record, rehash, and publicly ruminate over thoughts, emotions, aspirations, and events. It is no surprise that others are privy to our take on things. Often enough, whether they are interested or not, we tell them.

Words require interpretation. So the epistemic access our words afford is available only to those who interpret them correctly. And for all our verbosity, much that is required to understand our words inevitably remains unsaid. We can only say one thing at a time. But no locution is so perspicuous that it interprets itself. To interpret any utterance involves locating it in a vast, complex array of linguistic and social conventions. When those conventions are our own, or near enough, we invoke them automatically and interpret the locution straightway. Because we need not, and often cannot, articulate the assumptions our construal is based on, we may be unaware that we are making them. But where we are—or suspect we are—on unfamiliar turf, the assumptions that underwrite a construal come to the fore.

Our predicament presents itself starkly in the case of radical interpretation, where the object is to interpret utterances and inscriptions of a wholly alien tongue.[4] The linguist begins by correlating spontaneous native utterances with conspicuous features of the environment. But a vast gulf separates the situations that prompt most remarks from the significance that attaches to them. To make sense of such utterances requires locating them in a context and filtering them through a mesh of attitudes and assumptions. Only then will the bearing—if any—of local conditions emerge.

Attitudes are interdependent, each being demarcated by reference to others. Grossly oversimplifying for the purposes of illustration, suppose a speaker's intentional stance has just three parameters: belief, desire, and meaning.[5] Given any two, we can generally solve for the third.[6] If, for example, we know that Fred believes that neutrinos have mass and that he wants to say as much, we can pretty safely interpret his utterance as

[4] Ibid., 26–79, and passim.

[5] In fact, an intentional stance has more. Values, ideals, preferences, and the like, also play a role. So in actual cases the interdependence is more complicated than in my illustration.

[6] We can generally solve for the third but not inevitably. We must allow for oversights and slips of the tongue. Even if Fred believes that neutrinos have mass and has every intention of saying so, he might, through nervousness, carelessness, distraction, or whatever, say 'Neutrinos have moss' instead.

'Neutrinos have mass' or words to that effect. If we know that Fred believes that neutrinos have mass and that his utterance is correctly construed as saying so, we can reasonably impute to him the desire to say that neutrinos have mass. And if we know that Fred wants to voice his views on neutrino magnitudes and that his utterance is correctly interpreted as saying that neutrinos have mass, we can normally ascribe to him the belief that neutrinos have mass. The difficulty is that ordinarily we are not given any two. "There is no assigning beliefs to a person one by one on the basis of his verbal behavior, his choices, or other local signs no matter how plain and evident, for we make sense of particular beliefs only as they cohere with other beliefs, with preferences, with intentions, hopes, fears, expectations and the rest. . . . [T]he content of a propositional attitude derives from its place in the pattern."[7] So we need to solve for all three at once, constrained only by the behavioral evidence and such assumptions about rationality as we can in good conscience make.

Merely assuming that your interlocutor is rational may suffice to correlate 'rabbit' with 'gavagai'. But without shared cultural practices, it will not yield correlations for 'pop quiz' or 'passing grade' or 'homework assignment'. To interpret such phrases requires understanding the social institution they and their referents belong to, the norms that structure that institution, and the activities it supports. A Masai field linguist, unacquainted with Western educational practices, could not hope to make sense of such terminology independently of mapping the values, expectations, institutions, and objectives that constitute the practice. To interpret such locutions then, the linguist needs to delineate the norms, practices, institutions, and taboos that structure the speaker's social world. For the circumstances in which a speaker finds himself are thick cultural constructs.

The method the field linguist employs does not in any way favor the claims of natural science. It will yield access to the native's political, aesthetic, religious, and practical pronouncements as readily as to his scientific ones. A report of a rabbit sighting engages practical concerns about dinner options at least as directly as it engages zoological interests in indigenous wildlife. And a laughing child affords as solid a basis for the interpretation of the native locution for 'He's happy!' as a rabbit sighting does for 'Gavagai!'. Indeed, we may have the resources for interpreting the native's emotional vocabulary long before we have made much headway on his biology.

The field linguist's work is largely anthropological. She cannot devise a translation manual without simultaneously constructing psychological

---

[7] Donald Davidson, "Mental Events," in *Essays on Actions and Events* (Oxford: Oxford University Press, 1980), 221.

profiles of her informants and a sociological profile of their society. She provisionally ascribes beliefs, emotions, values, and preferences to her informants and institutional supports to sustain them. She then attempts to interpret their utterances in light of her ascriptions. She modifies her ascriptions to accommodate the evidence her tentative translations supply. Through a process of mutual adjustments, she reconciles her construals of the speakers' words, deeds, and attitudes with one another, with the reactions of other members of the community, and with the situations in which they occur. Only then can she purport to understand their utterances.

The problem of radical interpretation is not just an occupational hazard for field linguists. For radical interpretation begins at home. In learning his native tongue, a child has no more to go on than the linguist does. Like the linguist, the child observes the verbal behavior of fluent speakers. He establishes correlations between their utterances and the natural environment and notes regularities in usage. He forms conceptions of the institutions and practices that constitute his social world and of the activities they engender. He notes correlations between utterances and conspicuous features of the world so construed. He resolves complex constructions into repeatable elements and recombines those elements to form new constructions. He tests his constructions against the verbal behavior of fluent speakers and modifies them in response to the feedback he receives. He achieves competence when he speaks like a native.

The child, like the linguist, has to impute attitudes to those around him. The difficulty is that multiple, divergent complexes of attitudes accommodate the evidence equally well. Indeterminacy results. There is no saying absolutely what an agent believes, desires, values, or whatever. An attitude is fixed only within a network composed of other attitudes.

Throughout, child and linguist apply some version of Quine's principle of charity.[8] They limit their construals to ones it would be rational for the speaker to hold in the circumstances in which he finds himself. Little is inherently irrational. The rationality or irrationality of an utterance, action, or attitude typically depends on how well it fits into a relatively well-integrated whole. So the principle of charity constrains us to ascribe to a speaker statements, attitudes, and actions that, on the whole, mesh. The ascriptions we make to a single agent should, for the most part at least, be reasonable in light of one another. And if his compatriots treat the agent as rational, those ascriptions should mesh fairly well with the attitudes we ascribe to other members of his community.

The requirement that we construe our interlocutors as rational may seem unduly strong. Surely some people harbor irrational attitudes. But if

[8] Quine, *Word and Object*, 59.

the principle of charity is mandatory, there seems to be no way to ascribe them. We cannot, for example, interpret a native's report of an eclipse as saying literally that the moon ate the sun, for such a statement is crazy.

Part of the problem stems from an equivocation on the term 'rational'. The rationality of a self-consistent utterance, attitude, or action is assessed against a backdrop of commitments. The same item may receive different ratings depending on the backdrop it is measured against. When the issue is whether to adopt an attitude, we take our own commitments as the backdrop. But when our goal is understanding other people—particularly people whose commitments threaten to diverge considerably from our own—we need to consider how well it accords with their commitments, not with ours. It is irrational to claim that the moon literally ate the sun, if one believes, as we do, that celestial bodies are inanimate. We are not then tempted to accept the claim or even seriously entertain it as an explanation of an eclipse. But judged in terms of an animistic worldview, the claim is not obviously irrational.

This might seem to threaten the epistemological position I have been advocating. Surely we do not want to say that the native knows that the moon ate the sun or that his belief that it did so is tenable. But if it is rational, it is reasonable in light of the cosmology he endorses. And that cosmology could well be reasonable in light of his relevant antecedent commitments.

Obviously I do not want to say, nor am I committed to saying, that he knows that the moon ate the sun. It did not. So he knows no such thing. But whether to say that he harbors a tenable belief to that effect is a more delicate question. It turns on the relation of the native's cosmological commitments to the findings of modern science. If those findings are epistemologically inaccessible to him—as they might be if his culture is sufficiently isolated—his failure to accommodate them does not undermine his theory's tenability. Its defect lies in a lack of access to relevant information, not in a failure to accommodate the information it has access to. The native's belief displays some understanding of eclipses and may be the best construction available in the epistemic circumstances he finds himself in. Such probably was the situation of our remote ancestors. If, on the other hand, the native has access to the findings of modern science but screens his cosmology off from them, then his belief is untenable. For in that case it is not reasonable in light of the initially tenable commitments it ought to accommodate.

It may then be appropriate to construe the native as believing that the moon ate the sun and his statement as affirming it. But could we have evidence for such a construal? Davidson evidently thinks we could not—at least we could not take the utterance to be an expression of a thorough-going animism. "Whether we like it or not, if we want to understand others, we must count them right on most matters."[9] And right "by our own lights, it goes without saying."[10] So we must translate sentences they hold true as sentences we hold true, sentences they desire true as sentences we desire true, sentences they prefer true as sentences we prefer true, and so on. A little divergence is permissible. But we cannot construe them as holding true many sentences like 'The moon ate the sun', since we hold such sentences false.

Lest you think I am construing Davidson's principle uncharitably, let me remind you of his discussion of alien astronomical beliefs.

> How clear [are] we that the ancients—some ancients—believed that the earth was flat? *This* earth? Well, this earth of ours is part of the solar system, a system partly identified by the fact that it is a gaggle of large, cool, solid bodies circling around a very large, hot star. If someone believes *none* of this about the earth, is it certain that it is the earth he is thinking about? An answer is not called for. The point is made if this kind of consideration of related beliefs can shake one's confidence that the ancients believed that the earth was flat.[11]

Although I consider nothing certain, I confess that my confidence is unshaken. We have, I take it, ample reason to believe that the ancients—some ancients—believed that the Earth is flat, even though they believed none of the claims on Davidson's list.

Davidson's version of the principle of charity is too strong. We needn't assume that other people agree with us about most things. We need only construe them as rational. This requires crediting them with a system of mutually supportive, relevant, and contextually appropriate cognitive commitments. Granted, we need evidence to identify those commitments. But a far smaller base of agreement suffices to supply the requisite evidence.

Even if our commitments diverge from the native's, they are apt to overlap significantly at the level of banalities. These provide the linguist her entrée. Celestial animists and mechanists are likely to agree that the moon has phases, that the sun warms the Earth, that cows eat grass, and so forth. The linguist grounds her translation manual in uncontroversial statements like these, not because they constitute the majority of our beliefs or claims but because she has reason to consider them the least tendentious. She tests her tentative translations against further, relatively untendentious claims and, let us assume, confirms them. She then encounters a sentence that, according to her manual, says, 'The moon ate

---

[9] Davidson, "On the Very Idea of a Conceptual Scheme," 197.

[10] Davidson, "Mental Events," 222.

[11] Donald Davidson, "Thought and Talk," in *Inquiries into Truth and Interpretation*, 168.

the sun'. Assessed against her own astronomical commitments, the claim, literally construed, is clearly irrational. Should she take it to discredit her translation manual?

Maybe. The evidence is equivocal. It might tell against her translation manual. Or it might show that her informants believe something that is deeply at odds with what she believes, or that the utterance should not be construed literally. Further investigation is needed.

The linguist can conduct the requisite research because the native's utterance is nested in an elaborate network of presuppositions, implications, and implicatures. By tracking them through the web of belief, she can investigate whether the native harbors the other attitudes that routine utterance of 'The moon ate the sun' would seem to commit him to. For example, a speaker would not normally either affirm or deny that the moon ate the sun unless he presupposed that the moon is alive.[12] So, ceteris paribus, the linguist can ascribe to the native the belief that the moon is alive. By elaborating the presuppositions, implications, and implicatures of the sentence she ascribes, and of that sentence in conjunction with other commitments she has reason to impute to the native, the linguist stands to gain access to a cosmology fundamentally at odds with her own. If that cosmology is rational, the beliefs and other attitudes that constitute it are reasonable in light of one another, even if they are unreasonable in light of the linguist's own cosmology.

Translation of the native's utterance, together with the tracking procedure, provides resources for identifying a cluster of attitudes in the context of which the utterance would make sense. Once she has identified those attitudes, she can investigate whether the speaker harbors them. She knows what sort of evidence to look for. If her translation manual is adequate to the task, she can simply ask him. She can ask, for example, whether the moon is alive, what other actions it performs, whether other celestial bodies are alive, and so forth. And she can ask whether he means the remarks to be taken literally. Even if she lacks the resources to pose such questions, once she attunes herself to the relations of presupposition, implication, and implicature that link diverse sentences together, she can listen for spontaneous utterances that bear on the issue and perhaps maneuver her informant into situations in which he is likely to make such utterances.

Tracking then tells the linguist where to look for further support, not what she will find. It is entirely possible that the native will reject enough of the presuppositions, implications, and implicatures in question to discredit the proposed translation.

---

[12] See Robert Stalnaker, "Pragmatic Presuppositions," in *Semantics and Philosophy*, ed. M. Munitz and P. Unger (New York: New York University Press, 1974), 197–213.

Of course, the situation is more complicated than I have made out. Pragmatic presuppositions and implicatures are hedged by generous ceteris paribus clauses. But ceteris are not always paribus. So in any given case, an expected connection may fail to hold. That is one reason for investigating each sentence's position in a web of interconnections. No single link decisively confirms, nor does any single gap decisively disconfirm, a proposed translation.

Another caveat is this: I have been speaking as though each interpreted utterance belongs to a unique cluster of presuppositions, implications, and implicatures. This is obviously an oversimplification. There may be several clusters, any one of which would make sense of the utterance under the interpretation the linguist gives it. So the native's refusal to assent to elements of a given cluster does not by itself refute her proposed translation. Another cluster might validate it.

As these complications show, the linguist's lot is not an easy one. Still, they raise no difficulties of principle. The job the linguist sets out to do can be done. With luck, ingenuity, skill, and time, she can translate a foreign tongue, even if those who speak it harbor attitudes quite alien to her own. And a good thing too. For we do not have to travel to distant lands to find opportunities to ascribe attitudes we consider irrational. We regularly impute them to one another.

Religious tenets often seem irrational to nonbelievers, yet we readily and reasonably ascribe them to their adherents. Even though I consider it irrational to think that death is reversible, I take many of my compatriots to believe in personal resurrection, to say as much, and to orient their lives around this belief. Actions, choices, priorities, and words that otherwise make little sense form a mutually supportive worldview when interpreted in light of a belief in resurrection. Like field linguists and anthropologists, each of us ascribes what she takes to be irrational attitudes when doing so seems the best way to make systematic sense of an agent's or community's words and deeds. And like linguists and anthropologists, we can track the presuppositions, implications, and implicatures of our ascriptions and thereby generate further evidence to test them against.

INDETERMINACY

The problem of radical translation is that a variety of separately acceptable but mutually incompatible translation manuals can be constructed. Since nothing favors one of those manuals over the rest, translation is indeterminate. A translation that is right according to one acceptable manual is wrong according to another.

Propositional attitude ascriptions suffer the same fate. To be correct, ascriptions must accommodate the subject's verbal and nonverbal behavior and dispositions. But divergent constellations of ascriptions prove equally accommodating. Under one, although not without reservations, the subject believes in personal resurrection, hopes for eternal salvation, and therefore speaks and acts so as to maximize her prospects of heavenly reward. Under another, the subject has doubts about personal resurrection but considers Pascal's wager a good bet, hence speaks and acts so as to maximize her prospects of heavenly reward. Whether to say that the subject believes in personal resurrection thus depends on which constellation of attitudes we impute to her. If both constellations make equally good sense of her behavior and dispositions, there is no basis in fact for favoring either over the other. Like translation, ascription of propositional attitudes is indeterminate.

Elsewhere I have argued that Quine's behaviorist assumptions are not responsible for indeterminacy. So we cannot evade it simply by employing a more robust methodology.[13] Indeed, Hilary Putnam's model theoretic argument shows that there is nothing we can do to evade it. The question is, how can we live with it?

Quine copes by espousing a double standard. He concedes the utility of intentional idioms but accords them a sort of second-class status. They have, he insists, no place in science, strictly so-called: "If we are limning the true and ultimate structure of reality, the canonical scheme for us is the scheme that knows no quotation except direct quotation and no propositional attitudes but only the physical constitution and behavior of organisms."[14] Since he considers it the goal of science to limn the true and ultimate structure of reality, it follows that intentional idioms are to be excluded from science.

Conceivably we could eschew intentional idioms in the statement of fundamental physical theories. But without the resources such idioms supply, we could not do science. For science is a collaborative endeavor. Experimentalists report their results to theorists and take theoretical findings back to the lab. Nor is this division of labor just a matter of convenience. The requirement of variety of evidence practically necessitates collaboration. Rarely is it feasible for an individual scientist single-handedly to amass enough evidence to support her own theory. Nor can she calibrate all the instruments, validate all the methods, or calculate all the constants she uses.

Collaboration relies on testimony. And to treat an utterance or inscription as testimony, we cannot merely report it as we do a birdcall. We must assign it an interpretation and construe it as something its author

---

[13] Catherine Z. Elgin, "Facts That Don't Matter," in *Meaning and Method: Essays in Honor of Hilary Putnam*, ed. G. Boolos (Cambridge: Cambridge University Press, 1990), 17–29.

[14] Quine, *Word and Object*, 221.

believes, supposes, or hypothesizes, and wants to convey.[15] 'The litmus paper turned pink' is significant for chemistry if it can be construed as saying that the litmus paper turned pink, as providing its audience with reason to believe that the litmus paper turned pink, and if the litmus paper's turning pink is relevant to and informative about the issue under investigation.

Relevance and informativeness are of course contextual matters. They depend on what is accepted and what is at issue in the circumstances at hand. If the interlocutors all know and know that one another know that in such circumstances litmus paper always turns pink, or if the paper's turning pink has no bearing on the matter under investigation, the sentence token 'The litmus paper turned pink' is an idle aside that makes no contribution to the inquiry. If, on the other hand, the reaction of the litmus paper was initially in doubt and makes some difference to the investigation, the utterance functions as a report of a scientific finding. The scientific community's standards of relevance, appropriateness, adequacy, and significance thus underwrite the chemist's report that the litmus paper turned pink. As a string of uninterpreted squiggles or the human equivalent of a birdcall, her remark has nothing to contribute to chemistry.

It is disingenuous to think that by excluding intentional idioms from the canonical statement of fundamental physical theories we show the intentional stance to be eliminable from or peripheral to science. Science involves collaboration. An individual scientist can neither formulate, test, support, nor evaluate a theory without drawing on what other scientists think and say and intentionally do. To eliminate all dependence on intersubjective support would be to eviscerate science. To think that intentional idioms are just convenient labor-saving devices is to overlook how integral they are to intersubjective support. Even if a theory in fact limns a true and ultimate structure of reality, without the intersubjective, normative resources the intentional stance supplies, an individual scientist would have no reason to accept it. She might, of course, accept it without reason. But taking theories on faith is hardly an epistemically creditable stance.

Quine's double standard is then ill-advised. It is also unnecessary. For indeterminacy is not a form of skepticism. Radical translation succeeds. And it is easier than armchair philosophers are apt to think. Multiple mappings from one language onto another satisfy all the constraints on correct translation. The skeptical reading of Quine's conclusion derives from the mistaken assumption that there is at most one *really* right interpretation of

---

[15] If the situation warrants, we can of course construe our informant as unreliable and modify our take on her utterance accordingly. But if we are limited to treating her remarks as the human equivalent of a birdcall, we cannot construe them as about anything or construe her as an informant rather than, say, a measuring device.

a speaker's words, but the linguist lacks the resources to figure out which one. In fact there are several, each as good as the others.

Relativity results. Because multiple, divergent translation manuals can be constructed, there is no saying absolutely whether 'gavagai' means 'rabbit' or 'undetached rabbit part'. Relative to one acceptable manual it means 'rabbit', relative to another it means 'undetached rabbit part'. The English translation of 'gavagai' is then absolutely indeterminate. But relative to each acceptable translation manual—each manual, that is, that satisfies all our theoretical and methodological constraints and accommodates the behavior and dispositions of native speakers—'gavagai' has a determinate English translation.

A regress threatens, since radical translation begins at home. Relative to one acceptable manual, 'gavagai' means 'rabbit'. But means 'rabbit' in what sense of 'rabbit'? There are multiple, divergent mappings of English onto English, all of which respect our verbal behavior and dispositions. So, one might wonder, does 'gavagai' mean 'rabbit' in the sense of 'rabbit' or in the sense of 'undetached rabbit part'? It avails us nothing to go around muttering, "By 'rabbit', I mean 'rabbit' in the sense of *'rabbit'*," for one can always ask, "And what sense of 'rabbit' is that?" and the regress begins anew.

The regress is real but not vicious. For we can terminate it at will,[16] relativizing to a background language that we take for the nonce as unproblematic. We need not even specify (explicitly or tacitly) which one. Since the available alternatives are all viable, I need only commit myself to the claim that 'gavagai' means 'rabbit' in some acceptable sense of 'rabbit'.

Obviously such a maneuver would be illicit if the regress posed a skeptical challenge. We cannot, after all, discredit Cartesian skepticism by telling Descartes, "Just don't worry about demons." But radical translation succeeds. So long as the candidate pool consists only of translations sanctioned by acceptable manuals, whatever sense of 'rabbit' we settle on, 'gavagai' means 'rabbit'.

Nor does the indeterminacy of propositional attitude ascriptions give rise to skepticism. Propositional attitudes are demarcated by their place in a psychological schema—a network that fixes the identity conditions on the psychological states it recognizes. Multiple schemata apply to the same realm, drawing their lines in different places. Such schemata, moreover, are apt to employ much of the same terminology. Thus, for example, 'believes that neutrinos have mass' occurs in several schemata and has different compliance conditions in each. So whether to say that Fred believes that neutrinos have mass depends on which schema is in effect. Under

[16] Quine, "Ontological Relativity," 49.

one, he does, even though he recognizes that his reasons are less than conclusive. Under another, owing to his recognition of the inconclusiveness of his reasons, he does not quite believe that neutrinos have mass, although he strongly surmises that they do.

It might seem that Fred, at least, should be able to settle the matter unequivocally. But he cannot. No more than other objects do attitudes dictate their own descriptions. So even Fred has to invoke a schema to determine whether his attitude toward neutrinos amounts to believing or merely surmising that they have mass. And Fred, like the rest of us, might easily invoke any of several, individually adequate but divergent schemata.

Independent of all schemata, whether Fred believes that neutrinos have mass is indeterminate. But it does not follow that what Fred *really* holds is somehow ineffable. Rather, until criteria for the individuation of attitudes are in effect, it makes no sense even to ask what someone really holds. Like the criteria for believing, those for *really holding* need to be fixed.

Relative to each acceptable schema, it is determinate whether Fred believes that neutrinos have mass. To ascribe an attitude is to ascribe it as part of a schema. The indeterminacy of propositional attitude ascriptions arises from our failure to fix all the relevant parameters. It is no more mysterious than the indeterminacy that arises when we ask whether Houston is bigger than Chicago without specifying the magnitude that concerns us. If 'bigger' is a measure of surface area, Houston is bigger; if it is a measure of population, it is not.

The assurance that there exist determinate facts of the matter relative to a translation manual or psychological schema may seem less than wholly consoling. We rarely specify such a framework. If determinacy required us to do so, the ascriptions and interpretations we actually provide would remain indeterminate, despite the discovery that we could, in principle, do better.

In the absence of a schema, I said, there is no fact of the matter as to whether Fred believes that neutrinos have mass. But it does not follow that in the absence of an express specification of a schema there is no fact of the matter. For the requisite schema may be presupposed. Is there any reason to believe it is?

There is. As David Lewis recognizes, "It's not as easy as you might think to say something that will be unacceptable for lack of required presuppositions. Say something that requires a missing presupposition, and straightway that presupposition springs into existence, making what you said acceptable after all."[17] Normally, I suggest, interlocutors remedy one

---

[17] David Lewis, "Scorekeeping in a Language Game," in *Philosophical Papers*, vol. 1, 234.

another's failure to specify a suitable framework by presupposing one that will do the job.

But, one might demand, "Which one?" One that takes us to speak of rabbits or undetached rabbit parts? Can we revive the skeptical worry, through our inability to tell exactly what is being presupposed? We cannot. For ordinarily it does not matter exactly what is presupposed. Only acceptable frameworks will do the job the presupposition is needed to do. So only acceptable frameworks will be presupposed. Among the acceptable frameworks, one is as good as another.

If it matters—if, for example, the issue under discussion is just how confident Fred is that neutrinos have mass—we can insist that the schema in effect be specified. But where such precision is unnecessary, we tacitly concede that an acceptable framework is in place and proceed from there. It simply does not matter which one.

Not that we are always ready, willing, and able to grant the requisite presupposition. The ardent theist's contention that deep down, everyone really believes in God requires a schema that assigns the predicate 'believes in God' enormous scope. We may balk at presupposing such a schema on the grounds that it would distort other attitudes—by, for example, convicting avowed atheists of self-deception or inconsistency, without any evidence of either. The proud parent's claim that her infant believes that Sidgwick was a major moral philosopher requires a schema that specifies what it would take for a baby to believe such a thing. Having no idea what such a schema could be, we are incapable of presupposing it. The point then is a fairly modest one. Absent impediments, the requisite presuppositions get made.

It does not follow of course—nor should it—that the ascriptions in whose service such presuppositions are made will turn out to be true. The availability of a suitable framework insures that whether Fred believes that neutrinos have mass and whether the native said that rabbits are plentiful will be determinate. But they may turn out to be determinately false.

It is worth emphasizing that nothing I have said bears on the question whether acceptable psychological theories have to be framed in terms of beliefs, desires, preferences, and the like. That is a substantive question for the science of psychology to decide. My point is epistemological. We cannot (now at least) collaborate without ascribing attitudes to and interpreting utterances and inscriptions made by one another. And we cannot do science (or much of anything else) without collaborating. So intentional idioms are integral to epistemology, whether or not intentional states are eliminable from psychology.

This is not so alarming as it first appears. Any number of crucial epistemological notions—evidence, justification, explanation, and the like—make no pretense of answering to discriminable psychological states. They are none the worse for that. We have to be able to tell whether a claim is believed, just as we have to be able to tell whether it is justified. But it need not be psychology that tells us.

Still, Quine cannot sustain his position by barring intentional notions from psychology while allowing them free rein in epistemology. For if, as he contends, philosophy is continuous with natural science,[18] philosophy is not exempt from scientific strictures. Whether or not they are underwritten by psychology—which is, after all, just one science among many—acceptable epistemological concepts and devices are subject to the rigorous standards of science. Nor is this just a problem for Quinean physicalists. We need not consider philosophy continuous with natural science to recognize that it would be both intellectually dishonest and futile for a discipline to depend for its results on means that it repudiates. If science faces the tribunal of experience as a corporate body, methodological and theoretical commitments stand trial together. There is no premium in being willing to use concepts or devices one's theories are forbidden to mention. For whether a commitment is central or peripheral, it is implicated in the fate of the sciences that depend on it. When science stands trial, there are no unindicted co-conspirators.

Advancement of understanding in the sciences, the humanities, and less structured settings is of a piece. We come to understand the natural world by understanding what others make of it. We come to understand social practices, political institutions, ethical requirements, and works of art in the same way. This is not to say that we must agree with one another. But unless we impute attitudes to one another, we cannot communicate, cannot collaborate, cannot draw on one another's expertise or build on one another's findings. Nor can we dispute, disconfirm, or distance ourselves from received opinion. An iconoclast must recognize icons before she can smash them. We need not and should not be complacent about the assumptions of the communities we live in. They provide starting points, not end points of inquiry.

The traditional problem of other minds is miscast. We cannot hope to understand the material world without understanding what other people make of it. And our theories of nature, ourselves, and each other inform one another. As we learn more about a domain, we learn more about which methods, values, and categories advance our understanding of it, which intellectual abilities are useful, and about whose judgment deserves to be trusted. As we refine our talents, judgments, and methods, we discover more about the domain. Each tenable theory provides a platform from which to launch new investigations. None affords a permanent resting place. The task is endless.

[18] Quine, "Two Dogmas of Empiricism," 42–46.

INDEX